The Fit Shall Inherit the Earth

The Fit Shall Inherit the Earth

A Theology of Sport and Fitness

Erik W. Dailey

PICKWICK *Publications* • Eugene, Oregon

THE FIT SHALL INHERIT THE EARTH
A Theology of Sport and Fitness

Pickwick Publications
An Imprint of Wipf and Stock Publishers
199 W. 8th Ave., Suite 3
Eugene, OR 97401

www.wipfandstock.com

PAPERBACK ISBN: 978-1-5326-4925-7
HARDCOVER ISBN: 978-1-5326-4926-4
EBOOK ISBN: 978-1-5326-4927-1

Cataloguing-in-Publication data:

Names: Dailey, Erik W., author.

Title: The fit shall inherit the earth : a theology of sport and fitness / Erik W. Dailey.

Description: Eugene, OR : Pickwick Publications, 2018 | Includes bibliographical references.

Identifiers: ISBN 978-1-5326-4925-7 (paperback) | ISBN 978-1-5326-4926-4 (hardcover) | ISBN 978-1-5326-4927-1 (ebook)

Subjects: LCSH: Sports—Religious aspects—Christianity. | Sports—Religious aspects—History. | Sports—Moral and ethical aspects.

Classification: GV706.42 .D35 2018 (print) | GV706.42 .D35 (ebook)

Sections of chapters 1, 2, and 3 have appeared in Erik W. Dailey, "On the Body and Liturgical Practices: Why Don't Presbyterians Dance in Worship," Studia Liturgica 45 (2015) 93-109, and Erik W. Dailey, "Sport and Transcendence through the Body," International Journal of Public Theology 10, (2016) 486–506.

Manufactured in the U.S.A. 10/12/18

Contents

Acknowledgments

My sincerest thanks go to my mentor, Bill Dyrness, for his help, patience, and guidance through this process. I would also like to thank my other mentors, official and otherwise, Ben Houltberg, Robert Ellis, Ron White, Todd Johnson, Rob Johnston, Hak Joon Lee, and Bob Covolo. This project was only possible because of the love, support, personal sacrifice, and editing help of my wife, The Rev. Millason Dailey. Thanks also for all the proofreading from my mother, Donna Dailey, and all the encouragement from my father, Robin Dailey. I am indebted to the members of Occidental Presbyterian Church, who have allowed me the space and time away to work on this. Finally, my thanks go to Chad Durieux, coach of the Rose Bowl Masters swim team, who has shown me that fitness and speed can still be a part of one's athletic career, even twenty years past one's prime.

Introduction

IN 1986, ANDY WARHOL showcased his final series of paintings, the "Last Supper" collection, at the Credito-Valtellinese bank in Milan, right across the street from the Church of Santa Maria della Grazie, which houses Leonardo DaVinci's own famous Renaissance era work "The Last Supper" (1498). In his typical fashion, Warhol utilized commercial reproductions of DaVinci's masterpiece to create the works on display. One piece, of particular note, features a close-up of Jesus—taken from a nineteenth-century encyclopedia—sitting at the last supper table and offering bread to the disciples. Immediately next to it is a reproduction of a bodybuilding advertisement, which features a shirtless, muscular, and proud looking man surrounded by the words "Be a Somebody with a Body." This painting plays with ideas surrounding having and being a body, as well as notions of the Eucharist and sacrifice. As Christ offers his body through the institution of communion, and the bodily death that is to come, the body builder finds purpose and value in his own muscular physique. One body is broken; one body is built up. One body returns in resurrection, and the other faces eventual decay and death. While this work reveals Warhol's own struggles with his body, sexuality, and faith, it also reveals the difficulties that the Christian church has had in understanding embodiment, and, in the modern age, what it means to pursue physical fitness.[1] What does it mean, as a person of faith, to have, maintain, and even strengthen one's physical body? What does it mean to "glorify God in your body" (1 Cor 6:20) in a time when bodily perfection is popularly defined by advertising firms and food degradation has led to the worldwide obesity epidemic?

This book will address those questions and many others through theological engagement with sport, though it will pay particular attention to physical fitness as a subcategory of sport.[2] What is lacking though

1. For a more thorough analysis of Warhol's religious art, see Dillenberger, *The Religious Art of Andy Warhol*; Anderson and Dyrness, *Modern Art and the Life of a Culture*.

2. Theology of sport has seen increased attention in recent years, but little has been

is a critical examination of the theological implications and theological intersections of sport and fitness. Where is God in sport and fitness? What value might sport and fitness have for the Christian Church? Is there a good to be found?

My central thesis here is that the pursuit of physical fitness is an integral part of the life of Christian discipleship, and it can serve as cooperation with God's redemptive purposes in creation. This is not to deny the often-destructive impact that sports, fitness, and the diet industry have had, and that will be addressed. What I do wish is to give a theological framework for the life-giving experiences many people have had with sport, fitness, and embodied pursuits. So first, there is a need for definitions.

Physical fitness, in the modern age, is assessed by a number of metrics, including VO_2 max, lactate threshold, heart rate variability, and bodily composition. These are empirical methods that have developed through research with athletes, astronauts, and other personnel for whom it was necessary to be in top physical shape in order to perform specific tasks. I will not be saying much about these metrics, but rather about the pursuit of physical fitness, as it is made up of these and other metrics, and what it means in light of Christian theology to strive for a state of fitness. Physical fitness has obvious overlap with notions of health. A common definition of health is a state of being free from illness or disease. One is healthy if one is not sick.[3] However-

said specifically about physical fitness. The first crucial book looking at the intersection of religion—or we might say religious affections—and sport was Michael Novak's *The Joy of Sports* (1967/1994). Shirl Hoffman, an emeritus professor of kinesiology and a former basketball coach is also recognized as a pioneer in the field, having edited many theologically astute volumes including *Sport and Religion* (1992) and more recently *Good Game* (2010). Lying underneath all discussions of sport and religion is a philosophy and theology of play. Plato and Aristotle both wrote on play, as did Hans-Georg Gadamer more recently in *The Relevance of the Beautiful* (1986). The most seminal work on the subject, especially as a segue into spiritual matters, is Johan Huizinga's *Homo Ludens* (1950), which was followed by Jürgen Moltmann's *Theology of Play* (1972) and Robert K. Johnston's *The Christian at Play* (1984/1997). Johnston's book serves as an excellent source for beginning a theology of sport. No researcher into sport can ignore sport's presence in popular culture. Hoffman's volume *Sport and Religion* contains a number of notable essays that look closely at sport's religion-like exterior and it's role as both a folk religion and a civil religion. As for actual constructive theologies of sport, two recent titles have emerged: Lincoln Harvey's *A Brief Theology of Sport* and Robert Ellis's *The Games People Play*, both of which were published in 2014, although they are not in dialogue with one another. These two works offer vastly different understandings of God's role in sport. The emerging literature on exercise and health often focuses on idolization of the body through fitness regimes, as is seen in William Hoverd's *Working of My Salvation* (2005). Marie Griffith looks at the odd intersection of evangelicalism and dieting fads in *Born Again Bodies* (2004). For a thorough review of literature, see Watson and Parker, *Sport and the Christian Religion*.

3. Foucault, *The Birth of the Clinic*.

ever, since 1948, the World Health Organization has defined health as "a state of complete physical, mental and social well-being and not merely the absence of disease or infirmity."[4] This is a more holistic, and I would argue, agreeable definition that shows the lineage of contemporary understandings of fitness. For my purposes here then, physical fitness will be defined as a state of high physical functioning, where the body is cultivated and honed so that it expresses its full potential, within in the limits by which it was created. This definition locates physical fitness as part of human thriving, flourishing, and well-being—that is, doing well in a particular environment and context.[5] And that is to say that any understanding of physical fitness is highly contextual. The gold medal decathlete has attained a level of fitness that most of the world could never attain, no matter how hard one might strive to do so. To engage theologically with physical fitness then implies asking what it means to pursue fitness in a particular context, and what role fitness might have in God's work in the world.

This book will look at fitness in the context of sport, and selections from the previously-mentioned literature on sport theology.[6] I will define sport as the bureaucratized and competitive form of play that heavily utilizes the human body.[7] Kicking a ball between two people is play. Setting up goals and identifying and universalizing a set of rules around the kicking of a ball, is to create a sport. I will distinguish also between sport and sports: sport is the social phenomenon, as it exists in communities of people, while sports are the individual contests and forms of bureaucratized play. To study the history of sport is to look at how sport has played a role in societal formation, while studying sports history means analyzing scores, records, and historic performances. Asking, "How did the ancient Olympics function within Greek and Roman cultic practices?" is to ask a question about sport. Asking, "Who won the Super Bowl in 1983?" is to ask about sports. Sport

4. World Health Organization. "Basic Documents."

5. It should be noted that "well-being" is an often discussed yet vaguely defined term within health and psychological literature. For a more thoroughly nuanced understanding of the term, see Mehta and Davies, "The Importance of Psychiatry in Public Mental Health"; Dreyer, "Practical Theology and Human Well-Being."

6. The broader concept of well-being, which I will touch on, is usually discussed outside of sport, more often in literature related to health.

7. This definition does not include competition, which is often considered an integral part of sport. For my purposes here, I will not be discussing competition, as sport-related fitness pursuits are less explicitly competitive. For discussion of competition, sport, and the Christian faith, see Stuart Weir, "Competition as Relationship" in Deardorff and White, *Image of God in Human Body*; Hoffman, *Good Game*; Linville, *Theology of Competition and Sport*.

is the preferred term of scholarship, although not all of the sources quoted here will use the term in the same way.

Physical fitness is linked to sport, and, I argue, can be analyzed as a subset of sport, in conversation with larger dialogues on the topic. How is this the case? Let me offer some examples. Two friends are out in the hills of Griffith Park in Los Angeles, riding their high-end, carbon fiber road bicycles. They are both arguably engaging in the sport of cycling, the exact same sport that is featured every year in the Tour de France. They both pay close attention to their speed, heart rate, cadence, and distance travelled, as they both hope to chart their improvement as cyclists. Neither of these men will ever compete in the Tour de France, nor are they anywhere near capable of becoming professional or even sponsored cyclists—they are recreational athletes. One of the friends though has entered a century race (a standard 100 km endurance event), in which he will compete later in the month, and hopes to challenge himself and do well in his age bracket. The other has no desire ever to race, but rather wants to lose some weight, stave off some potential cardiovascular health issues, and improve his overall quality of life. For the latter, cycling is the most enjoyable means for the ends of improved fitness and health. For the man who will race, he needs to improve his fitness, like his lactate threshold and VO_2 max, in order to do well in the race. Fitness plays a role for both men, even as they have different goals. And yet, they engage in the same sport.

Think also of two women in a 24 Hour Fitness gym, lifting weights and exercising on the elliptical machine. One woman hopes to increase her muscle mass and lose fat mass in order to promote health, longevity, and better equip herself to play with her young daughter. She seeks improved health and quality of life. The second woman wants to increase her muscle mass in order to compete in a body-building contest, which requires highly defined and pronounced muscle striations over functional strength. After her workout, the latter takes a number of dietary supplements that are not regulated by the FDA, and when at home, she injects herself with illegal steroids that imbalance her hormones. Her overall health and longevity are of little concern. Before her competition, she will again use the elliptical machine to dehydrate herself, thereby creating greater muscle definition. These two women use the same devices at the gym, yet they have very different goals for fitness and health.

What these examples show is that sport, play, physical fitness, health, and personal life goals are highly interwoven and, in many situations, it is difficult to isolate each element. The recent fitness movement known as

CrossFit has yielded the CrossFit games, where contestants compete at the exercises that make up a CrossFit workout. The games are marketed as "the ultimate proving grounds for the Fittest on Earth."[8] Whereas the soccer player lifts weights and runs laps to increase fitness and become a better soccer player, the CrossFit Games participant has fitness—not a game—as a goal, and participates in a game to demonstrate that fitness. So, these various teloi of sport and fitness have a pull and influence on each other, even when a particular participant might have a goal in one area that diminishes the end of another. In some senses, fitness is for the sake of sport, but it also can be understood as its own entity with its own narrative and teloi, even if the play dimension is often undeveloped.[9] Because of this then, I will be utilizing and analyzing arguments from conversations on sport theology, health and wellness, human thriving, and the fitness industry in order to build a theology of fitness.

To that end, perhaps the most pressing issue, in terms of health and fitness, that the United States and arguably the industrialized world as a whole face today is the global obesity epidemic. It is important in this discussion because it is a crisis of health and it is also the driving force behind many people's physical fitness and recreational sporting pursuits. So, one of the focuses here will be the causes and theological implications of the global obesity epidemic. To best understand it, I will analyze the history of food along with the macro-level phenomena that shape and impact the human body. This book will focus less on elite or professional athletes (or fitness personalities) and more on recreational and non-professional athletes, that is, those who pursue sport and fitness as a passion and as part of the perceived abundant life. Now, there is certainly a place within theological discussions of sport for analysis of elite athletics. However, the questions at hand here deal with humankind as a whole, and even the nature of being human. Recreational sport provides a better focus for our concerns. Take for example just the sport of swimming. The United States sent forty-nine swimmers—the elite amongst the elite—to the 2016 Olympics.[10] In that same year, 58,000 people were registered with U.S. Masters Swimming, the competitive swimming organization for adult recreational athletes.[11] While they might be heroes and role models, elite athletes do not represent the wide body of people who engage in sport. Therefore, as we move toward

8. "2017 Reebok CrossFit Games Tickets."

9. In recent years weight-lifiting, a fitness endeavor that does not have a play element, has found greater prominence in golf, a sport that is often considered a "lesser" sport. See Matuszewski, "Rory McIlroy's Weightlifting Prompts Fears."

10. USA Swimming, "2016 U.S. Olympic Team Roster."

11. "U.S. Masters Swimming Fact Sheet."

a theology of fitness that takes into account the very nature of our created selves, it is appropriate to focus on recreational athletics, which is pursued by a much larger population. I will however make many references to elite athletes for the sake of illustration.

Now, I should say a bit about what this book is not. It is not a workout or fitness guide for Christians, nor is it a manual for sports and fitness ministries, although there will be some discussion of the latter. This is not a work of ethics, or a recommendation for how athletes should behave. This is a theological work, but while it will touch on the doctrines of creation, eschatology (eternal life and the end times), theological anthropology (what is a human being in relation to God), hamartiology (sin), and soteriology (salvation), it is not a thorough explication of any of these. It will bring in conversations from neuroscience, nutritional science, globalization, psychology, and other fields, but it is not a thorough explication of any of these either. This book, rather, attempts a theology of culture, specifically one that asks how God is at work in the cultural practices of sport and fitness. There are a number of themes that flow throughout this work, but ultimately the arguments here are rooted in the nature of relationship. I am indebted to William Dyrness's work on the Trinity, its internal relationship, and the impact that has on the human relationships. Tending to the body is ultimately a question about tending creation, as the body is part of creation. Dyrness points out that

> If the distinctive work of Christ is to reveal the love of God for creation, that of the Holy Spirit is, through Christ, to perfect creation. As Christ offers up to God the renewed life of God's human creation, so the Holy Spirit bears up the whole created order and moves it toward the perfection to which creation is directed. Resurrection, ascension, and Pentecost are the opening up of relations between God and the creation, and, at the same time, a reaffirmation of its value to God.[12]

The implications of this statement for sport and fitness will be expounded upon in the ensuing chapters. But, at its core, physical fitness is an issue of relationship, within ourselves, between each other, and with God, as we strive toward and cooperate in God's vision for the perfection of creation.[13]

12. Dyrness, *The Earth Is God's*, 15–16.

13. Now, God is working to perfect all of creation, but I am aware of how ideas of perfection and the human body can be highly problematic. The two terms together bring up notions of magazine covers, diet book, and other sources that shape perceptions of what the human body is supposed to look like. Ensuing chapters will go into great detail about the diversity of the human form. So, know here that when I mention the body and God's desire for perfection, this does not equate to the perfection upheld in *Men's Health* or *Shape* magazine.

Chapter 1, "Creation Is Good," will give an overview of the doctrine of creation and how I will be using it throughout this work. I argue that yes, creation is good, and that has tremendous implications for how humankind treats both the natural world and ourselves, our physical bodies. The chapter will pay particular attention to food—its formation and, in modern society, degradation—as an often-unrecognized aspect of creation care. Food is part of God's abundant provision and it is intimately tied to our use of the earth and the formation of our physical bodies. I will also show how humankind's own acts of creation are good, and are part of fulfilling God's mandate for humankind. Overall, God's creation is not to be escaped, even as it is compromised by sin. The project of God rather is to redeem and renew creation.

Chapter 2, "The Body Is Good," will build off of the first chapter and argue that the human body is also part of creation and is therefore good, while still yearning for that time of re-creation. I will look at historic Christian understandings of the body, particularly in relationship to theological anthropology and notions of the soul or spirit. These first two chapters will serve as an entry point into discussions of sport and fitness.

Chapter 3, "The Basics of a Theology of Sport," will give an overview of sport theology and the language and principles that are used in existing literature. I will argue that sport is not a religion, and should not be conceived as a competitor to religion, but rather that sport is an aesthetic endeavor, and that is the place where it finds kinship with religion. I will also analyze two recent entries into the sport and theology literature, looking at how they deal with transcendence. I will argue that sport theology needs to give greater importance to the role of the body, even when dealing with notions of transcendence. Bridging from this then, chapter 4, "Sport Is Good," will make exactly that claim. I will look at the two dominant arguments for why sport is good: the instrumental claim, that it is good because it produces other goods, and the intrinsic claim, that it is good in and of itself. I will contend that neither of these positions fully shows the goodness of sport. Rather, I will argue that sport is good because it has the capacity to bring about human flourishing as part of and cooperation with God's redemptive work in the world.

Chapter 5 contains an analysis of qualitative data from a study conducted with adolescents who ran a marathon through Team World Vision (TWV). TWV recruits adolescents and adults to run marathons as a means of raising money for clean water projects in African countries. These youths engaged in an event that was both sport and fitness related, and was framed in Christian mission and philanthropy. Using sociologist Christian Smith's basic goods of human flourishing, I will show how this sporting endeavor manifested flourishing—including spiritual growth—in the lives of the youth who participated.

In chapter 6, "Groundwork for a Theology of Fitness," I will unearth some historical understandings of exercise, bodily shape, and food, especially as they intersect with issues of morality and virtue. By bringing these to light, and assessing them adequately, I believe it will prepare the way for a more robust and measured theology of physical fitness. Chapter 7 will then engage in that theology of fitness, and look particularly at doctrines of sin and salvation, with special attention on the obesity epidemic.

It is my hope that these seven chapters will show that the human body, a part of God's good creation, should be tended to and appreciated as part of the life of Christian discipleship. This should be done not just for a more pleasant life in the here-and-now, but it should be done as part of the redemptive project of God, part of God's working toward the perfection of all things. I wish too that this work will move the scholarship on sport to recognize the place of fitness, and find a groundwork for the pursuit that so many people find life-giving.

1

Creation Is Good

"The world is charged with the grandeur of God," proclaimed nineteenth-century poet Gerard Manley Hopkins in his poem "God's Grandeur" (1877). Certainly, the snow-capped mountains and endless oceans, in all their beauty, tell of God's goodness. But what of the human form? Or the marathon runner who has set a new personal best? Are those charged with the grandeur of God? One of the enduring criticisms against sport and physical fitness is that they do not matter. Why should one work to strengthen muscles when those very muscles will decay at death? One should focus instead on spiritual or eternal matters. The mountains are beautiful, but the higher spiritual matters alone are truly important, at least for humankind. At the root of this notion though is a misunderstanding of creation, the good world and order that God has made and that God continues to sustain, and eschatology, that is, what will happen to creation—ourselves included—when Christ returns. So, to show that sport and fitness are good, and that they should have a place in the life of Christian discipleship, we need to start at the very beginning, at God's first creative act, when all of the Earth and Heavens came into being. The biblical creation myths tell a great deal about who God is, how God works, and how God sees the world, which by extension informs how we should see the created world. This chapter is by no means a complete examination of the doctrine of creation.[1] Rather, I will highlight the aspects of the doctrine of creation that are necessary to move toward a theology of sport and fitness. In this chapter I will argue that creation is good. I will give a brief overview of the theological imperative for creation care (more commonly known outside of theological conversations as environmentalism), and I will give special attention to one often-overlooked aspect: food, which is an important component in the obesity epidemic and people's understandings of fitness. I will show how food, including its production and consumption,

1. For that, see Gunton, *The Triune Creator*.

are integral parts of creation care. I will also elaborate on another sense of the goodness of creation, that is, how humankind's own creating activity is also good and pleasing to God.

Being Created

Throughout the creation narrative of Genesis 1, God creates and declares that these creations, including light and dark, the heavens and the earth, all the animals—even the sea monsters—are good (טוֹב). And after creating humankind, God looks at everything and declares it all *very* good (טוֹב מְאֹד). These works of God's hands, created in freedom and love for divine purposes, are seen as pleasing, fair, worthwhile, and meaningful. This is an important distinction to make whenever discussing the doctrine of creation and its implications for aesthetics, culture, and human activity. God saw creation as good, and God treats it as good. The seven days of creation also show the orderliness of God's work, and that God has formed the earth with an order. At the most basic level, this order includes God, at the foremost authority over all, and the earth and all of its creatures. One is not the other: God is not creation and the creation is not God.

Creation though, because it exists for divine purposes and was created good, raises the possibility of a source and end of the created order, which transcends this order. Creation implies that there is something beyond it, something bigger, which the believer knows as God. Now, I want to give some definition to this term transcendence, as it is a difficult word that often gets used vaguely, especially when speaking of human achievement and sport.[2] In a generic sense, transcendence is anything beyond human understanding. Douglas Cowan states that transcendence "put simply, [is] the search for something beyond ourselves, the belief that outside the boundaries of everyday living something greater exists."[3] Filmmaker Paul Schrader notes the transcendent "is beyond normal sense experience," which means "that which it transcends is, by definition, the immanent."[4] So there are two spheres: the immanent and the transcendent. One is not the other, and both are defined by not being the other. As James Faulconer puts it, "It must be the case that certain 'realities' . . . withdraw from all

2. See Cronin, "Things That Made Kobe Bryant;" Murphy and White, *In the Zone*. The former uses the word transcendent to refer to Bryant's great achievements. The latter gives accounts of athletes experiencing extra sensory perception and out-of-body experiences.

3. Cowan, *Sacred Space*, 11.

4. Schrader, *Transcendental Style in Film*, 5.

presence, that they be given only in this withdrawal."[5] Adam B. Seligman notes that "the most 'not ourselves' that we can conceive is the transcendent. For transcendence is the most radical form of heteronomy, with heteronomy understood as subject to the authority of another, to an external law."[6] In short, the transcendent is beyond full human comprehension, and is beyond the authority of the immanent.[7]

All of this is to say that for our purposes here, I will be defining the transcendent as that which is and of God. God is transcendent and exists beyond the limits of creation, which is the immanent. In Paul's terms, God is "King of the ages, immortal, invisible, the only God" (1 Tim 1:17). Following then is the traditional Reformed understanding, particularly as explicated by Karl Barth: "God [is] the pure and absolute boundary and beginning of all that we are and have and do; God, who is distinguished qualitatively from men and from everything human, and must never be identified with anything which we name, or experience, or conceive, or worship, as God."[8] Humankind then is created and is a part—although a special part—of God's created order, and is meant to fulfill purposes that God has for this order. No part of humanity exists outside of creation. Everything that makes up humans—our minds, our thoughts, our souls, our feelings, our languages, and our physical bodies—is part of creation. Everything that we interact with, even time, is creation. So, I will be using the term transcendent primarily to refer to the transcendent God, who works in freedom and sovereignty and is not bound by creation.

Now, this touches on issues of revelation: how can the creature know or communicate with the transcendent God? This question is ultimately beyond the scope here.[9] But, what I will affirm is that humankind's understanding of God, our understanding of the transcendent, will always be mediated through creation. That is, even in an experience of direct revelation, God is mediated through language, the physical capacities and limitations of the eyes, ears and brain, and the cultural constructs of the age. Humans, as part of creation, know God through the created order. The great mystery of the gospel then is that the transcendent God became human and entered

5. Faulconer, *Transcendence in Philosophy and Religion*, 107.

6. Seligman, *Modernity's Wager*, 10.

7. Faulconer and Seligman are particularly interested in philosophy and law, that is, how does a modern society, which does not necessarily give referent to a transcendent God, build a law which is recognized as transcending the whims of individuals, and will be treated as authoritative?

8. Barth, *The Epistle to the Romans*, 330–31.

9. For some contemporary answers to this, see Gill, *Mediated Transcendence*; Johnston, *God's Wider Presence*.

creation as the person of Jesus Christ, both fully human and fully God. After Jesus's ascension, God remains present in creation through the Holy Spirit, revealing God's continued commitment to the good creation, and working to bring it to the perfection for which it is designed. So, affirming God's transcendence does not mean that God is absent from creation (as the Deists believed) but that God is separate in substance, even as God is present and working through substances. And again, affirming God's transcendence means that God works in freedom, as God chooses, as sovereign.

As mentioned before, the term transcendence often arises in conversations about sport. Sport is of course replete with feats that transcend—that is they transcend what was previously thought possible. A new world record in a swimming event transcends all other previous performances, as does a perfect 10 vault done with a previously-unattainable degree of difficulty. So, it is fair to say that there are transcendent moments in sport, but not as they reference a direct experience with the transcendent God, or break out of creation into the transcendent realm.[10] God works in sovereignty and humankind does not on its own volition pass beyond the created order without God's active choice for such. I would argue though that those transcendent moments in sport are in fact instances of joy, thankfulness, and appreciation, that echo or point toward the higher transcendence of God.[11] They are moments when we see the possibilities that lie within humankind, what humankind can be. Going forward then, I will differentiate between those experiences that transcend previous performance, yet stay well within creation, and those experiences that are encounters with the transcendent God, who exists beyond creation.

Note here though that even as humankind is part of creation, God sets humanity apart as distinct from all other creatures. Even as humankind is part of creation, God has made us special within creation:

> So God created humankind in his image, in the image of God he created them; male and female he created them. God blessed them, and God said to them, "Be fruitful and multiply, and fill the earth and subdue it; and have dominion over the fish of the

10. See Watson and Parker, "The Mystical and Sublime in Extreme Sports." They state that, "As to whether extreme sport experience provides access to the mystical realms of the Holy that Rudolph Otto, St Paul, Jonathan Edwards and St John of the Cross refer to, our answer is an emphatic no. That said, we wish clearly to articulate our endorsement of sports such as mountaineering, surfing and snowboarding. Within a balanced theology of leisure, they can be seen as forms of deep play, an avenue to well-being and growth, even spiritual expression in an aesthetic, creative sense that provides opportunities for meaningful, therapeutic and exhilarating wilderness experience."

11. For a philosophical and non-theological take on the thankfulness and joy that sport elicits, see Gumbrecht, *In Praise of Athletic Beauty*.

> sea and over the birds of the air and over every living thing that moves upon the earth." (Gen 1:27–28)

Humankind, as created in the image of God (commonly referenced with the Latin term *imago Dei*), has both a special relationship with God, by being the only creature to bear God's image, and because of that, humanity has a unique responsibility to tend and steward the rest of creation. Humankind, even its specialness, is rooted in the physical world, in God's good creation.

Now, the biblical witness makes it clear that humankind has difficulty accepting its place in creation. In Genesis 3, part of the very first temptation is to be "like God," that is, transcendent: "But the serpent said to the woman, 'You will not die; for God knows that when you eat of [the forbidden fruit] your eyes will be opened, and you will be like God, knowing good and evil'" (Gen 3:4–5). The serpent offers the opportunity to be equal to God, at least in terms of knowledge. Eve is tempted to step beyond her place in God's good creation. Later, after the Exodus, as God instructs the Israelites on proper worship, the command against idolatry again highlights the separation between the immanent and the transcendent. God declares, "You shall have no other gods before me. You shall not make for yourself an idol, whether in the form of anything that is in heaven above, or that is on the earth beneath, or that is in the water under the earth" (Exod 20:3–4). The Israelites, members of creation, are not to worship creation. Proper worship is pointed only toward the transcendent.

This leads to the understanding of sin that I will be using in this work. William Dyrness notes, "that the human creatures sin by violating the relationships into which they have been introduced and misusing the agency they have been given."[12] Adam and Eve attempted to step out of their place in creation; the Israelites who made the golden calf attempted to lift up a part of creation and declare it as God. Adam and Eve tried to be like God and the Israelites tried to define and control God. Both groups violated the order of the relationship in which they had been created. Sin corrupted their relationships with one another and with the rest of creation. Lovingly endowed with agency by God, they misused that gift for selfish ends. The ramification of sin then, as Cornelius Plantinga puts it, is that life in the world "is not the way it's supposed to be," as sin "saws against the grain of the universe . . . it doesn't fit the design for shalom."[13] Sin distorts God's vision for holistic well-being and human thriving.

12. Dyrness, *The Earth Is God's*, 41.

13. Plantinga, *Not the Way It's Supposed to Be*, 114. In the quoted passage, he is speaking specifically of murder, an act that any moral framework will find as reprehensible.

Now, it's important to note that the existence of sin does not deny or override the implicit goodness of God's creation. God still sees the creation, humankind included, as good. As Colin Gunton states, "In affirming that the creation, because it is the work and gift of God, is good, it is necessary to conclude that evil—in so far as we are sure that we know what that is—is not intrinsic to the creation, but some corruption of, or invasion into, that which is essentially good."[14] Relationships are still there, although disordered; desire is there and is good, although it too becomes disordered. Sin is the disordering of that good creation, the rejection of its goodness, and the movement toward that which is limited, toward death. Ensuing chapters will look particularly at the relationality of humankind, and how current health dilemmas stem from a violation of relationship. God gave humankind the ability to do and to make, to exercise agency. Under sin, that agency is misused, and instead of bearing life, it bears death.

Creation and Eschatology

The Christian tradition has, at many times, fought against heresies and other neighboring faiths that deny the goodness of creation. The Gnostics taught that the material world was evil and inferior to the spiritual world. Early church father Tertullian, in one interesting instance, countered the Gnostics by analyzing the role of the scorpion in God's good creation.[15] Augustine rallied against Manichaeism and its dualistic cosmology of light against dark. The medieval Cathars taught that the God of the Old Testament, the creator God, was in fact Satan, having created the evil physical world—the God of the New Testament, the creator of the spiritual, non-material realm, was superior. Pope Innocent III however brought Catharism to a violent end with the Albigensian Crusade.[16]

A proper doctrine of creation— one that affirms the goodness of what God has made—by extension then, impacts eschatology, namely, issues over the eternal fate of humankind and the destination of a person at death. The question then is whether the hope of the Christian faith and eternal life is one of removal from the created order (as was practiced by the heretical groups named above), or whether there is a hope for something to be done with this created order, even as it is mired in sin. I will be advocating here for the latter. The hope of the Christian faith is not an escape from the physical world, or an escape from creation and the material life. Current folk

14. Gunton, *The Triune Creator*, 202–3.

15. See "Antidote for the Scorpion's Sting (Scorpiace)" in Dunn, *Tertullian*.

16. Stoyanov, *The Other God*.

eschatologies, particularly in the evangelical tradition, focus on the escape of the soul and its eternal existence in another realm, ostensibly the transcendent realm of God.[17] This is certainly affirmed every year as Christians sing the classic carol "Away in a Manger": "I love thee Lord Jesus, look down from the sky . . . and fit us for heaven to live with thee there." I will say more about this escapist eschatology in chapter 2, but what is important here is that the doctrine of creation affirms both the goodness of creation and the goodness of humankind's place in creation, both now and in eternity. We need not escape. That is, we need not believe in the destruction of creation or our removal from creation in order to conceive of a pleasing eternal life. As the biblical witness affirms, eternal life is found in resurrection, as evidenced by Jesus. And this resurrection extends into the re-creation and the flourishing of all of creation. The hope of the Christian is for a new, resurrected, embodied life in the New Earth (Rev 21), where humans don't move to God's home, but "the home of God is among mortals" (verse 3).

Bridging off of this though, one does need to take into account the post-Enlightenment notions of transcendence and how this impacts eschatology today. As Seligman points out, "Modernity as a civilizational project is predicated on the wager that transcendence can be represented as no more than transcendental reason yet still maintain its authoritative nature and sacred aura: Immanuel Kant's 'starry heavens above and moral law within' or the 'self-evident' truths of the Declaration of Independence being this benchmark of modernity."[18] Humankind need only look inward to find value and authority. In Charles Taylor's terms, Enlightenment-driven secularity has led to "a new context in which all search and questioning about the moral and spiritual must proceed. The main feature of this new context is that it puts an end to the naive acknowledgment of the transcendent, or of goals or claims which go beyond human flourishing."[19] That is,

17. I borrow the term folk theology from Grenz and Olson, *Who Needs Theology?* They define folk theology as "a kind of theology that rejects critical reflection and enthusiastically embraces simplistic acceptance of an informal tradition of beliefs and practices composed mainly of clichés and legends" (loc. 208–9, Kindle edition). Also, see chapter 3, "Is Christianity to Blame: The Ecological Complaint Against Christianity" in Bouma-Prediger, *For the Beauty of the Earth.* Bouma-Prediger gives an excellent exegesis of 1 Thessalonians 4 and the popular notion of the rapture, which seems to indicate a destruction of the Earth by God. Rather, he claims, "When Paul writes in 1 Thessalonians 4 that we—the living and the dead—will meet the Lord in the air, this does not refer to some rapture. It refers, rather, to those in Christ joining the royal procession of Jesus the king coming to reign on a renewed and renovated earth," (loc. 150, Kindle edition).

18. Seligman, *Modernity's Wager*, 29.

19. Taylor, *A Secular Age*, 21.

secularity has led to an age where human progress, human good, needs no reference to a transcendent being, but can be defined purely in terms of immanent human flourishing. However, for the Christian believer, according to Taylor, "the account of the place of fullness requires reference to God, that is, to something beyond human life and/or nature."[20] So then, the question is, does an eschatology that affirms the goodness of creation and eternity's rootedness in creation simply affirm the secular notion that life is nothing more than human flourishing? I would argue no. Taylor's notion that for the believer, fullness must reference something beyond human life and/or nature, is true, in part. The life of faith must always make reference to the one transcendent God, but that does not deny flourishing within creation. Rather, the goodness of creation is theologically grounded in God, in that God made it, redeemed it in Christ, and is busy restoring it by the Spirit. So, the flourishing of creation is in fact only made possible by God. Flourishing is ultimately a reference to God and God's good ends. The purposes of God, and therefore the purposes of humankind, are in fact tied to and connected to nature, or more broadly, creation. Where this leads us then is to the creation-minded purposes of God. Human fullness is not about self-transcendence, but rather self and community-fulfillment toward that which God intended creation. And as those created in the *imago Dei*, humanity has a special role in creation and God's purposes for it. Dyrness makes it clear, stating,

> Created from the dust as part of the organic life of creation, humans are also called to responsibility for creation before the Creator . . . For humans carry out this tending and keeping from within the order, not from outside of it. Their leadership will in its human way reflect God's own non-coercive servant-like presence, working to bring creation to its highest end, as a vehicle for God's glory. Just as God both dwells within creation and is also sovereign over it, so the human creature has a special role both within and over creation, even if he or she does not constitute the final purpose for creation. That role is to be responsive to the call of the Creator, to work to bring out of creation the goodness the creator has hidden there.[21]

And therein lies the key to a contemporary eschatology that affirms the goodness of creation, the transcendence of God, and humankind's rootedness in creation. We are working not to find our place outside of creation, but to find the fullness of our place within creation. This is human

20. Taylor, *A Secular Age*, 8.

21. Dyrness, *The Earth Is God's*, 127.

flourishing, but it is not just human flourishing. It is human flourishing as designed by God, rooted in and springing from God's good creation and the work of redemption being done there. It is flourishing that does the difficult work of finding, underneath the layers of sin and corruption, the goodness that exists in creation. The project of God is not about the destruction of the world, but rather its redemption and renewal, about retrieving what God originally intended. As Dyrness continues, "The work of reconciliation, which is put on display in the resurrection, involves a perfecting, not the denial, of bodily life in this world . . . Christ died not to make us angels, but to make us human."[22] And so we are starting to see here how this relates to sport and fitness: the physical life, here in the created order, is a good life. It is not one that requires escape. Maintaining and honing our physical selves just might be concordant with God's ends on earth.

Humankind's Contemporary Role in Creation

God's creation is good, and should be treated as such. Yet, humankind has reached a unique place in history, in that we can now see the ecological effect that our past actions and current actions have had in damaging creation. We are in a place where decisive changes will be needed, should we hope to stave off future ecological disaster. Steve Bouma-Prediger makes it clear: from a theological point of view that affirms the goodness of creation, "authentic Christian faith includes care for the earth. Earthkeeping is integral to Christian discipleship."[23] The Christian's role in creation care at this point is well established, especially in mainline theological conversations. What I hope to highlight here is one category that relates particularly to sport and fitness: food. Food and its impact on the body will be discussed in chapters 6 and 7, especially as food relates to obesity and health, but I want to raise it here as an issue of creation care.

To begin, all food that humans eat comes from the earth, so food and its production is part of the relationship that humankind has with the created order. Food—second only to perhaps the air we breathe—is the most immediate and ever-present means by which human life is supported by and engaged with creation. Humans need food to live, and that food comes from the creation. There is, in a sense, a covenantal relationship: the way we care for the land impacts the quality of our food, which then impacts the health of our bodies. But if we take care of the land, it will take care of us.[24]

22. Dyrness, *The Earth Is God's*, 22.

23. Bouma-Prediger, *For the Beauty of the Earth*, loc. 150, Kindle.

24. Dyrness, *The Earth Is God's*, 126–27.

Again, there is an order to creation. Since the advent of mechanized food production, citizens of industrialized countries, particularly city dwellers, have come to live at a greater distance from food sources.[25] In other words, we live disconnected from the land, a point that Wendell Berry makes very clear in his 1978 essay "The Body and the Earth." He states that "the most dangerous tendency in modern society . . . [is the] severance, once and for all, of the umbilical cord fastening us to the wilderness or the Creation. The threat is not only in the totalitarian desire for absolute control. It lies in the willingness to ignore an essential paradox: the natural forces that so threaten us are the same forces that preserve and renew us."[26] This power and comfort-driven disconnect from the land, this alienation from the sources of our food, heightens our role as consumers over and against caretakers or stewards. Berry argues that there is a problem in the

> extreme oversimplification of the relation between the body and its food. By regarding [the body] as merely a consumer of food, we reduce the function of the body to that of a conduit which channels the nutrients of the earth from the supermarket to the sewer. Or we make it a little factory that transforms fertility into pollution—to the enormous profit of "agribusiness" and to the impoverishment of the earth.[27]

Those who partakes in the modern industrial diet eat like a consumer, disconnected from the land and its yields. This disconnect fosters an environment of overproduction, overconsumption, and eventual obesity and illness (which will be discussed at length in chapter 6). Apart from the land, apart from the wider creation and our place in it, we become ill. This view, that personal health and humanity's treatment of the environment are linked, has gained increased attention, particularly in terms of overconsumption of food and the resultant obesity epidemic. Environmental degradation—like that which leads to climate change—and degradation of the physical body intertwine with one another. Scholars reason that

> tackling obesity and tackling climate change can both be characterised as "ecological" in form and share a number of similar underlying drivers and characteristics. Both have been years in the making, both involve the interplay between similar factors—overuse of energy derived from fossil fuels and underutilisation of human energy, overproduction and waste, and lack

25. For a thorough explanation of the history of industrialized food, see Winson, *The Industrial Diet*; Pollan, *The Omnivore's Dilemma*.

26. Berry and Wirzba, *The Art of the Commonplace*, 124–25.

27. Berry and Wirzba, *The Art of the Commonplace*, 130.

> of sustainability—and both, in public policy terms, are insufficiently recognised and require long term framework of action, implying a thorough redirection of society.[28]

All of this is to say that as the world tackles issues of health and environmental degradation, the two arenas should be seen in conversation with one another. Abuse of the environment leads to illness in the body. There is a relationship between the overarching health of creation and the specific health of humanity.

What this then leads to is the necessity of a theology of food, particularly its production and consumption as an aspect of creation care.[29] Discussions of food have never been absent from Christian theology, though. The ancient Christian ascetic tradition, while diverse, did give great attention to food. Desert fathers were lauded for eating very small amounts, and while their food selections were not any different from those of their nearby communities, they showed their spiritual fortitude by choosing not to eat.[30] But these decisions had nothing to do with environmental care or maintaining a trim figure. Rather, they stemmed from a view of food as a gateway into the desires of the former life. Evagrius of Pontus, in his treatise to Eulogios, put gluttony at the top of his list of vices, as it "suggests to the monk the quick abandonment of his asceticism."[31] Basil of Caesarea's rule though, compiled around 350 CE, stressed not denial of food but rather simplicity of diet.

> We ought to choose for our own use whatever is more easily and cheaply obtained in each locality and available for common use and bring in from a distance only those things which are more necessary for life, such as oil and the like or if something is appropriate for the necessary relief of the sick—yet even this only if it can be obtained without fuss and disturbance and distraction.[32]

This platform of simplicity and harmony with the surrounding environment sounds incredibly similar to contemporary food activists and those who stress "eating local."

Medieval Scholastics debated the impact and role food had on the physical body. Hugh of St Victor, Gilbert of Poitiers and Peter Lombard

28. Rayner et al., "Why Are We Fat?," 4.

29. For a thorough theology of food, see Wirzba, *Food and Faith*.

30. Grumett and Muers, *Theology on the Menu*, 5.

31. Grumett and Muers, *Theology on the Menu*, 10–11; Corrigan, *Evagrius and Gregory*.

32. Silvas, *The Asketikon of St Basil the Great*, 215.

all believed that food, when ingested, was not assimilated into the "truth of human nature." Growth of the body came about by a quasi-miraculous process based on multiplication of the original seminal material. Eaten food was simply expunged as spittle and other fluids. Under this belief, it makes sense then that a desert mystic could survive or even thrive without significant amounts of food. Food does not shape life. This view came under the scrutiny of Thomas Aquinas, who argued instead for an "assimilationist" view of food, in that the body is in fact dependent on food for growth and nourishment.[33] This view eventually won out, but it did not lead to a greater stress on the role of food in the Christian life. Rather, as David Grumett and Rachel Muers argue, Aquinas's work

> directed theological attention away from both food and the body towards an understanding of human identity as abstract and spiritual. This scholastic idea of the spiritual soul emerged in the context of discussions about food and eating, and against a background of shifts in Christian dietary practice. These practical origins were soon forgotten, however, as the abstractions generated from theological reflection on material activities developed increasing complexity and coherence in isolation from the practical concerns that had originally produced them. Theologians less frequently engaged medical authorities and those in the other natural sciences. Questions of diet, which pertained to the mutable physical body, were increasingly secularized.[34]

This is to say that when food became associated with the physical body, which of course it is, it exited theological conversation and became secularized. This, I would argue, persists today.

So, what is needed is a greater sense of the interdependencies of the created order. Humankind, a part of the created order, eats food produced by that order. When humankind neglects its responsibilities for proper stewardship of the earth, in particular the stewardship of its food production, then humankind becomes ill.[35] Grummet and Muers put this well, asking,

> Can alternative Christian food practices be identified which express and inculcate hope for the renewal and transformation of embodied life and for just and sustainable relationships? The practice of giving thanks to God for food expresses not only the goodness of creation as gift but the hope for a way

33. For a lengthy discussion of this debate, see Reynolds, *Food and the Body*.

34. Grumett and Muers, *Theology on the Menu*, 52.

35. Norman Wirzba even argues that industrialized food production is idolatrous. See Wirzba, *Food and Faith*.

> of living and eating which would properly honour creation. Eating what would now be described as sustainable food, as in the Rule of Basil, and fasting in order to reflect and live out a vision of social and ecological peace, can also be seen as a sign of goodness and hope.[36]

As members of creation, given a special relationship and responsibility, humankind must look particularly at food and its production, as it is an aspect of wider creation care. Neglect of God's gift has yielded harm to our physical bodies, showing just how interconnected humankind is within creation.

In summary, humankind is created and is part of God's good creation. Humankind though, unlike all other creatures, was created with a special relationship to God and a special responsibility. We are the stewards, the caretakers, of God's work. Miroslav Volf nicely notes that creation care is rooted in relationship.

> Now think of the world as a gift—the entirety of it and all individual things in it . . . To think of a gift, you must, of course, think of a giver. That would be God, the creator and sustainer of worlds . . . And then there is you, the recipient. We name a giver (God), a recipient (you), and a gift (the world). A gift is not the object given as such. Little trinkets on the shelves of gift stores are not gifts; they become gifts when somebody gives them to somebody else. In other words, gifts are relations. If the world is a gift, then all things to which you relate—and may to which you don't—are also God's relation to you.[37]

Creation care is not just about avoiding melting ice caps or saving polar bears (although those are important things). Creation care, at its core, is about living out a relationship with God and a relationship with one another. Creation is a gift from God, and therefore our abuse of it—whether through pollution or unhealthy food production— is a denigration of that gift and a reflection of a poor relationship. In further chapters, we will look particularly what this means for our bodies and our physical beings

Humankind's Own Creative Activity

I want to make a slight turn here and look at another aspect of the goodness of creation, that is, how it is good for humankind to create, further utilizing God's creation. God is at work in the project of redeeming all of creation,

36. Grumett and Muers, *Theology on the Menu*, 139.
37. Volf, *Flourishing*, 204.

humankind included, and moving it toward that perfected time in the New Earth. That is the "not yet" of our eschatological hope. It is to come, and we live with it in sight. At creation though, God gave numerous instructions to humankind: to be fruitful and multiply, fill and subdue the earth, and have dominion over all that lives on the earth (Gen 1:28), and to till and keep the garden (Gen 2:15). These are the mandates of creation, or we might say creating, that God has placed on humankind. For the Christian believer then, these are seen in harmony with Jesus's instructions to be "salt of the Earth," (Matt 5:13), to bring about God's glory through our activities in creation. This is the "already" of our eschatological hope. It is what humankind, and particularly those of the Christian community, is already supposed to be doing, here in this time before Christ's return.[38] All of this means that humankind has something to do. It has instructions from God. We do not just sit and relax, or hide, or keep to ourselves until God fulfills God's promises, as Paul warns against in 2 Thessalonians 3. We have a calling. What we make and do then, in the broadest sense, is called culture. Culture "is what we make of creation. Our making is a response to—indeed it engages with—who God is and what God has done and continues to do in creation."[39] We are called to be culture-makers. Being human means being creative.

The act of creating though is not independent of or unimportant to God's ultimate renewal of all things. In fact, it is part of it. The formation of the New Heavens and New Earth does not mean that God will wipe away all that humanity has done. Again, our eschatology is not one of escape or destruction. Rather, in the New Jerusalem, "the kings of the earth will bring their glory into it . . . People will bring into it the glory and the honor of the nations" (Rev 21:24–26).[40] What we make here on Earth, during our time in the "already" as we wait for the "not yet," will in some form be carried over into the next age. As Dyrness states, our lives, here and now, as they are shaped by Christ, "are meant to bring about something altogether fresh: a fellowship reflecting the Trinitarian life of God producing works that will not be lost but brought into the heavenly Kingdom. All human life in the world is meant to find its orientation in the project that God has inaugurated in creation and embodied in Christ."[41] Journalist Andy Crouch echoes this, stating "we will find the new creation furnished with culture. Cultural goods too will be transformed and redeemed, yet they will be recognizably

38. For a more thorough explanation, see Dyrness, *The Earth Is God's*, 72.

39. Dyrness, *The Earth Is God's*, 58.

40. For a thorough analysis of these verses and their impact on culture, see Mouw, *When Kings Come Marching In*.

41. Dyrness, *The Earth Is God's*, 160.

what they were in the old creation—or perhaps more accurately, they will be what they always could have been."[42]

This sense of the eternal permanence of (worthy) cultural goods has a tremendous impact on how the Christian believer engages in culture making. The relevance of this argument for the fine arts is well captured in numerous places.[43] The interest of this project here though is what does this mean for the athlete and more generally, the human body? Certainly Van Gogh's "The Good Samaritan" will be on display in the New Jerusalem, and maybe Delacroix's earlier version as well. But what about the U.S. national record in the 200-yard freestyle swim, which will ostensibly be broken numerous times before Christ's return? Looking again at art, Gunton states, "In so far as art aims at perfection—producing something as good as possible— it aims to anticipate the redemption of things brought about through Christ by God the Holy Spirit."[44] So, I argue, that applies to sport as well, and the perfecting of a particular sport performance. For every person who has made a record performance, he or she has accomplished what is arguably a cultural feat that is in pursuit of perfection and has thereby anticipated the redemption of all things. More will be said about this in ensuing chapters, which will focus on how sports and fitness fit even more into the creational, eschatological, aesthetic, and culture-making system presented above.

Conclusion

I have outlined here the creational theology from which I will be engaging sport and fitness. God has created good, and that includes humankind—which is inextricably part of creation. Humanity's falleness—sin—is displayed through disordered relationships, both with God and with one another, and the improper use of human agency. But the presence of sin does not override the goodness of creation. It does not justify the anti-matter or anti-physicality of past (or current) heresies and the presence of sin does not condone the destruction of the environment. As Hopkins declares, "Nature is never spent . . . because the Holy Ghost over the bent/ World broods with warm breast and with ah! bright wings." In the here and now, we both wait for and participate in God's plans of redemption, which means tending to and stewarding the Earth, as well as engaging in culture making. Humankind has a calling to do, make, and create. As Dyrness says, "if we believe that God is creator of this world and that Christ holds all things

42. Crouch, *Culture Making*, loc. 1978–81, Kindle.

43. See Dyrness, *Poetic Theology*; Fujimura, *Culture Care*; Wolterstorff, *Art in Action*.

44. Gunton, *The Triune Creator*, 234.

together through the ministry of the Holy Spirit, we can insist that God has a stake in what we are making of the world."[45] We can now turn to look more specifically at what this means for the human body.

45. Dyrness, *The Earth Is God's*, 11.

2

The Body Is Good

On August 4, 2013, pastor Chris Towsend of Emmanuel Lutheran Church (ELCA), a congregation of 210 members in Lodi, California, delivered his sermon while power walking on a treadmill. The next week he gave his sermon while riding a stationary bicycle. His goal was to encourage physical fitness in his congregation, as he himself had recently lost a great deal of weight.[1] What's interesting though is that this non-traditional method of homiletic performance in a mainline church made the national news! Why was this sermon series worthy of or even interesting to national news sources? Why was this important? I would argue that he broke an unspoken rule in the Protestant church: while in worship, he brought the congregations' attention to their physical bodies. From a place of spiritual authority, he spoke on bodily matters. In a setting that focuses on the soul and the spirit, he focused on the physical. And all of this serves to highlight that Christians have a difficult and confused relationship with their bodies. Within the Christian tradition, it is difficult to enunciate a clear understanding of the body. Returning again to Dyrness, he points out that Christians, particularly evangelicals,

> have tended to feel that human life as embodied beings, and the created order generally, is somehow less important than the life of the spirit and soul, which, in the Gnostic view, came from God and was meant to be reunited with God. Since the realm of our bodily life is of lesser importance, the theological significance of the body is never subject to serious theological scrutiny.[2]

What I propose to do here is outline some historical theological understandings of the body, paying close attention to John Calvin, and how these understandings are manifested in worship and religious practices. Moving

1. Fishbein, "Pastor Gives Congregation a Workout."
2. Dyrness, *The Earth Is God's*, 3.

forward, I will look particularly at how the Christian notions of embodiment relate to sports and fitness.

The Problem of Dualism

In the 2008 *Doctor Who* episode "Forest of the Dead," the Doctor "rescues" his friend River Song from imminent death by uploading her consciousness into a computer where she can then live forever, free of the embodied world.[3] Underlying this story is the belief that the human person is made up of distinct and possibly separable parts: the mind—or in spiritual terms, the soul—and the physical body. Generally, this understanding of the person is called dualism, and it has a lengthy history in the fields of philosophy,[4] psychology, and even neuroscience,[5] and it is a perennial plot device in Western films.[6] Our interest here though is in how dualism has affected and has been a part of the Christian theological tradition. As I will show, dualism has had a particular impact on eschatology, liturgical practices, social class, and the general treatment of the physical body. The effect of dualism, I will argue, is a denigration of the body and an elevation of that which is non-tangible or purely interior. Dualism is fundamental to what I have referenced previously as an escapist eschatology—that is, the soul, the better part of the human, escapes from the body at death and enters into another realm. This view is ultimately contrary to the goodness of creation.

So how did the understanding of the human person come to be, especially in the church? One can look to ancient Greek dualistic philosophies such as Platonism and Aristotelianism and their impact on early Christian theology. As Frank Bottomley notes,

> The Roman world into which the Church came was decadent in both philosophy and life. The former was increasingly emphasising a dichotomy between body and soul, and abstract thought tended to denigrate the body in order to free the soul

3. *Doctor Who*. "Forest of the Dead."

4. In philosophical language, dualism refers to the existence of two kinds of reality: the material and the immaterial, namely the body and the physical world and the mind or consciousness. In contemporary philosophy, it falls under the category of philosophy of the mind.

5. See Brown and Strawn, *Physical Nature of Christian Life*.

6. Disney's 1959 movie, *The Shaggy Dog*, features a man's consciousness being transferred into a dog's body. *Freaky Friday* features minds being swapped. In the Marvel film *Doctor Strange*, the titular character affords extra time for study as his spiritual "astral" self exits his body and continues to read while his physical body sleeps.

> for the contemplation of higher things on earth and to facilitate its ascent, when disburdened of the body, to the realms above.[7]

In Plato's *Phaedo* (360 BCE), Socrates, on his deathbed, speaks with Simmias, who asks, "Is [death] anything but the separation of soul and body? And being dead is the attainment of this separation; when the soul exists in herself, and is parted from the body and the body is parted from the soul—that is death?" to which Socrates replies, "Exactly: that and nothing else."[8] Death, in the Platonic tradition, means the rending of soul from body, to the benefit of the soul. That body is to be escaped. To be fair though, the anti-embodiment stance explicated by Greek philosophy was the position of the educated class. One need look no further than the embodied nature of many Greek and Roman pagan rites, as well as athletic festivals and coliseum events, to see that the majority of citizens led highly physical lives. I mention this here and will note again how bodily notions and social class are intertwined and are often in conflict throughout history.

The early church had the difficult task of building a new Christian theology that held intellectual credibility and also demarcated itself from pagan religiosity, which perceived as unintellectual, lower class and embodied. Building this theology meant selectively borrowing from the language and methods of Greek philosophy, the "substitute religion for thoughtful aristocrats."[9] Aristotelianism in particular lent the understanding of God as the Unmoved Mover.[10] Elochukwu E. Uzukwu points out that at this time, "God-like immobility or the absence of emotion was preferred to the 'un-disciplined' flexing of the body. Immobility symbolized perfection."[11] That is, contemplation and stillness were preferred over physical engagement or use of the body.

This is not to say that Christian leaders were uncritical of the Greek philosophical tradition or unaware of its dualistic anthropology. For example, the first chapter of Tertullian's (155-240CE) *A Treatise on the Soul* is in fact titled "It is Not to the Philosophers that We Resort for Information About the Soul But to God!" In the treatise he makes direct reference to the *Phaedo* and argues that body and soul are in "conjunction." He does not however deny the existence of both a body and a soul, or that there will be

7. Bottomley, *Attitudes to the Body*, 14.

8. Plato, *Phaedo*, circa 360 BCE. Benjamin Jowett translation, http://classics.mit.edu/Plato/phaedo.html.

9. Bottomley, *Attitudes to the Body*, 2.

10. Found in Book 12 of Aristotle's Metaphysics.

11. Chauvet and Lumbala, *Liturgy and the Body*, 73. He is referring particularly to the early church's condemnation of dance.

a time of separation after death. However, "souls are to receive back at the resurrection the self-same bodies in which they died."[12] So, early Christianity was not anti-body, in the sense that hope of eternal life rested purely in escape from creation. Rather, eternal life would eventually be found in the resurrection at Christ's return. But, Tertullian's view was emblematic of a shifting view of eschatology. Caroline Bynum argues that,

> During the patristic period, millenarian [impending end time] expectation gradually abated. The bodily resurrection hoped for by Jews and Christians in the centuries just before and after the beginning of the Common Era was supposed to occur in a reconstituted universe—a "new heaven and new earth." . . . Such hopes had not disappeared by the fifth century, but few any longer expected the millennial age to come soon and eschatological yearning was increasingly focused on heaven, to which soul might go while the bones still reposed underground . . . by late antiquity Christian theologians held soul to be immortal but defined body as that which falls and must therefore rise again.[13]

So as the Christian community moved further away in time from Christ's resurrection and ascension, the hope for an impending resurrection of the dead moved further back in the Christian imagination. Hope for the resurrection was never abandoned, but other notions of the immediate afterlife developed. There became greater concern for what is known as the "intermediate state," the time between death and the resurrection. This then had an effect on the understanding of the person, or what makes up a person. Bynum continues:

> To put it a little simplistically, the awakened resurrection body *was*, to early Christians, the person; to later theologians it was a component (albeit an essential component) of the person. Early Christians expected the body to rise in a restored earthly paradise, whose revival was imminent. Most late medieval Christians thought resurrection and the coming of the kingdom waited afar off in another space and time.[14]

12. Tertullian, *Ante-Nicene Fathers*.

13. Bynum, *Resurrection of the Body, 200-1336*, 13. I personally would argue that this springs from a pastoral issue that the church has continually dealt with: where are my loved ones after they die? "They have been planted like seeds and will come back to life in the future" is less appealing than, "They have gone to a better place and they are *now* with God." Dualism is then encoded in pastoral language: "Your loved one has *passed on*, and they are in a *better place*."

14. Bynum, *Resurrection of the Body*, 14.

Ancient and medieval Christians never abandoned the hope of resurrection for a purely dualist and escapist eschatology. Rather, they lived with an uneasy alliance between the ascent of the soul and the eventual resurrection, which had an impact on the theological understanding of the human being, and by extension, treatment of the body.

Calvin and the Body

Moving ahead, amongst the Reformers, John Calvin showed a very interesting and complicated understanding of the body that is still largely present in the Reformed tradition (which is my own background). In his *Institutes of the Christian Religion*, first published in 1536, he argues that the belief that "man consists of a soul and a body ought to be beyond controversy," and that the soul is "the immortal yet created essence, which is his nobler part." At death, the soul is "freed from the prison house of the body," and anyone who denies this understanding of the body and soul is "stupidly blundering in this opinion."[15] It would appear here that Calvin is adamantly in line with the tradition of Platonic dualism, as he utilizes Plato's own imagery.[16] The soul is good and the body, a prison, is bad. Twentieth-century theologian T. F. Torrance, in his commentary on Calvin's doctrine of humankind, states that "compared to the body the soul must be regarded as having *something essential* by which it survives the body and is distinguished from it, as that which inhabits or is imprisoned by the body."[17] This implies that the soul is held back by the body, that it is ultimately superior.

However, like his early Christian predecessors, Calvin was not entirely anti-body or anti-physicality. In his discussion of the resurrection, he states that

> it would be utterly absurd that the bodies which God has dedicated to himself as temples (1 Cor 3:16) should fall away into filth without hope of resurrection! . . . What madness is it for that part of man, deemed by the Heavenly Judge worthy of such shining honor, to be by mortal man reduced to dust beyond hope of restoration?[18]

15. Calvin, *Institutes of the Christian Religion*, 184.

16. The body as the "prison house of the soul" is an allusion, although not a quote, from Plato's *Allegory of the Cave*.

17. Torrance, *Calvin's Doctrine of Man.*, 26. Italics in text.

18. Calvin, *Institutes of the Christian Religion*, 998-99.

The body is, in fact, created by God, and it is something special, something that will be preserved by the resurrection. Why would God create it just to destroy it? While Calvin shows a preference for the soul, he does not reject the idea that there is some value in the body, however difficult it might be to find that value. God has some bit of honor for it.

During Calvin's time, it was hotly contested as to where the image of God (*imago Dei*) resides in humankind. Many of his contemporaries took a highly dualist and Platonic (or Neo-Platonic) stance: the image of God is only in the soul. Calvin, however, in his final version of the *Institutes* argues, "Although the primary seat of the divine image was in the mind and heart, or in the soul and its powers . . . there was no part of man, not even the body itself, in which some sparks did not glow."[19] He takes a stance that is less body-denying than other theologians of the time, offering some small glimmer of God's Image even in the body.[20]

What's more, in his personal life, Calvin had ample reason to despise the body. He was constantly in ill health, suffering from stomach problems, migraines, and arthritis. Further, the bubonic plague often reemerged during Calvin's time—it even struck his close friend and colleague Theodore Beza. To a plague victim, the body can certainly feel like a prison house. Contextually then, Calvin shows an unusual accommodation for the body. He certainly holds it in no high esteem, but he is not an outright Platonist. Mary Potter Engel argues therefore that the "meaning of the image of the body as the prison house of the soul has to do not with the evils of matter but the servitude of sin. In many places Calvin joins these two ideas together, the prison house of the soul and the servitude of sin. He is clear that the word body can be used as a synecdoche for the sinful condition of humankind."[21] While the body may not be entirely bad, it is rather the place where sin is bred.

Because then of this assumed connection between sin and the body, Calvin's view of humankind's religious life is highly disembodied. He states that, "Man was made for meditation upon the heavenly life . . . the chief activity of the soul is to aspire thither."[22] The approach to God is not one of physical movement, but rather a mental exercise. Torrance again comments on Calvin and reinforces the disembodiment of the spiritual life, saying that "is why God made man a living soul, not only in the sense in which he has a living body, but in the sense that he has a mind in order

19. Calvin, *Institutes of the Christian Religion*, 188.

20. Van Vliet, *Children of God*, 258–59.

21. Engel, *John Calvin's Perspectival Anthropology*, 179.

22. Calvin, *Institutes of the Christian Religion*, 192.

to meditate on the heavenly life in which he finds the true destiny of his being in the image of God."[23] For Calvin, the quest for God is contemplative and meditative. It resides in the upper body, in the mind and soul. God might not despise the body, but it's certainly not the place from which humankind reaches for God.

Calvin was arguably following the intellectual cultural momentum of his time. In 1530, just prior to the first edition of the *Institutes*, Desiderius Erasmus published *Manners for Children*, a practical guide that gave physical instruction on how to enact the upper-class tenets of Neo-Platonism. The book became incredibly popular throughout Europe and brought about the idea of codified civilized behavior, much of which conflicted with Catholic religious and festival behavior. Edward Muir states that "with the rise of manners the upper body triumphed over the lower body. The reason and restraint represented by the upper body took precedence over the emotions associated with the lower body, both through the spread of self-control and through attempts of church and state to obliterate carnivalesque rituals."[24] The views of the body held within the upper class were becoming codified. Theologically speaking, what was catalyzed at this time, amongst elite church leaders, was a view of the body as a place for sin—the body must be controlled.

Putting his theological precepts into action, in 1547 Calvin banned dancing throughout Geneva. It was, for him, "an incitement to lewdness."[25] Ami Perrin, who was one of those who invited Calvin to come and lead Geneva, was arrested for dancing with his wife at a betrothal party.[26] Again, it should be noted that the Protestant reformers were like the Early Church: just as the first Gentile Christians wanted to demarcate themselves from Roman paganism, Calvin and the other Protestant reformers strove to remove themselves from the perceived corruption of Roman Catholic culture and popular ritual practices, especially those of Carnivale. Overall, Calvin's doctrine of humankind reinforced the dominance of the upper body, further codifying the body ethics of the educated class. What we have seen so far in this brief history is the belief that while the body does play some role in God's ultimate purposes, it is of small consequence for the life now and for any sense of eternal life prior to Christ's return. The physical body is rather the locus of sin. Its use in religious rites should be highly controlled and

23. Torrance, *Calvin's Doctrine of Man*, 31.

24. Muir, *Ritual in Early Modern Europe*, 151.

25. Davies, *Liturgical Dance*, 29.

26. Bottomley, *Attitudes to the Body*, 145. Bottomley however names him as Pierre Ami. To be fair to Calvin, Ami was a member of the Libertine party that opposed Calvin's leadership. Most likely, the arrest was a result of political issues, not just dancing.

moderated. What's more, excessive embodiment, especially as seen in pagan and later Catholic religiosity, is for the low-class and uneducated.

The Body in the Age of Enlightenment —and Slavery

Calvin remarks that "the more anyone endeavors to approach to God, the more he proves himself endowed with reason."[27] This fetishization of the mind, which marked much of the Protestant movement, fed directly into the Age of Enlightenment, further denying the body as a place of spirituality. Bottomley points out that in this time "the human body became an instrument only, a tool . . . The human body was not only an instrument for work, it was also an instrument apt for diabolic utilisation and therefore all its activities and manifestations required strict policing and censorship."[28] This negative view of the body, I argue, is particularly well illustrated in the Protestant Church's view of dance and embodied worship practices. J. G. Davies points out that

> this continuing negative approach to dance on the part of the churches was, as it had been in the patristic age, more a product of Western culture than of Christianity *per se*. This was the period of the Enlightenment with its dogma that the way to truth is exclusively through pure reason. Rene Descartes had prepared for this rationalism with his thesis that *cogito, ergo sum*. Where Plato had divided body and soul, to the detriment of the former and therefore of dance, Descartes divorced body and mind with the apotheosis of the intellect, and the consequent disparagement of the physical.[29]

Through the Enlightenment, the Protestant tradition became mind, reason, and word-heavy. Faith and the intellect were inseparable as faith is primarily transmitted through written texts and creeds. Spirituality is cultivated through contemplation, reasoning, listening, and rigorous control of the body. Dance scholar Maria-Gabriele Wosien sums this up by noting that "with the progressive development of reflection and the intellect, spontaneity diminishes. Worship shifts increasingly from active physical participation—as in dancing—to contemplative looking-on, and towards a conscious meditative internalization which excludes physical activity and even renders

27. Calvin, *Institutes of the Christian Religion*, 193.

28. Bottomley, *Attitudes to the Body*, 145.

29. Davies, *Liturgical Dance*, 33.

it unnecessary."[30] This disembodied faith was then imported into the United States and codified by historic European-rooted denominations.

There is however an alternative vision of the body displayed in the African-rooted culture of America. Between 1620 and 1865, nearly 600,000 African people were forcibly imported into North America as slaves. Having not been traditioned in Western philosophy and religion, they held a very different understanding of the body and movement. Uzukwu states that,

> The African experience of body and gestures displays humans in the universe grasped as a totality. The body is the center of the total manifestation of person in gestures. In gestures (verbal and nonverbal) the self reveals itself, from head to toe, as one complex reality—visible yet invisible; corporeal-incorporeal; part of, but also the center of a complex universe of interaction. The rhythm of interaction in this universe is discovered, re-created, and expressed bodily by humans.[31]

There is a one-ness in the African understanding of the body—it is not dualistic. There is no separation of body and soul. And because of this, the body is not seen as a place of sin, a place of wrongdoing to be controlled—it is not a prison for the soul. Embodied gestures and movements are a vital and integral part of communication, religious or otherwise. Uzukwu states that bodily movement "reveals the person," and therefore bodily engagements, especially dance, feature "prominently in diverse experiences of the human community in its contact with the universe."[32] Put simply, bodily movements are an integral part of African personhood.

African slaves brought this understanding of the body into the United States, and it became present in the slave-led practices of Christianity. The most notable of these practices was the Ring Shout, where slaves would move in a circle, shuffling and stomping their feet and singing praise songs. It was primarily practiced away from white-led religious spaces. Sterling Stuckey states that for slaves,

> in their desperate situation, [highly embodied worship] was their greatest spiritual and political resource, enabling them to recall the traditional African community and to include all Africans in their conception of being African in America . . . Just as they crossed actual boundaries in being brought to America, enough were able to make an imaginative retreat to

30. Wosien, *Sacred Dance*, 30.

31. Uzukwu, *Worship as Body Language*, 10.

32. Uzukwu, *Worship as Body Language*, 73.

> the ancestral home to discover, in the Ring Shout, the ground of cultural oneness.[33]

To the slaves, who were told that their bodies were no longer their own, embodied worship was a means to reclaim some aspect of ownership and personhood. Even while facing potential punishment, slaves danced and, in this way, restored some small bit of spiritual renewal. While many slaves were converted to Christianity—the religion of their owners—their ritual practices of the faith were uniquely African. Author Zora Neal Hurston, writing in the early twentieth century, states that "in fact, the Negro has not been christianized as extensively as is generally believed. The great masses are still standing before their pagan altars and calling old gods by a new name. As evidence of this, note the drum-like rhythm of all Negro spirituals. All Negro-made church music is dance-possible."[34] Hurston might be a bit hyperbolic in arguing that African-American Christianity is simply African paganism by a new name, but she does show that this enactment of the faith owes much to native African culture.[35] Slave Christianity is Christianity expressed through a distinctly African worldview, and an African understanding of the body. Unsurprisingly, white Christians were very hostile to this body-centric form of the faith, and many anti-body criticisms were unleashed: it is sexual, barbaric, and uncivilized. But of the slave conversions that happened, the majority was in the context of the Ring Shout.[36] The faith of the Unmoved Mover, of the Western upper-class tradition, held little appeal for slaves.

After the Revolutionary War, the excitement of democracy moved into the church, and the hegemony of traditional denominations, like the Episcopalians, Congregationalists, and Presbyterians, came into question. Through the two Great Awakenings, members of the working class founded numerous evangelical denominations and organizations that "seemed more authentic and self-evident."[37] Christianity grew among blacks as insurgent religious movements like the Baptists and the Methodists gave slaves and freed blacks the opportunity to create their own faith communities and traditions, which looked and acted very differently from European ones.

33. Defrantz, *Dancing Many Drums*, 44.

34. Hurston, *The Sanctified Church*, 103.

35. In the language of liturgical scholar Anscar Chupungco, Hurston recognizes the process of acculturation, "which is a juxtaposition of two cultures" that "do not go beyond the external forum or enter into the process of mutual assimilation. They do not affect each other's inner structure and organism." Chupungco, *Liturgical Inculturation*, 27.

36. Defrantz, *Dancing Many Drums*, 47.

37. Hatch, *The Democratization of American Christianity*, 34.

And yet, "well into the nineteenth century Episcopalians and Presbyterians were still wringing their hands about their failure to Christianize their own slaves," even after they had routinely denied them the opportunity to live out their faith in an embodied manner.[38]

Over time, these denominations and Christian groups, finding membership primarily in lower-class people, dispersed out into the larger American culture—and the world—taking with them their practices of embodied worship. Today these groups are broadly known as the enthusiast tradition, which includes the global powerhouse Pentecostalism. Liturgical scholar Scott Haldeman states that

> at its roots and in its vitality, all Pentecostal worship remains indebted to African-American liturgical traditions. African-American Pentecostals continue to practice a visible form of slave religion. While adapting to new circumstances in modern, urban America, Pentecostal worship reflects the participatory, ecstatic, and holistic performance styles of the "Invisible Institution" [the slave-led church].[39]

But today, as enthusiast worship, with its embodied and dance-ready forms, has become a powerful force in American and World Christianity—with deep influences on Pentecostal worship practices—it is not purely relegated to the "black church." People of many ethnic backgrounds engage in bodily worship.

This overview of the Enlightenment-era theological tradition and its impact on the body shows that our understanding and utilization of the body, particularly in worship practices, intertwines with notions of class and race. Depreciation of the body is found not only in Christian circles, but in the wider post-Enlightenment culture as well. Rodney Clapp posits, "It seems clear that modern individualism emphasizes the noncontingency and hence the self-determination of the nonphysical, essential self. The body, as well as all other things nonvolitional and merely physical, is nonessential and instrumental, to be directed and used by the deeper, real self."[40] To the modern person—or more specifically, the modern, educated, upper-class person—right thinking comes from the mind, and the true person, that deeper self, resides somewhere unconnected to the body.

38. Hatch, *The Democratization of American Christianity*, 102.

39. Haldeman, *Towards Liturgies That Reconcile*, 42. Haldeman offers an excellent graphic that illustrates the various "streams" of worship styles in the United States and their mutual influence on each other.

40. Clapp, "Tacit Holiness."

The Body Today

This legacy of body-soul dualism, and all its attendant class issues, is apparent today in the mainline American church. In her book *The Worshiping Body*, Presbyterian liturgical scholar Kimberly Bracken Long notes that current worship leaders in American mainline churches "present themselves as people with capable minds and faithful spirits who are utterly detached from the torsos and arms and feet that reside somewhere below their necks."[41] This is a valid and worthwhile critique. But she then lists the tasks involved in a faithful ministry whereby the whole self is utilized, that is, those tasks that are thoroughly embodied. These include: "watching and listening, praying and preaching, baptizing and breaking bread and pouring wine, anointing with oil, laying on hands, moving before and among the people, [and] raising hands in blessing."[42] Those are certainly meaningful bodily movements that are part of mainline worship leadership. But in light of the worship practices of churches in the wider Christian tradition, like the enthusiast churches, it is difficult to argue that these small motions comprise our whole selves. Those on the list that compromise actual movement are brief gestures in an otherwise intellect-heavy form of worship—one that also arguably represents the bodily notions of its middle and upper-class congregants. Long shows how deeply ingrained disembodiment is in the mainline American church. And this disembodiment has had a clear influence on American Christianity's often-apathetic view about physical fitness. We see now why a pastor preaching from a stationary bicycle makes the national news.

Having argued in the previous chapter that creation is good, and that the hope of humankind rests not in escape from creation but rather the redemption of all things, it should be said then that the Christian must resist these notions of disembodiment. As James K. A. Smith points out, "The Christian affirmation of the goodness of creation entails the affirmation of the inherent goodness of materiality and the body in a way that makes embodiment an original, essential, creational aspect of being human."[43] Being human and created by God means being embodied—it means living in a body, dealing with a body, forming, appreciating, and even refining a body. To strive for that which is wholly outside of the body, a consciousness that stands beyond the body, is not to live fully as a created human.

41. Long, *The Worshiping Body*, 12.

42. Long, *The Worshiping Body*, 33.

43. Smith and Olthuis, *Radical Orthodoxy and Reformed Tradition*, 71.

So then, how can the Christian tradition recover an appreciation for the body? From a theological point of view, I would argue that it is necessary to recover a biblical and therefore Jewish theological anthropology, particularly one that reads Paul without Platonist preconceptions. A thorough exegesis of all the biblical texts that reference the body and the soul/spirit is beyond the scope here, but I will offer a few key points that illuminate this discussion.[44] First, let us return again to the creation story, and the birth of Adam: "Then the Lord God formed man from the dust of the ground, and breathed into his nostrils the breath of life [(םיּיַח תָמְשִׁנ); and the man became a living being (הָיַּח שֶׁפֶנ)" (Gen 2:7). This passage is often seen as the place where God gives humankind its soul—that special part that only exists for humanity. The Septuagint translates שֶׁפֶנ (nephesh) as ψυχή (psyche), which in English is often rendered as soul. This is the same word that is translated as soul in English versions of Plato. However, the text previously mentions that the animals also have this special breath of life: "And to every beast of the earth, and to every bird of the air, and to everything that creeps on the earth, everything that has the breath of life (הָיַּח שֶׁפֶנ) . . . " (Gen 1:30). This is to say that if this breath of life is the soul, it's given to animals just as it is given to humans, and it's given as part of creation. It is not in any way the seat of reason and intellect, nor is it that which ascends to heaven at death. Rather, it's something humanity has in common with the other creatures. John Swinton therefore interprets these passages with a greater creational ethic: "Whilst humanity gains its existence from God, the constituent elements of the human body all belong to the world. Human beings are thus seen to be 'as one' with the world . . . the enlivening principle, the soul, which marks out the animate from the inanimate, life from non-life, is given to human beings in precisely the same way as it is given to other creatures."[45] These passages show that the creation of humankind is not about some metaphysical advantage or detachable component given by God. Rather, humans and animals are both enlivened by this breathe of life.[46] Even in this moment, when the first man receives life from God, it is clear that humanity is connected to the earth, that it shares something with the other creatures. Humanity is not distinct or separable from creation and its physicality.

44. See Brown, Murphy, and Malony, *Whatever Happened to the Soul?*; Green, *Body, Soul, and Human Life*; Murphy, *Bodies, Souls, or Spirited Bodies?*; Schnelle, *The Human Condition*; Burns, *Theological Anthropology*; Cortez, *Theological Anthropology Guide for Perplexed*; Schwarz, *The Human Being*.

45. Swinton, *From Bedlam to Shalom*, 27.

46. And it is literally that, the breathing that indicates life. For the ancient person— before CPR, defibrillators, and incubators—breathing meant being alive.

A further word study will reveal the complexities surrounding the body and the soul (as well as spirit), and how different biblical writers use them.[47] But Bottomley sums up well the Jewish understanding of the person, stating that,

> Jewish thought sometimes distinguishes body and soul, but it does not separate them. It neither over-emphasises the body nor despises it, nor does it neglect the soul or cleave it from the body as the essential element of [hu]man[kind]. Both body and soul are essential elements in the constitution of [hu] man[kind] who is the only true image of God . . . Man (sic) is also at a kind of *junction* between God and creation in that he shares both in the natural life of the created order and the supernatural life of God—he is linked to both physical and spiritual in his ground and destiny.[48]

So, yes, humankind is special, but not because it is outside creation. Rather, humankind has a special place within creation. Christ then is the redeemer of all creation, proven by his resurrection in bodily form, which serves as a first-fruits of the eternal life to come. Therefore, when Paul discusses the tension between flesh and spirit (Romans 8, Galatians 5–8), he is not declaring the superiority of spirit or soul over flesh, or that the body is filled with lower and reprehensible urges that are the source of all sin, but rather that the life of redemption, found in Christ, is rooted in that which is eternal, in that which will not die—and the bodies of the redeemed will not die. More will be said on these passages of Paul's in chapter 7.

I would argue then that the human person must be recognized as a unified whole, not a collection of separable parts. Bible scholar Joel Green and theologian Nancey Murphy have approached the concept of the unified person from a scientific perspective. After thorough analysis of current scientific studies on how the brain and the rest of the body interact, and keeping in mind the historic Jewish understanding of the unified body, Murphy concludes, from a theological point of view, that

> we are our bodies—there is no additional metaphysical element such as a mind or soul or spirit . . . [This] "physicalist" position need not deny that we are intelligent, moral, and spiritual. We are, at our best, complex physical organisms, imbued with the legacy of thousands of years of culture, and, most importantly, blown by the Breath of God's Spirit; we are Spirited bodies.[49]

47. See Green, *Body, Soul, and Human Life*.

48. Bottomley, *Attitudes to the Body*, 30.

49. Murphy, *Bodies, Souls, or Spirited Bodies?*, 55.

If the idea of a separable soul, the eternal and perfect soul or mind, is neither scientifically accurate nor biblical, we must conclude that our body is who we are.

So then, if there is no separable part such as the soul, no specific antenna that reaches God, then we meet God as embodied human beings. Our bodies are what we have for approaching God, and God approaches us as we are, in our physical, created selves. In the previous chapter I mentioned that our encounters with the transcendent God will always be mediated through creation, and this includes our bodies. So, if we are our bodies, and we meet God in our bodies, then physical activities are potentially spiritual activities. What affects the body is deeply correlated to our spiritual lives, as it is in the body that we come into contact with God. This might not seem particularly revelatory to a Christian from a traditional Roman Catholic Church, or someone from an enthusiast church—those traditions have always engaged the body. But this is where we begin to see how issues of embodiment are crucial to a theological understanding of sport and fitness. Moving forward, my contention will be that as we utilize all the physical capabilities that our bodies contain, we strengthen this bodily gift that we have from God and we literally strengthen this means by which we have for encountering God—we strengthen our physical and created selves, which impacts the whole person.[50] God works with humanity where humanity is, in this world as created beings. Physicality, and the use, maintenance, and honing of our physicality, is activity connected to God and God's work in the world.

Dealing with Dualism

As I mentioned before, dualistic anthropologies are a running trope in Western films and TV shows. Dualism is entrenched in the Western cultural imagination. The question might be now, if body/soul dualism is neither scientifically nor biblically valid, why does it endure? Since this is a work on sport and fitness, I would like to address this by looking at some occurrences in sport. Athletes, particularly those in endurance sports

50. Again, there are issues of revelation present here that cannot be addressed in the scope of this work. However, there are certain similarities to James K. A. Smith's argument for bodily posture and habitations of the Spirit. Bridging off of Merleau-Ponty's insight that we cannot choose to fall asleep, but only choose to put ourselves into a posture that promotes sleep, Smith argues that "sleep is a gift to be received, not a decision to be made. And yet it is a gift that requires a posture of reception—a kind of active welcome. What if being filled with the Spirit had the same dynamic? . . . What if we need to first adopt a bodily posture in order to become what we are trying to be?" Smith, *Imagining the Kingdom*, loc. 1536–40, Kindle.

like marathon running, long-distance cycling, and triathlon, are particularly prone to framing their experiences in dualistic language. Finishing endurance events is often heralded as a victory of "the will," that part of the person, related to the mind, that is able to push the body—the other part of the person—beyond what it can or should do. I am particularly inspired by Julie Moss, a college student, who at the 1982 Ironman Triathlon World Championship was in the lead of the women's competition going into the last few miles of the marathon run. With just a few hundred yards left, the win in sight, her body shut down and she collapsed on the pavement. Quickly though, she got back on her feet, only to fall again. Walking and then running, she collapsed once more, just feet away from the finish line, just as the second-place runner passed her and took the win. Moss then, with crowds cheering, crawled across the finish line on her hands and knees. Her body had quit but her will—or mind, or spirit, or even soul—had not. ABC's *The Wide World of Sports* was covering the Ironman for the first time that year, and Moss's finish was, for many viewers, a first encounter with triathlon.[51] Her performance solidified the mythology of the sport: It's one of human accomplishment, willpower, and testament to human possibility over the perceived limits of the body. The body can be conquered by the mind and the will. Jef Mallett, author of a memoir about his obsession with triathlon, echoes these sentiments, stating that, "We're still awfully impressed by the guys who come in first, make no mistake . . . But it's the Julie Mosses we relate to."[52] It was Julie Moss's will that got her over the finish line, even as her body gave up.

Are athletic endeavors then proof of dualism, and a counter to the argument for the unified-person which I have been presenting here? I would argue, no, and there is a scientific explanation for Julie Moss's performance and for other perceived battles between the mind and the body. Many exercise scientists subscribe to the theory of the central governor, a fail-safe mechanism in the brain that tells the body to shut down and cease activity as a means for self-preservation and avoidance of death through over-exertion. The central governor, however, is incredibly stingy and conservative, telling the body to stop even when the true point of over-exertion is far away.[53] The trained athlete knows how to ignore the central governor, that is, how to exert the will over the body. But our lived experiences do lead us to believe that we are, as James calls it, "double-minded"

51. Gonzalo de Abreu, *Julie Moss Competing in Triathlon*.

52. Mallett, *Trizophrenia*, 39.

53. "Mind over Matter?" *Runners Connect*, accessed May 30, 2013, https://runnersconnect.net/running-training-articles/central-governor-theory.

(Jas 1:7). Paul laments, "I do not understand what I do. For what I want to do I do not do, but what I hate I do" (Rom 7:15 NIV). Anyone who desires to live justly and make good decisions comes into conflict with their own being. But there is a scientific explanation for this as well. Journalist Jonah Lehrer gives an excellent layman's understanding of the role of the prefrontal cortex, the part of the brain responsible for willpower and wise decision-making. This part of the brain is small and weak in comparison to the rest of the brain, and its influence is easily defused by distractions, hunger, and simple tasks.[54] Hence, people give into temptation even when they know it is wrong. We do not do what we want to do. We are, in a sense, double-minded on a physiological level.

So, I posit, that we affirm that multiple voices, multiple influences, exist in our singular person, but that these influences are all part of the one person. Maurice Merleau-Ponty makes an interesting contribution here, arguing for the "body schema." He pushes against notions that our bodies are driven by our mind (intellectualism) or that our bodies are purely made up of reactive neurons and cells that are determined by our physiology (naturalism), which ultimately makes humans into just really advanced animals. In other words, my mind tells my hand to pick up a ball (intellectualism). But if I pick up that ball and throw it at someone's head, that person will duck without any conscious thought on their part (naturalism). We as humans exist as a hybrid of both of these poles, with the conscious and unconscious working together. A runner's conscious mind says, "I can push through and finish this marathon," while the "voice" of the body, the central governor, says, "Stop!" And yet, this happens within one, unified person. James K.A. Smith adopts this body schema as a way to understand liturgical practice and its place in the Christian tradition and faith formation. Once again looking at God's presence mediated through creation, Smith argues that,

> Our incarnating, accommodating God meets us in and through these creaturely conditions. Just as God's revelation accommodates itself to the hermeneutical conditions of our finitude, so the transforming Spirit of God meets us as the finite creatures of habit we are. The sanctifying Spirit condescends to meet us as narrative, imaginative, ritual animals, giving us practices and liturgies for our sanctification.[55]

Christian faith should be both a process of reflection and thought, but it should also be encoded into our habits, our storied bodies, our ways of being

54. Lehrer, "Blame It on the Brain."

55. Smith, *Imagining the Kingdom*, 849–52.

in the world. Christian faith should, through liturgical practices, engage in the pre-rational part of our being (that same part that catches the ball, or tells the runner to stop). Faith formation can occur through habit formation and ritualization, which help shape and direct all the different "voices" that one might hear within oneself. As Richard Zaner puts it, "my own body is an alien presence, something radically *other* than me yet *mine* most of all."[56] The appearance of dualism, while technically inaccurate, is a facet of lived experience and it is a part of how God created us.

The Resurrected Body

Let us deal with one more obvious element of this conversation: all people will die. That is, all human beings and all of God's creatures will one day expire, their hearts will stop beating, and the breath of life will leave them. Their bodies will decompose and their constituent elements will be infused into other parts of creation. That fact alone should lead to some desire for a disconnect from the body, a hope that there is some part that will survive. Or, rather, one might ask, why should we pay much attention to something that will inevitably expire and fall apart? Why even worry whether or not the body is good if it will die?

In the Christian tradition, the answer is that yes, there will be death, particularly as the result of the compounded sins of humanity, but that God does not end the relationship with creation at the time of a creature's death. God's relationship with creation extends beyond an individual's death. The hope of the Christian then is resurrection, a reconstitution in the physical world, made out of the elements of creation. This hope is certified in Jesus Christ, who was fully a human being, while simultaneously fully God. After a sacrificial death, Jesus was resurrected, brought back to life, not in an ethereal, ghostly, or angelic form, but as a human person. The gospel writers go to great lengths to show that the resurrected Jesus was embodied: Jesus encourages his disciples to touch his resurrected body (Luke 24:39), and he even eats breakfast with them (John 21:9-14). Joel Green states that,

> This is not resurrection understood as escape, but as embrace; in his career we find Jesus embracing the whole of God's work, from creation to exodus to exile and, now, New Exodus, as God's purpose working itself out in the world. Jesus's identity is lodged profoundly in the grand story of God — which, then, can only be grasped in reference to his crucifixion and resurrection. Resurrection is not soul-flight, but the exclamation point and

56. Zaner, "The Alternating Reed," 63.

> essential affirmation that Jesus has placed on display for all to see a life of service, even the service of life-giving death, and that this life carries with it the divine imprimatur, actualizing as it does God's own redemptive project.[57]

It is therefore not escape from creation that marks the culmination of God's project in creation, but the redemption and renewal of creation.

The question might be then, what will my resurrected body look like? What age will I be? If I'm supposed to care about it now, what will it be like in the time to come? Anticipating some of the fitness-related questions to come, will my resurrected body be in top physical form? We see in the gospels and Acts that Jesus's disciples and followers didn't recognize him after the resurrection, at least at first, but that his body still carried the marks of the crucifixion (John 20:26-29). So, there is something different even while there is something continuous. Paul responds to the question, "With what kind of body do they [the resurrected] come," in 1 Corinthians 15. His answer revolves around imperishability, made so by the power of God, serving as a culmination of God's work. The question "what will I look like," is then in error. As noted before, humankind does not exist outside of relationship with creation, and the individual human does not exist apart from relationships with other humans. The better question might be then, "How am I living out my relationships in the world today, with God, the creation, and others, that will impact my resurrected form?" This is to say, our personhood, which will be carried over into the resurrection, is not independent of the rest of creation. As Green puts it, "Our personhood, is inextricably bound up in our physicality, and so is inextricably tied to the cosmos God has created, and in the sum of our life experiences and relationships."[58] The resurrected body is not about a particular physical form of the human person, but rather the human person in relationship with God, others, and creation. So, all of this is to say that just because we will die we should not deny the value of the body. This is because the value of the body is found in its relationality, with God and creation, and that relationship carries on into the next life.

Conclusion

As a pastor, having worked with many people suffering from physical ailments, I have seen firsthand how often people feel alienated from their

57. Green, *Body, Soul, and Human Life*, 169–70.

58. Green, *Body, Soul, and Human Life*, 179.

physical bodies, asking questions like, "Why is my body failing? Why is my body not healing like it should?" and often concluding, "I don't want my body to be me." This is to say, we often live with a perceived estrangement from our bodies, and that is understandable. But denying our creatureliness—that we are part of creation— is not the answer. Dualistic anthropologies are actually damaging and can lead to further alienation from our bodies. Again, the biblical witness affirms the goodness of the physical body, even when suffering, and that the hope God presents is not escape but redemption. John Y. Fenton claims, "Once we can affirm the goodness of our creatureliness, we no longer need the idolatry of the immortal soul . . . If we could lose our desire to be something other than what we are, then the way could open to appreciate what we are as human beings, as creatures of God."[59] Ultimately, the biblical message is one of reconciliation with both God and with ourselves, including our bodies, which often hurt. But if creation is good, which includes our bodies, then living fully into God's purposes means abandoning dualistic anthropology and living as the creatures God created us to be. The way is now open to see how care for the body, in the form of sport and fitness practices, can serve as spiritual exercises that draw us closer to God.

59. Fenton, "Bodily Theology," 136–37.

3

The Basics of a Theology of Sport

From the Olympics, to the weekly golf outing, to the children's t-ball game, sport captivates and enthralls. Few aspects of human culture have been so consistently present throughout history. Sport has a pull on our lives, whether we are participants or spectators, which is often impossible to describe. Literary theorist Hans Ulrich Gumbrecht states that sport is "a phenomenon that manages to paralyze the eyes, something that endlessly attracts, without implying any explanation for its attraction."[1] Yet despite that lack of explanation, millions of people continue to cheer for a team, train to exhaustion, and seek athletic glory. As Philosopher Michael Novak states, with a bit of knowing hyperbole, "Sports are the high point of civilization . . . very few philosophical-religious texts have as clear a ring of truth as a baseball smacked from the fat, true center of a willow bat."[2] It is no wonder then that discussion of sport has entered into religious and theological conversations. The goal of this chapter is to offer the basics for a theology of sport and fitness that progress from and build upon the previously discussed theologies of creation and embodiment. This chapter will offer some of the introductory concepts of sport philosophy and theology. I will also analyze two recent voices in the conversation, Lincoln Harvey and Robert Ellis, looking particularly at their understandings of transcendence and God's place in sport, and offer further reflection on a theology of sport that takes into account the place of the body.

1. Gumbrecht, *In Praise of Athletic Beauty*, 16.

2. Novak, *The Joy of Sports*, 42.

Basic Principles in Philosophy of Sport and Play

First, a clarification of terms. By sports (plural), I mean actual events and contests, such as soccer or swimming. By sport (singular), I mean the cultural phenomenon, the competitive athletic element in society. Sport (singular) is the generally preferred term for academic analysis, but often the two words are used interchangeably, as can be seen in many of the sources quoted below.

Before beginning any discussion of sport, one must first look at play, which serves as the root of sport. In his classic text *Homo Ludens*, Johan Huizinga defines play as

> a free activity standing quite consciously outside "ordinary" life as being "not serious," but at the same time absorbing the player intensely and utterly. It is an activity connected with no material interest, and no profit can be gained by it. It proceeds within its own proper boundaries of time and space according to fixed rules and in an orderly manner.[3]

This category of human behavior, which is often judged as frivolous or unproductive, carries great weight and importance for humanity. Hans-Georg Gadamer states that "play is so elementary a function of human life that culture is quite inconceivable without this element."[4] There are a number of philosophical aspects of play that are important to highlight. First, it transpires in its own place, in a sense, in its own separate world. It is bounded by its own arbitrary but agreed upon rules and boundaries. For example, when a family sits down to play Monopoly, they use the money provided by the game. Real, internationally recognized currency is not used, nor would it be appropriate to do so, based on the rules of the game. And Monopoly money is of course valueless outside of the game. The economy of a game of Monopoly exists only in that game. As Roger Caillois puts it, "Play is essentially a separate occupation, carefully isolated from the rest of life, and generally is engaged in with precise limits of time and place . . . Nothing that takes place outside this ideal frontier is relevant."[5] Play makes its own world.

This leads into a second important point about play: it is autotelic, meaning it has an end only in itself. When the family's game of Monopoly is finished, nothing has been accomplished, no harvest has been reaped, no masterpiece created. The game itself was the only end. As Caillois states, "The game is ruined by the nihilist who denounces the rules as absurd and

3. Huizinga, *Homo Ludens*, 13.
4. Gadamer, *The Relevance of the Beautiful*, 22.
5. Caillois, *Man, Play, and Games*, 6.

conventional, who refuses to play because the game is meaningless. His arguments are irrefutable. The game has no other but an intrinsic meaning."[6] Therefore, for play to happen, all of the participants must "play along," they must agree to the set rules, boundaries, and limitations. They must implicitly agree that the game is an end in itself.

Now, the rational and pragmatic mind might bristle at the idea of autotelicity. Something that is an end in itself cannot be of great value. But, as philosopher Drew Hyland asks, "Are we so mired in a functionalist and utilitarian mentality that we can no longer see any value in an activity apart from its practical consequences?"[7] Gadamer shows that the very essence of beauty, especially in relation to fine arts, also revolves around autotelicity. He states that "we cannot expect any advantage from the beautiful since it serves no purpose. The beautiful fulfills itself in a kind of self-determination and enjoys its own self-representation."[8] There is more to be said about autotelicity and some problems with its place in sport. I will look at those in the next chapter.

So, if play is an important and autotelic cultural act that exists in a parallel, self-contained realm, then sport is the bureaucratized and competitive form of play that heavily utilizes the human body. As Robert Ellis puts it then, "sport is an embodied contest of physical and mental exertion."[9] For example, when two people are throwing a Frisbee on the beach they are playing. When they decide to see how many times they can throw and catch the Frisbee without dropping it, they have created a game out of their play. When the rules of that game expand to include boundaries, time restrictions, and a specific number of players, they are moving toward a sport. When everyone on the beach agrees to the rules of this game, an international governing body is formed to enforce these rules, and rule-abiding competitions are enacted, then, after this process of bureaucratization, there is a sport—this one is of course known as Ultimate [Frisbee]. To make a further distinction, Monopoly is a game, and it requires mental exertion. While it does require some use of the body to move pieces and roll the dice, the body is not a crucial element—intense training of the muscles in the hands and forearms will not yield an advantage in the game—hence, it's a "board game." Now, in football, there is certainly

6. Caillois, *Man, Play, and Games*, 7.

7. Hyland, *Philosophy of Sport*, 29.

8. This is one of the many similarities between play, sport, and art. There is a perennial question in the literature of sport philosophy around whether or not sport is art. I will not delve deeply into that here, but refer the reader to the excellent discussion of the question in Hyland, *Philosophy of Sport*, chapter 5.

9. Ellis, *The Games People Play*, 124.

mental exertion, as players must enact plays and follow the rules, but there is also physical exertion. Proper physical training *will* yield improvement and advantage in the game. So, sport is a contest that requires both mental and physical exertion and training. While sport grows out of play, not all play is sport. Sports generally utilize the body.[10] Notions of physical fitness however further complicate these definitions. Physical fitness benefits the physical and embodied aspect of sport and play. However, pursuit of physical fitness often exists without an element of play. The person on the treadmill is running in place with the goal of a higher lactate threshold. He or she is not running down the field in a soccer game and is not engaging in play. For my purposes here then, I am defining physical fitness as a subset of sport, an activity that can have its own telos while also being interwoven with the telos of a game or an instance of play.

Bridging from the "bounded" aspect of play, it can be said that sport brings us into a direct encounter with our own finitude. For example, a baseball game ends after nine innings, and the whole game must take place within the baseball field. Soccer, basketball, football, and hockey games all end after periods of a determined length, and they also take place in a specific and outlined area. Sport is limited and delineated, and these limitations are an essential part of the play. The winner of the game is determined within the prescribed time limit, and never outside of it. And it's here in this agreed upon limited-ness that participants encounter finitude. Hyland remarks that, "Sport is a strange human invention indeed. For in sport we take our finitude in its various modes and make an explicit theme of it. We constitute our games so as to bring to the forefront those modes of finitude which we usually try to avoid and force us to encounter them head on."[11] Perhaps this is most apparent in combat sports like boxing and mixed martial arts (MMA). The combatants fight until one is no longer conscious, no longer able to perform any action.[12]

Another important aspect of sport is the state of intensity and/or hyper-awareness, often colloquially referred to as "flow" or "being in the zone." Many athletes describe being in the zone as a time of effortlessness,

10. I'm not particularly concerned here with parsing out this definition any further, as it suits my purposes. But there are relevant questions surrounding whether or not darts and horseshoes and other games that are less bureaucratized and less physically intense are in fact sports. I am of the mind to be more open and permissive with the definition. The cyclist in the illustration in the Introduction, who only wants to improve health, is in fact still engaging in the sport of cycling.

11. Hyland, *Philosophy of Sport*, 129.

12. To be fair, boxing and MMA also have time limits, but the contest can end before the prescribed time.

synchronicity, or acute intuition. There is ease in every move, as actions occur on a nearly unconscious level. What exactly occurs when an athlete is in the zone? Gumbrecht, who refers to this state as "focused intensity" says it is when "our physical and emotional capacities are operating close to their maximum. *Focused* intensity encompasses not just the ability to exclude a multiplicity of potential distractions but also a concentrated openness for something unexpected to happen."[13] Hyland also seeks to describe this state, calling it "responsive openness," saying that "one feels especially open, aware, and capable of responding to whatever happens. So it is not literally an experience of being 'unconscious' (though we may describe it as such for lack of a better word), but, if anything, a heightened level of consciousness of a qualitatively different sort."[14] The flow state is where all the faculties work in harmony and one's full potential comes into view—and it is sport that so readily effects this state. As Hyland puts it, "Play and sport are activities which in a particular and explicit way call upon us, not just to be 'normally' responsively open, but to be so in a heightened way."[15] It's here then, in the flow-state, that sport first begins to court the spiritual—in the flow-state, something happens that surprises even those with great self-knowledge. Again, Hyland remarks that "one sees the teamwork, self-discipline, concentration of the athlete in a way which is simply not as manifest for the businessman in his office, or the doctor in her hospital. On this argument, it is not only the physical but also the spiritual qualities which the athletes exhibit that leads us to admire them so."[16] The flow-state has a spiritual aspect. Catholic theologian Patrick Kelly, student of psychologist Mihaly Csikszentmihalyi, who did a thorough ethnography on the topic, shows how the flow state mirrors many human goods applauded in spiritual communities, such as a disconnection from self or "ego-lessness" and autotelic enjoyment.[17] Much more can be said about or drawn from this phenomenon of flow, but I present it here to introduce the beginnings of the spiritual qualities recognized in sport—what's often identified as "transcendence."[18]

13. Gumbrecht, *In Praise of Athletic Beauty*, 52.

14. Hyland, *Philosophy of Sport*, 80.

15. Hyland, *Philosophy of Sport*, 126.

16. Hyland, *Philosophy of Sport*, 27.

17. Csikszentmihalyi, *Flow*."Flow, Sport, and the Spiritual Life," in Parry, Nesti, and Watson, *Theology, Ethics and Transcendence*.

18. It should be noted Nick J. Watson, who looks closely at extreme sports and instances of flow, gives an "emphatic no" to the idea that these instances give an athlete access to the holy, in the sense of the holy as Wholly Other. At root here are really issues of revelation. I bring up flow merely as an entry point to larger discussions of the spiritual leanings of sports. See Nick J. Watson, "Nature and transcendence: The mystical and sublime in extreme sports," in Parry, *Sport and Spirituality*.

A number of scholars, who comment on the intersection of sport and religion, identify sport as an opportunity for transcendence. Craig Detweiler and Barry Taylor state that "fans flock to stadiums for a touch of the divine. Sports unite communities, inspire prayers, and offer transcendence."[19] Michael Novak even argues that "among the godward signs in contemporary life, sports may be the single most powerful manifestation."[20] In chapter 1, I noted that the theology of sport and fitness that will be presented here understands transcendence to refer only to God, who exists as wholly other to creation. Transcendent experiences then are ones that go beyond expectations while still remaining within creation—they show us what we did not think was possible. More will be said later about transcendence and its place in a theology of sport, but it is important first to recognize that in sport there is an element of "getting beyond" normal life.

But where is God in all of this? Certainly, play and sport dance with spiritual themes. Is there something theological to be said here? To begin to answer that I must first address one of the perennial questions that arises when speaking of religion and sport: "Is sport a religion?" For my purposes here, I will argue that no, it is not.[21]

Sport Is Not a Religion

British track and field sprinter Eric Liddell was highly criticized for his refusal to compete in the 100-meter race at the 1926 Summer Olympic Games in Paris. While it was his best event, he chose not to race because the qualifying heat was held on a Sunday. Liddell, a devout Protestant Christian, would not run on the Christian Sabbath. To his credit, he went on to run the 400 meters, an event that was not his best, and win by setting a world record. His story is recorded in the classic film *Chariots of Fire*, and while he is lauded as a hero amongst many Christians, it should be remembered that he was chastised by the media and even the British Parliament. Honoring the Sabbath was not a valid excuse to refrain from running. In 2011, Pakistani-American weightlifter Kulsoom Abdullah was eliminated from American Open qualifications because of her clothing—a full-body covering in compliance with her Muslim faith. Judges said her clothing restricted their view of her elbows, which should not be locked, in accordance with the rules of competitive weightlifting. The

19. Detweiler and Taylor, *A Matrix of Meanings*, 247.

20. Novak, *The Joy of Sports*, 20.

21. There are however arguments that have been made that sport serves not as a traditional institutional religion but rather as a folk or civil religion. For detail on this, see Evans and Herzog, *The Faith of Fifty Million*.

International Weightlifting Federation has since changed their policies to better accommodate full-body coverings.

These are just a few of the many stories where sports and religious practice have collided and caused controversy. Which should take priority? Which is more important? Many religious leaders, particularly youth pastors, can tell stories where youth have had to make decisions between attending important church functions or competing in high-level sporting events. The students' confusion and indecision were matched by their parents' own uncertainty. The level of devotion with which many people now approach sport has led some to wonder if sport has become a religion. Has practicing or watching sports now become a religion of its own? Or have sports even replaced religious devotion, unseating the once dominant force in global culture?

I've already mentioned the various roads by which one might identify divine engagement in sport—the flow state, the necessity of play, and the increased openness. But in a more metaphorical sense, one can see how the sporting life mirrors the religious life. There are high holy days, like Super Bowl Sunday or the NBA draft. There are massive celebratory festivals like the World Cup and the Olympics. There is rigorous ascetic devotion shown in the training regimens of elite athletes, who have to monitor closely their diets, sleeping habits, and non-sporting activities, all of which might separate them from their non-athlete peers. Overall though, there is a love and zeal for sport that is matched by few other human activities. Novak states that sport flows "from a deep natural impulse that is radically religious: an impulse of freedom, respect for ritual limits, a zest for symbolic meaning, and a longing for perfection." He continues "I don't mean that participation in sports, as athlete or fan, makes one a believer in 'God,' under whatever concept, image, experience, or drive to which one attaches the name. Rather, sports drive one in some dark and generic sense 'godward.'"[22] This is a knowingly high estimation of sports, but Novak hits on what many who love sports feel: there's something great there. There's something to be cherished and treasured, cultivated and appreciated, just as there is with religious faith. Historian William J. Baker states that "for all their differences, religion and sport seem to have been made in the image of each other. Both are bathed in myth and sustained by ritual; both reward faith and patience; both thrive on passion tempered with discipline."[23] So then, is it right to call sport a religion, or even a form of religious practice? To answer this, one must look closely at what constitutes a religion.

22. Novak, *The Joy of Sports*, 19–20.

23. Baker, *Playing with God*, 2.

Sociologist Émile Durkheim offers a classic definition of religion that, while highly critiqued, can serve as a starting point. He states that a religion is any "unified system of beliefs and practices relative to sacred things, that is to say things set apart and forbidden—beliefs and practices which unite into one single moral community called a Church, all those who adhere to them."[24] How might this definition work with sports? Take, for example, a baseball game. It could be argued that the codified rules of baseball—the bureaucratized play that forms boundaries— create a unified system of beliefs, as those participating believe that those rules are the best way to play the game. Sacred things might consist of the field, where only the players may go, or the dates of major games, like the World Series. The single moral community might comprise all of the fans who laud, or even worship, the players and events taking place on the field. But even in Durkheim's broad definition, it is difficult to shoehorn baseball into his categories and markers for a religion. There is something bigger missing.

I would argue rather that even though sport and religion look and feel very similar, sport is not a religion, and should not be referred to as such for one main reason: the two have different ends. Joan M. Chandler asks whether or not "people who would consider themselves religious and people who are sports fans expect the object of their devotions to meet the same needs."[25] Does the person who attends the baseball game have the same expectations there as the person who attends church on Sunday morning? It is most likely that they do not. While the baseball fan might find community, camaraderie, and even a sense of purpose at the game, he does not find what Chandler identifies as the key elements to religious life. Religions, even highly divergent religions, offer "detailed explanations of the origin and purpose of the world, clear statements about questions of ultimate concern (what many would call 'the supernatural'), and continuing attempts to explain and cope with the existence of pain."[26] In other words, sport does not tell us where we came from, who we are, where we are going, or how to deal with the difficulties of life. While to many people sports might be of intense concern, sports do not attempt to explore matters of ultimate meaning. Sports don't explain the biggest parts of life, even if they might be an organizing or dominant force in someone's life. It has long been the place of religion to make sense of life's biggest questions, and in that it differentiates itself from sports. To put it doctrinally, sport does not offer an eschatology, much less an understanding of creation.

24. Durkheim, *Elementary Forms of Religious Life*, 62.

25. "Sport is Not a Religion," in Hoffman, *Sport and Religion*,55.

26. "Sport is Not a Religion," in Hoffman, *Sport and Religion*,56.

That being said, there is still some deep relationship between sport and religion, and here, I believe, it is helpful to look at the work of anthropologist Clifford Geertz. He proposed an understanding of culture through the metaphor of "webs of significance."[27] Cultural forms and products, like both sports and religion, exist in an intertwined web of meaning. Philosophers Jeffrey Scholes and Raphael Sassower continue this line of thought, saying that

> we may think of sports and religion as two spiders on the same web. They are different spiders but when one moves on the web, the other is affected by the movement of the thread. And because, according to Geertz, the web is one of cultural significance and meanings, both sports and religion must, at times, utilize the same pathways and channels on the web to get where they are going.[28]

So, we see the kinship of sports and religion because they are made out of the same elements, they travel on the same roads and on the same web of interconnected meanings. But even though they are made out of many of the same elements, they are not the same, primarily because of their functions and their different ends.

It is important, I would argue, to show that sport is not a religion, because to claim otherwise would be to allow for a certain competitiveness. As mentioned in chapter 1, sport can elicit moments of joy and thankfulness that mirror or even speak of a larger frame of being, that is, the transcendent. But, if sport is a religion, it is in competition with the Christian faith. Granted, there are times when a church function is in direct competition with a sporting event, at least in terms of attendance. But to approach sport as a competitor is to buy into what Merold Westphal calls the "hermeneutic of suspicion."[29] In the late eighteenth and early ninteeenth centuries, revivalists, like John Wesley and his Methodist followers, were particularly hostile to sports. As Dominic Erdozain points out, this hostility "reflected the evangelical connection between faith and the emotions and the conviction that Christianity should claim the whole person, body and soul. Christianity was supposed to provide its own pleasures, and this fuelled suspicion of non-Christian activities and amusements."[30] What is apparent here is that sport and the Christian faith clashed on aesthetic terms. It wasn't simply whether or not one was a religion, but rather how both affected the emotions, how

27. Geertz, *The Interpretation Of Cultures*, 5.

28. Scholes and Sassower, *Religion and Sports in American Culture*, 157–62.

29. Westphal, *Suspicion and Faith*, 284.

30. Erdozain, *The Problem of Pleasure*, 69.

both elicited love. Because of this then, I believe it is much more helpful to approach sport and its relationship to religion in terms of aesthetics.

Aesthetics and Sport

Frank Burch Brown defines aesthetics as "all those things employing a medium in such a way that its perceptible form and 'felt' qualities become essential to what is appreciable and meaningful."[31] That is, something aesthetic can be only be understood when one pays attention to how it pulls on feelings, or how it moves and engages people. In 2016 the Chicago Cubs won their first World Series since 1908. It had long been understood that the Cubs were cursed, eternal underdogs and perpetual losers. After the win, 5 million people came out for a parade in downtown Chicago. Quite interestingly, a number of fans found third baseman Kris Bryant's wedding registry online and bought him all of the gifts on the list.[32] That is, fans showed their love to this player in a manner usually reserved for family members and close friends. What I want to argue here is that sport, like religion, is an aesthetic endeavor. The Cubs' World Series win captured the emotions of fans so record numbers of people came out for a parade and some even bought a player wedding gifts. But how further might we see sport as an endeavor with appreciable and meaningful felt qualities?

First, sports are undeniably sensuous—they appeal to our senses. Historian Donald Kyle argues that the allure of sports is "visceral and elemental—more subliminal than cerebral."[33] Jumping off the couch and shouting is not a rational activity. Granted, there is a great deal of mental work to all sports (plays in football, strategy in baseball), but the goal of the participant and the viewer is to experience those great feelings, like the joy of winning, completing a great play or record breaking achievement, or witnessing an amazing, and arguably beautiful, accomplishment. Sport grabs us on that basic, often unexplainable level.

Second, there is the aspect mentioned above, that is found in play, called "responsive openness." Both playing and watching a sport require comportment to the world that is more responsive and aware than other everyday activities. Walking down the street requires focus out ahead, but little focus on other items in the vicinity. The soccer player however needs to have a different comportment and level of awareness. She needs

31. Brown, *Religious Aesthetics*, 22.

32. "Inside Look," NBC Sports. http://vplayer.nbcsports.com/p/BxmELC/chicago_article/select/media/V4CleUAvviaS.

33. Kyle, *Sport and Spectacle in Ancient World*, 340.

to know where the other defenders are at all times, where the ball is, what potential avenues there are for moving toward the goal, and the ways the goalie might choose to defend the goal. The long-distance swimmer must be responsively open to the language of his body, how much energy is being expended, and how much distance remains in the race. The engaged spectator stands in openness to the possibility of witnessing an amazing feat, like a World Series win or a new world record time. She must know the rules and of the game and be looking for great acts as they are accomplished within that bounded area of the game—hitting a ball 450 feet with a bat means very little outside of a baseball game. Sport requires that type of comportment to the world, one of responsive openness. And the same is true of other aesthetic endeavors, particularly art. The artist must be responsively open and in a state of heightened awareness when picking out colors and creating a composition. The art appreciator enjoys a visceral and emotional response to a work of art while also being open to and appreciative of its place within the grander conversation of an artistic movement. As Gumbrecht states, "Athletic experience—and aesthetic experience in general—is not qualitatively different from our experience in other less marked situations. What is different is that our physical and emotional capacities are operating close to their maximum."[34]

There is more that can be said about sport as an aesthetic endeavor.[35] But like religion, sport offers a shared openness that includes feelings of joy and celebration. Both aesthetics and religion offer such experiences, in their own way, and these provide possible openings for God's presence and work. They are both valuable for human flourishing. I would argue then that encountering sport with a hermeneutic of suspicion denies the opportunity to see how God might be working within a cultural medium to bring about God's good ends within creation. Again, God's redemptive work is mediated through creation and culture, and therefore cultural endeavors, like sport, should be approached from a stance of appreciation. Dyrness argues that

> the aesthetic sense is fundamental to humanity. People seek to create beauty, to make something of their lives, not because they are educated or economically privileged, but because they are created to reflect God. Since symbolic practices are fundamental to human flourishing, any project of human betterment will seek to appreciate and celebrate the aesthetic impulse that is already present in the community.[36]

34. Gumbrecht, *In Praise of Athletic Beauty*, 52.

35. Another worthwhile conversation stemming from these points is around whether or not sports can be considered art in Hyland, *Philosophy of Sport*.

36. Dyrness, *Poetic Theology*, 254.

The role of sport in human flourishing will be discussed in detail in the next two chapters. But it has become clear here that sport and its kinship to faith practices is ideally found in aesthetics.

Theologies of Sport

Having outlined the basic principles and language for sport theology and philosophy, we can now begin to ask the theological question, where is God in sport? Theologian Robert K. Johnston argues that there is in fact a possibility for God's presence in play, which, as stated prior, is at the root of sport. Approaching the question from the direction of work's relation to play, he states that, "In a time when work is proving increasingly sterile and defective, could it not be through our play that the serendipity of God's presence might most easily be experienced?"[37] Is Johnston right? Is it here that we find within the intense allure and pull of sport a theological language? To answer this question, I will analyze here two recent theologies of sport, particularly as they deal with transcendence.

Lincoln Harvey, a lecturer in systematic theology at St. Mellitus College in London and an ordained priest in the Church of England, begins his analysis with the question "why have sports been so popular throughout history?" Even when the church has deliberately outlawed public games and sport, Christians have still participated. His argument is that "sport is to do with our true nature. It is to do with who we really are. It is a question of our created *being*."[38] He begins this argument by stressing the autotelicity of sport and play, in that "the game is simply the game. It is radically non-productive, a passing event in which time, energy and skill are invested for no apparent reason. Therefore, playing is a strange economy of gratuitous waste. It is barren. It is *for nothing*."[39] While this sounds like a denigration or even judgment of play, Harvey stresses that autotelicity does not denote meaninglessness. Rather it is an "unnecessary-yet-meaningful activity," and autotelicity "does not devalue it. We do not have to spend time looking for a worthier reason [to play]. We should simply accept that play is what it is: it is radically unnecessary but internally meaningful. It is genuinely free from the serious business of life."[40] As I mentioned previously, play is often seen as frivolous. An activity that does not produce something is not worth

37. Johnston, *The Christian at Play*, 81.

38. Harvey, *A Brief Theology of Sport*, xi. His emphasis.

39. Harvey, *A Brief Theology of Sport*, 68. His emphasis.

40. Harvey, *A Brief Theology of Sport*, 69.

doing. But Harvey argues that autotelicity does not strip play and sport of meaning. Rather, it is meaningful in and of itself.

Building on this, Harvey shows how the autotelicity of sport mirrors the autotelicity of creation. The whole act of creation was unnecessary but meaningful.

> God has not created us as part of some extrinsic economy between rival gods. God did not create us because he had to prove himself to someone who was judging his work. God did not create us for any purpose beyond or outside the event of Jesus Christ. The reason for creation is therefore intrinsic to the creature, because it *is* Jesus Christ and he is fully human. This is what the Church believes.[41]

God created as an act of autotelic play, rooted in the incarnation of Christ. Humankind and the world are unnecessary. God's creation was not necessary but it was meaningful. From this view of creation, Harvey argues, "When we play—unnecessary but meaningfully—we are living out our deepest identity as unnecessary but meaningful creatures. Simply put, we reverberate with ourselves. We chime with our being." Therefore, sports have remained popular throughout history because they ring with our being, they mirror who we are as the creation of God.

So, because sport reverberates with who we are—not who God is—then there is no place for transcendence in sport. Sport is not worship and it does not draw humanity closer to God. Harvey argues that "worship is the liturgical celebration of who God is with us. Sport is the liturgical celebration of who we are by ourselves."[42] What's more, God does not participate in humankind's sport, but "God instead steps back, evacuating the space created by the liturgical action, enabling the creature to be somehow at a distance in its own integrity. In effect, in worship, God transcends the difference. In sport, God establishes the difference. He is in one. He is out of the other."[43] Now, this is not to label sport as "God forsaken," idolatrous, or even wrong. Harvey writes from a place of great love for sport. But in his argument, sport is about humanity. It's about who we are as the creation—unnecessary but meaningful. It's not about God. But I don't believe this is all there is to say.

41. Harvey, *A Brief Theology of Sport*, 83.
42. Harvey, *A Brief Theology of Sport*, 94.
43. Harvey, *A Brief Theology of Sport*, 95.

Criticism of Harvey

Harvey has certainly crafted a theological argument for sport's popularity. We love it because it reverberates with who we are as created beings. But his conclusions land as harsh, and I believe this is a result of an over-insistence on the autotelicity of play and a conflation of sport and play. Play, in a strictly philosophical sense, is an end in and of itself, and it exists in an alternate realm. But it rarely ever works out that way. The reality is that the boundaries between our play and our everyday lives are often blurred, as are the ends of both realms. This is well illustrated in a story from an episode of *This American Life*.[44] Journalist David Hill loves playing the game Diplomacy, a strategic board game where players form and break alliances in an effort to gain control of all the countries of the world. Heads of state have been known to be fans of the game, and large tournaments are held around the world. Central to the play is "stabbing people in the back," and betraying allies. Hill found though, that as he played the game, complete with many vicious betrayals, his relationships with other competitors were suffering outside the game. People told him that he was just too vicious, even as he followed the rules of the game. When the opportunity came to compete in the World Diplomacy Championship, he decided he needed some outside help so he enlisted real-life diplomat Dennis Ross, who was President Clinton's Middle East envoy and an advisor to President Obama. Ross helped Hill for the first game of the tournament, and quite interestingly, the first game ended in a six-way draw. This is an acceptable but extremely rare outcome in the game. Normally one player will gain control of every country, which is advantageous in a tournament as decisive wins accumulate tournament points. And yet, the game ended in a tie. Building from the theories of play presented earlier, it can be seen here that the ends of the game Diplomacy (to conquer the world inside the game) was superseded by the ends of real diplomacy (ostensibly, real-world peace). The ends of the actual world came into the play-realm of the game through a real diplomat. The "ideal frontier," in Caillois's language, was breached.

We see here that our games, while they might ideally exist in a separate space, do not exist in a vacuum. In other words, even if a game has its own rules and it exists in its own realm, these rules still observe the wider rules of creation. We all must follow the rules, the bounded-ness, by which we have been created. And so, our games can never fully escape everyday life. This is all the more true in sport, and one of the reasons that sport cannot

44. *This American Life*. "Got Your Back." Accessed April 25, 2015. http://www.thisamericanlife.org/radio-archives/episode/531/got-your-back.

be completely conflated with play. If you break your arm during a football game, your arm is still broken when you get home.

Getting back to Harvey, it is clear now that his reliance on the autotelicity of play and sport handicaps his argument, as he does not take into account the lived experiences of people who play and participate—the phenomenology of sport. In reality, our love of sport is so much more complex than a simple resonance with our created nature. Most recreational athletes, when asked why they participate in their sport, will give a whole host of reasons, ranging from fitness goals to time spent with friends. A boy loves going to a baseball game because he gets to spend quality time with his dad—and eat some popcorn. A young woman loves practicing mixed martial arts because it empowers her. A triathlete craves races because it's the only time he feels as if he's accomplishing something. So, is God unable to be present there? Does God compete with these ends?

What's more, Harvey's conclusions, which spring from his theology of sport, are unsettling. Because of autotelicity, he argues, "We need to recognize that professional sport is not true sport. It mimics it at best, it destroys it at worst. The professional sportsperson is simply an actor or a prostitute. Either way, they are not a player."[45] Certainly there are many ethical issues plaguing professional sports, issues that often turn away critically minded fans. But Harvey's criticism is, at its core, a misunderstanding of work and its relationship with play.[46] This will be discussed in greater detail in the next chapter.

Harvey also criticizes those who see sport as a means for praising God. "As with idolatrous self-importance, instrumental use of sport to the 'glory of God' should be resisted. Christians should simply play sport for sport, not for the opportunities it presents."[47] This is a valid criticism for the demonstrably Christian athlete who equates victory with God's favor. But too much is lost here, and it stems from a defect in Harvey's view of creation. Creation is certainly non-instrumental and autotelic, but that does not eliminate its capacity to serve higher ends, such as glory to God and human flourishing. Rather, it supports those higher ends. Perhaps it is better

45. Harvey, *A Brief Theology of Sport*, 104–5.

46. The work–play relationship is another avenue for exploring religion and sport. Johnston argues that "our central task as Christians is not to maximize either our work or our play while minimizing the other, nor to merge our work with our play. Instead, Christians are created and called to consecrate both their work and their play. As we have seen, play is God's appointment, his gift to humankind which is meant to relativize and refresh our endeavors, putting them in their God-intended perspective. But work too is from God, his appointed means of service to '[hu]man[ity]' and nature alike." Johnston, *The Christian at Play*, 134. Both work and play can be consecrated for God.

47. Harvey, *A Brief Theology of Sport*, 113.

to call Harvey's theology of sport a "non-theology" in that there is no place, no role, for God. For Harvey, sport is a celebration of who humanity is, as created freely by God, but it is not a celebration of the creating God.

Robert Ellis's Theology of Sport

Robert Ellis is a member of the faculty in the Theology and Religion Department in the University of Oxford and an ordained minister in the Baptist Union of Great Britain. His book, *The Games People Play*, was published the same year as Harvey's *A Brief Theology of Sport*, and while they both often reference the same literature, it is clear that the two are not in direct conversation with one another. Ellis has a very different approach to sport. First, he insists that something happens in play. Again, referencing creation, he states that "play is not simply the mode of God's act of creation; it is also a means by which creatures become open to receiving life as the Creator's gift and so become open to the Creator in relationships and potentiality."[48] Play brings about an openness to God. It opens humans up to a divine encounter. Sport, then, is a "particular form of play, institutionalizing play in its bureaucratizing of it, and so takes it seriously in a new way."[49] In other words, sport is a systematic form of play. From the beginning then, Ellis makes space for a transcendent experience in sport and play. He writes, "If play and sport can be (though are not necessarily) a participation in God's playful creativity and even in God's self, then one might expect such goods to follow."[50] There is a real possibility in humankind's practice of sport to grow closer to God, to have Godly goods flow from sport. Here he makes play and sport much more akin to aesthetic experience.

Like other writers, Ellis agrees that play is an escape into a new world, with different boundaries and chronologies. However, unlike Harvey, he does not see this as a separate realm where humanity celebrates humanity, but rather a realm where one might encounter God. If play is a participation in God's creativity and an opening for receiving life, then the separate realm of play has the possibility "of being a vehicle for divine encounter . . . [it] may not simply be windows through which we can catch sight of another world, but might also be apertures through which the reality beyond comes in to encounter us."[51]

48. Ellis, *The Games People Play*, 147.

49. Ellis, *The Games People Play*, 147.

50. Ellis, *The Games People Play*, 147.

51. Ellis, *The Games People Play*, 157.

Next, quite importantly, Ellis brings in the notion of human achievement into his argument. He builds from an Irenaean understanding of the *imago Dei*, where humankind is not created complete but rather open to God and open to growth and flourishing.[52] Humans are created in potential. Therefore, "the image of God is the potentiality of maturity and fullness, and human persons grow into this potential (or, indeed, slip back from it)."[53] This combines with his understanding of transcendence, which he defines as "mundane moments of striving and reaching 'beyond' the present and its achievements, and also more elongated practices and dispositions that are oriented to this end."[54] So, humankind is always working to transcend itself by reaching out to God, by doing the necessary work to perfect itself, to live into the possibilities of the full *imago Dei*. And sport is a perfect example of this:

> This movement towards self-transcendence seems to be an essential element of all serious sport: players train for it, spectators wait for it and celebrate it. Humanity in the *imago* Dei is a dynamic creature of potential, reaching beyond itself to God, and sport exemplifies this human characteristic in a distinctive way. This human restlessness, this striving for better, is ultimately a striving after God.[55]

The athlete who strives to run faster or jump higher, and the spectator who cheers her on, not only seek glory in sport but also seek (even if unknowingly) God.

Discussion of Ellis

There are many strengths to Ellis's argument, especially since his conclusions spring from thorough ethnography with athletes and spectators. As I mentioned before, any theology of sport must look closely at the phenomenology—the actual experiences—of those who take part. However, while Ellis does argue for play as a place for an encounter with God, and the striving of an athlete as truly a striving after God, he seems finally to summarize sport as a symbolic activity. We strive in sport just as we strive for God. It's an analogy. But is sport purely an analogy? If the athlete is

52. While he does not engage with it in this book, Ellis's background is in the Process Theology.

53. Ellis, *The Games People Play*, 232.

54. Ellis, *The Games People Play*, 236.

55. Ellis, *The Games People Play*, 243–44.

truly striving after God by participating in a sport, is something actually happening?[56] To answer this, we need to return again to notions of transcendence. For Ellis, transcendence

> may include moments of flow, the moments that some will describe as mystical; but it also includes other kinds of experience much less mystical . . . [such as] the more mundane moments of striving and reaching "beyond" the present and its achievements, and also more elongated practices and dispositions that are oriented to this end.[57]

Depending on the definition of "mystical," this definition does not contradict that which I presented in chapter 1: God is transcendent, humankind is created, and we can have transcendent experiences in the sense that these experiences go beyond what is believed to be possible—but these experiences are still rooted in creation. They don't imply escape from our creatureliness, nor do they necessarily bring about contact or engagement with the transcendent God. For Ellis, sport is systematized reaching and growing, but this reaching is ultimately a reaching for God. Again though, this is, at its core, a symbolic understanding of the theological role of sport. This notion of reaching for God and seeking transcendence could be applied to any great human endeavors, particularly those with aesthetic components. But where is God active in sport? What are God's purposes for sport? Is there something about sport, theologically, that is unique amongst aesthetic endeavors? Those answers, I believe lie in a deeper understanding of embodiment and sport, and will be clarified below.

Further Theology of Sport

The missing component, I would argue, of both Harvey and Ellis's theologies of sport is that they pay very little attention to embodiment. Ellis also critiques dualism, but the physical body does not play a prominent role in his theological platform. As noted previously, sport sets itself apart from other forms of play by its integral use of the body. Checkers doesn't require physical training; running a 5k does. A robust theology of sport must account for the theological place of the body. So how then does an understanding of the

56. There are certainly shades of sacramental language. I will not be pursuing a worship-based argument here, but that is certainly a worthy avenue to explore.

57. Ellis, *The Games People Play*, 236.

body, particularly the theological platform that I presented in the previous chapter, expand a theology of sport?[58]

To begin, I offer the question of whether or not some sports are more moral than others. Anecdotal evidence might suggest that tennis players are more moral than football players as most tennis players don't take steroids (or it's not as well publicized) and are less often arrested for domestic abuse. And beyond those superficial assessments, it can be argued that tennis players don't damage their bodies like football players do, especially in light of new studies on the effects of football on the brain.[59] But perhaps posing the question about comparative morality between sports is problematic. Based on the basic principles of the philosophy of play presented earlier, this is a question that cannot even be asked. Each sport creates its own world, with rules, boundaries, and principles that exist only in that world. To be amoral within a sport would mean breaking only the rules of the game. The pitcher who uses sandpaper to scuff a baseball is amoral, but a person who scratches a baseball outside of gameplay is just damaging a ball. And yet, our experiences of sport do not uphold this principle. Tiger Wood's marital failings were highly condemned by both golf fans and many of his sponsors, although he did nothing to break any rule within the game of golf. Interestingly enough, after his failings became public, his game suffered. All of this is to say that sport does not create a full sub-world but rather a set of sub-norms. And these norms can never fully escape the macro-norms of our world, or the norms of creation that we all must follow.[60] So, since sport is a form of play that is embodied, the creational norms that most immediately come into perspective are those of the body. A broken arm in a game is also a broken arm at home. Therefore, any theology of sport must take a very close look at what happens in and to the athlete's body.

Second, a theology of sport that incorporates embodiment must look closely at human achievement, as it is arguably one of sport's primary draws. Take for example the medal winning women's vaults at the 1956 and 2012 Olympics. In 1956, Larissa Latynina of the U.S.S.R. won gold with a single cartwheel over the vault. Her body, straight and unbending, moved with grace and elegance and she stuck her landing perfectly. In 2012, American

58. For my purposes here, I will focus primarily on an athlete-centered theology of sport. This argument relates to those who participate in sport, with little reflection on those who watch, although the two aren't mutually exclusive. A theology of the spectator could be very fruitful, but this analysis will focus on those who engage in playing sports.

59. Bahrami et al., "Head Impact Exposure and Football."

60. In this sense then, some sports do follow the norms of creation better than others, which may or may not make them more moral.

McKayla Maroney executed a perfect vault (but took the silver due to a mistake in a previous run) by doing three layout flips, a full twist, and sticking her landing. One can watch these two performances side by side and immediately see how far the sport has advanced in just fifty-six years.[61] Sport serves as a phenomenal showcase for human achievement, especially as it pertains to physical, bodily achievement. But how do we theologically understand human achievement in the body? Again, Ellis looks back to Irenaeus and humanity's growth into a fully realized *imago Dei*. In reaching for God, humans develop and grow. But this doesn't necessarily account for the development of the vault exercise, or for a new world record in the 1500-meter run, but, bridging back to the previous chapter, where I argued that our bodies are unified wholes and that physical activities are therefore inherently spiritual activities, this development of human physical achievement must be acknowledged as having a place in God's purposes on Earth. Sport and its physical component, I have argued, are potentially part of God's redemptive purposes in creation.

But the legacy of dualism and its denigration of the body have at times limited the church's perception of the importance of sport. Roman Catholic Michael P. Kerrigan states that the Catholic Church takes an interest in sport because "she prizes everything that contributes constructively to the harmonious and complete development of the person, body and soul. She encourages, therefore, what aims at educating, developing, and strengthening the human body in order that it may offer a better service for the attainment of personal maturation."[62] So, the human achievement that is such a large part of sport is valuable because it helps people grow and mature, physically and spiritually. But the value of the body itself is still absent from these endorsements. Rather, benefit to the body is seen as eventual benefit to the higher faculties of the soul. As Carlo Mazza puts it, "in sport, the human body is the 'instrument;' the body is not an end in itself . . . As their more remote purpose, you have the use made, by the soul, of the body so prepared, for the development of the interior or exterior life of the person; that of contributing to its perfection."[63] In the Catholic—and arguably dualist—tradition that is represented here, the body is just a tool. In sport, there is no increase in being in the body itself. That increase only occurs in the soul.

But if the body is the location where sport takes place, and the human person is a unified whole, then something must be happening in the body itself. The body must be more than just a tool for the betterment of the

61. "The Olympics. Then and Now." Imgur. http://imgur.com/gallery/yVoV4.

62. Kerrigan, "Sports and the Christian Life," 253.

63. Mazza, "Sport Viewed From Church's Magisterium," 63.

higher faculties. As discussed in the previous chapter, the historic western dualistic (or even triadic) understanding of humans as made up of body and soul (and spirit) was adopted from Greek philosophy into Christian theology, and this is often labeled as "Platonism." I will continue to use that term in reference to dualism and the influence of Greek philosophy on Christian thought. Ironically though, a more thorough look at Socrates, as depicted by Plato and Xenophon, shows that he was what we might call today a "gym rat." He spent a lot of time at the gymnasium. Granted, the gymnasium of ancient Greece was not strictly a place for physical training as it is today—it was also part school, part park, and part social club. But Socrates spent a great deal of time there and he encouraged people to maintain and train their bodies. In *Memorabilia*, Socrates is quoted as saying,

> In everything that men do the body is useful; and in all uses of the body it is of great importance to be in as high a state of physical efficiency as possible. Why, even in the process of thinking, in which the use of the body seems to be reduced to a minimum, it is matter of common knowledge that grave mistakes may often be traced to bad health.[64]

That is not a denigration of the body in any way. Rather, what benefits the body benefits the whole person. Hyland argues that physical training, according to Socrates, "is part of the unified education of the whole person. A proper education in gymnastics makes one a better person, not just the body a better body." Therefore "Socrates seems already to appreciate this intimacy of the mental and the physical that the phenomenologists today emphasize."[65] The Socratic tradition is, in some sense, a strong supporter of sport and its value for the entire person. Philosopher Heather Reid then puts it that "athletics is the striving of whole persons to actualize their wholeness."[66] Recall the earlier discussion of "being in the zone," where it was shown that athletes experience a time where body, mind, and even spirit are all perceived to interact fluidly and harmoniously. Peak athletic performance requires a unified body. Sport is therefore an excellent means for reclaiming the understanding of the unified person.

64. Xenophon, Memorabilia 3.12.5–6, http://perseus.uchicago.edu/perseus-cgi/citequery3.pl?dbname=GreekFeb2011&getid=1&query=Xen.%20Mem.%203.13.1.

65. Hyland, *Philosophy of Sport*, 99.

66. Reid, *Introduction to Philosophy of Sport*, loc. 2251, Kindle.

Conclusion

It is encouraging that sport is being discussed in theological circles. There need be no fear that sport is a religion usurping the place of the church. Sport is not a religion but rather an aesthetic endeavor, and like all aesthetic endeavors, has the potential to promote human betterment. Finding God's place in sport proves difficult. Harvey argues that sport isn't really about God but about humanity and how it was created by God. There is no role for God in sport. Ellis however sees sport as a place, like play, for a transcendent experience. However, I argue, that if we truly recognize that transcendent experiences in sport do not take humanity beyond its created-ness, beyond its bounded-ness, then we must find the theological starting place somewhere else. I believe that the body is a better place to engage in theological discussions of sport, particularly as sport is dependent on bodily activity. If the body is taken seriously as a unified whole, then embodied activities and achievement are in fact places where God can be active. This leads us into the next chapter, how, in light of all the shameful and harmful aspects of sport, a theologian might claim that it is in fact good. That place, I will argue, is in its capacity to promote human flourishing.

4

Sport Is Good

Having outlined the basic principles and language for theological engagement with sport, I now want to make the claim that sport, like creation and like the body, is good. Now, this contention should generate some queries. To the successful athlete, who finds purpose and enjoyment, sport is unquestionably good. To those who have been alienated by sport, it presents many real problems, as it appears to generate prolonged pain in people's lives. The problems that sport presents should not be ignored. Performance enhancing drugs appear to be omnipresent; Lance Armstrong, once a cycling hero and lauded philanthropist, has been defrocked of all his Tour de France wins. In 2014, after a second DUI arrest, Michael Phelps, the most decorated athlete in Olympic history, checked himself into a rehabilitation clinic for substance abuse. If sport is good, it certainly seems to have a deleterious effect on many athletes. How then, using the concepts presented in the prior three chapters, can we argue theologically that sport is good?

In this chapter I will give an overview of the two prevailing theological arguments that posit that sport is good. The first of these is the instrumental view, that sport is good in that it can produce other goods, like health, clear thinking, and moral instruction. The second is the intrinsic or autotelic view, that sport is good in and of itself, a product of God's good creation and the creation mandate. I will argue though that neither of these arguments fully captures what is good about sport, especially in terms of its relation to God's purposes on earth, where God works in real contexts and situations. Rather, I will show that sport is good in that it is an exceptional means for promoting human flourishing as cooperation with God's redemptive purposes. The project of God in the world is to bring redemption to humanity and all of creation—as opposed to offering escape from the embodied world. Sport is an excellent avenue for this. It is when athletes—or spectators and fans—veer from the goal of human flourishing that sport becomes damaging. To aid in this, I will utilize sociologist Christian Smith's understanding of basic human goods, and show how sport, when rightly ordered, leads to human flourishing and God's redemptive plans, thereby making it very good.

The Christian Church, Leisure Time, and Sport

Before looking at the two prevailing theological arguments for the good of sport, it's worthwhile to show briefly how Christians have approached, what we would call today, leisure time, or free time, and its relationship to work. The historical views of leisure, by extension, affect the church's view of sport and its value. Since I am arguing here about the good of sport, it is important to show some of the historical precedents about sport and leisure's place in society and how people spend their time. First, the early church knew sport only in the context of Greek games and Roman spectacles. The Greek Olympics and other smaller sporting events were inextricably tied to paganism. They were wrapped up in cultic ritual and therefore were largely opposed by early church leaders. The violence of Roman spectacles turned many Christians away. Augustine, by his time, after the conversion of the Roman Empire, viewed the games and spectacles with apathy. He notes that "if passing, that coursing peradventure will distract me even from some weighty thought, and draw me after it: not that I turn aside the body of my beast, yet still incline my mind thither."[1] As Michael Shafer points out, for Augustine, "the problem with sport lies in the distraction it creates from the more important work to be done by the Christian, namely 'serious meditation.'"[2]

Leisure studies scholar Paul Heintzman points out that in Medieval Christendom there was a bifurcation between the active life and the contemplative life. This "resulted in the notion that the only true, or at least the highest, Christian calling was a priestly or monastic one that focused on the contemplative life."[3] To be truly faithful to God meant entering the priesthood or a monastery and not engaging in a trade or manual labor. In general, work was inferior to the God-centered and contemplative life. Aquinas however did lay groundwork for an instrumental view of non-work time, stating that "man needs bodily rest for the body's refreshment, because he cannot always be at work, since his power is finite and equal to a fixed amount of labor, so too is it with his soul, whose power is also finite and

1. Augustine, *Confessions*, 104.

2. Shafer, *Well Played*, 93–94.

3. Heintzman, *Leisure and Spirituality*, 69.

equal to a fixed amount of work."[4] For Aquinas, both physical and spiritual work required times of rest.

During the Reformation, Luther and Calvin stressed the value of vocation, noting that all work, whether inside or outside the church, can bring glory to God—all are called to an active life of obedience to God, whether clergy or not. Leisure time then became a new category of time, distinct from contemplation, and defined rather as the time spent not working. So, it "came to be considered in terms of recreation—time off work to re-create oneself to go back to work,"[5] similar to Aquinas's understanding. Again, leisure was valuable in that it refreshed mental and physical capacities, allowing one to return to work renewed and productive. The Reformers however saw work through a much more sacred lens.

These understandings of work continued to form in the United States under the Puritans, who further emphasized the sacredness of time. Puritans are often stereotyped as killjoys, bent only on simple and plain living, free from excess or pleasurable activities. While there is some truth to this, they were not adamantly against leisure time or leisure activities. Rather, they feared that recreation activities might be time poorly used, or even a distraction from the good things of God. As Heintzman states, "the Puritans were not opposed to recreation, as long as it was truly refreshing, was not a waste of time, was not done in excess, and was not immoral, sensual, or glorifying the flesh. As with all other activities, this seasonable recreation must contribute to the main goal of life, acting in obedience to God."[6] The Puritans enjoyed games and other recreational activities, but always in the wider context of God's purposes in the world.

This brief history shows that sport and its value are couched within wider questions of how one should spend one's time. Sport, for the most part, is a leisure activity, one done during free time—at least for the amateur athlete—and has therefore often been understood as unnecessary. But is it unnecessary? I will now show the two prevailing arguments for how sport is good, and perhaps even necessary.

The Instrumental Argument for the Good of Sport

The instrumental argument for the good of sport proposes that sport is good because of what it can create, because of what it can yield. Again, this

4. Aquinas, *Summa Theologica*, II–II, 168, 2.

5. Heintzman, *Leisure and Spirituality*, 69.

6. Heintzman, *Leisure and Spirituality*, 75–76.

originates in Aquinas, who makes it explicit in *Summa Contra Gentiles*, stating that:

> Even sports activities, which appear to be carried on without any purpose, have a proper end, namely, so that after our minds have been somewhat relaxed through them we may be then better able to do serious jobs. Otherwise, if sport were an end in itself, the proper thing to do would be to play all the time, but that is not appropriate. So, the practical arts are ordered to the speculative ones, and likewise every human operation to intellectual speculation, as an end.

For Aquinas, leisure serves the higher ends of spiritual and intellectual pursuits.

The Catholic Church has continuously upheld Aquinas's understanding of sport, but in later years extended its instrumental value to other forms of work as well, beyond just the spiritual. In his speech "The Sporting Ideal," given in Rome in 1945, Pope Pius XII states that

> sport is not an end in itself, but a means. As such, it is and must remain subordinated to its end, which consists in the perfect and balanced formation and education of the whole man, for whom sport is an aid in the ready and joyful accomplishment of his duties . . . If a sporting activity is for you a recreation and stimulus which aids you in better fulfilling your duties of work and study, then it can be said that it is being used in its true sense, and is attaining its true end"[7]

Again, it is claimed quite clearly that sport is not an end in itself. It is good if it produces something, namely aid in work and spiritual development. Pius XII though recognizes the physical component of sport and does not deny the value that it has for forming and strengthening bodies, but still warns of excess and indulgence. In another speech entitled "Fundamental Principles Governing Sporting Activity," given in Rome in 1951, he claims that with "sport being the care of the body, it must not degenerate into the cult of matter, becoming an end in itself. It is at the service of the whole man and, therefore, it must not only not obstruct man's intellectual and moral formation, but promote, aid, and second it."[8] He continues:

> What purpose would be served by the use and development of the body, of its energies, of its beauty, if it were not at the service of something noble and lasting, namely the soul? Sport which

7. Feeney, *A Catholic Perspective*, 32.
8. Feeney, *A Catholic Perspective*, 42.

> does not serve the soul is nothing more than a useless movement of the body's members, making show of something which attracts for a while, a fleeting pleasure.[9]

Pope Pius XII again makes it very clear that sport must never be an end in itself, that is, it must not be understood through its intrinsic value. Sport benefits the body, which then benefits the soul. Without service to the soul, it would not be good.

Present here again is a dualistic theological anthropology that hearkens back to the Platonic tradition (see chapter 2). Pope John Paul II, while giving a homily at the Olympic Stadium in Rome in 1984, repeated this theme, but broadened the benefit of sport to the development of persons. He notes that "great efforts have been made to ensure that the 'philosophy of sport' always prevails, the key principle of which is not 'sport for sport's sake' or other motives than the dignity, freedom, and integral development of man!"[10] Sport aids in human development. And so, in harmony with Aquinas, the Catholic Church has stayed with an instrumental view of sport, with its value lying in its ability to promote the growth of the soul and the person.

Protestants have also given value to sports and leisure for their instrumental purposes, as shown above in Calvin and the Puritans. But a more uniquely Protestant contribution, especially amongst conservative evangelicals, has been the instrumental use of sport for the sake of evangelism. That is, sport, and more specifically the heroes who excel at it, have remarkable platforms that are useful for evangelism. Rising out of the movement known as "Muscular Christianity,"[11] para-church organizations like the YMCA, Athletes in Action, and Fellowship of Christian Athletes (FCA), have all utilized sports and athletes for evangelistic purposes (more will be said about this movement and its impact in chapter 7). FCA's vision statement says that they desire "to see the world impacted for Jesus Christ through the influence of coaches and athletes."[12] These movements, while often very successful, have marginal and often vague theological underpinnings. Scholarly criticism of this instrumental view of sport will be shown later.

While there are both examples of avoidance and apathy, the church, for the most part, has chosen to approach sport as a means toward higher purposes. Whether the betterment of body for the sake of the soul, the refreshment of the person for more productive work, or the offering of a

9. Feeney, *A Catholic Perspective*, 50.

10. Feeney, *A Catholic Perspective*, 70.

11. See Ladd and Mathisen, *Muscular Christianity*; Putney, *Muscular Christianity*.

12. Fellowship of Christian Athletes. "Vision & Mission."

platform for evangelism, sport should yield something. The Christian's role in sport, therefore, is to ensure that these good ends are realized. If sport exists just for sport's sake, it is a waste of the precious time—time given by God. If these ends are neglected, then sport becomes damaging. But in more current discussions, this instrumental view has come under fire.

The Intrinsic Argument for the Good of Sport

The intrinsic argument for the good of sport is not fully dismissive of the instrumental view, but it searches for something deeper. Theologian and pastor Michael Shafer starts from a place of disappointment, in that sport is filled with corruption and destruction. His particular focus is the ethical problems surrounding doping and performance enhancing drugs. If sport is good because of what it yields, then its yields seem to speak overwhelmingly to the contrary. He argues that the

> instrumental understanding of sport, while not necessarily misplaced, does not speak to any intrinsic value of sport . . . Certainly, there have been immoral practices associated with sport and sport often serves as an instrument to some other good but the value of sport reaches much further than this. Such a thin view of sport fails to recognize the created goodness of games which God intends for humans to enjoy, not as a means to "serious" work but as a fundamental source of enjoyment and human flourishing.[13]

Sport must have some value that goes deeper than what it produces. It must be rooted in a theological understanding of the good of creation and human flourishing. To make this case, Shafer, as well as other proponents of the intrinsic argument, turn to an understanding of play. Play, as it is affirmed by many scholars, is an autotelic activity.[14] It does not produce anything and it is good in and of itself (see chapter 3). One might imagine a young child having tea with her dolls. There is no purpose for this activity, nor is there something that is created. It is just play, but it is extremely valuable as an "innate capacity given to us by God."[15] All games and thereby all sports are rooted in play, and Shafer argues that the spirit of play must be present, because without it

13. Shafer, *Well Played*, 4.

14. See Johnston, *The Christian at Play*; Caillois, *Man, Play, and Games*.

15. Shafer, *Well Played*, 225.

> at the center of our involvement in sport we overlook the deeper significance of the activity. Sport without play does not mean that it is no longer sport but it might suggest that our priorities in sport are misplaced upon the results of sport, (i.e., winning, health benefits, etc.) rather than on the act of playing.[16]

When play is taken out of sport, or the focus on play is lost, then sport deviates from its God-given goodness, and its results are damaging. The win-at-all-costs mentality that drives steroid use (Shafer's primary concern) bubbles up when the sense of play is neglected. Therefore, sports' value should not be found in its products, even as those often might be good, but in its God-given nature as play. In sum, Shafer argues that sport should be "enjoyed purely for its own worth, with no further end than itself . . . When we fail to move beyond these extrinsic goods we miss out on the good of what many call sport's purest form, the love of the game."[17]

Theologian Lincoln Harvey also supports the intrinsic argument for the good of sport. His primary motivation lies in understanding why people love sport so much. Also working from an understanding of play and sport as autotelic, he takes the argument even further and condemns any instrumental use of sport, particularly professional sports, saying

> sport should not be professionalized, any more than worship [another autotelic act] should be professionalized. This is because both sport and worship are for nothing, in that nothing is harvested, nothing is produced, nothing is earned. As a result, people should not be making a living leading worship, and neither should they make a living playing sport . . . We need to recognize that professional sport is not true sport. It mimics it at best, it destroys it at worst.[18]

These are harsh words, but they are a reasonable conclusion to an understanding of sport as autotelic, especially if that autotelicity is evidence of God's role in sports. For Harvey, any deviation from sport's autotelic nature is a corruption.

So what then is the role of the Christian athlete or sports enthusiast if sport has purely intrinsic value? For Shafer, who wants sport to reconnect to its sense of play, the Christian athlete should be

> an example of how to fit competition within the broader context of a God glorifying narrative. More so than abstaining from

16. Shafer, *Well Played*, 225.
17. Shafer, *Well Played*, 221.
18. Harvey, *A Brief Theology of Sport*, 104–5.

> sport, Christian courage is needed to participate in sport in the right way. What the modern sports culture, which is focused on self-made heroes, needs is a course corrective that is led by saintly athletes.[19]

These saintly athletes will not pursue winning at all costs. They won't damage their bodies in pursuit of victory. Rather, they will enjoy sport for what it is, an activity built on play that when rightly appreciated, serves as a joyful gift from God. Harvey gives a slightly different understanding of the Christian's role in sport, locating it more in the realm of the critic. For Harvey "the task for Christians is to commentate on sport. We can help people understand why it is so popular. We can explain what is so great about it."[20] The Christian works as an analyst, perhaps even a cleansing agent into the world of sport, which has defiled God's good gift of play.

The argument for the intrinsic view of sport, while not fully dismissive, gives considerable criticism to the instrumental view. Sport is not good just because it leads to another good, but it is good in and of itself, rooted in play, and a gift from God. We should therefore enjoy sport for sport's sake.

The Appeal of the Two Arguments

Having now presented both arguments, it would serve well here to state briefly the appeal to both lines of thinking. For the instrumentalist, there is the knowledge and assurance that if sport is producing something that is known to be good, then that time spent playing sports was not wasted. If good things come out of sport then it is time well spent. There is a simple but perhaps unsophisticated logic to this, especially in light of all the bad that is produced by sport. As shown above though, contemporary theologians are bristling at this interpretation. Their arguments show why they choose an autotelic interpretation, but I believe there is even more under the surface that can be revealed. First, in a post-Marxist world, there are heightened sensitivities to notions of production, or rather notions of something or someone's value being located solely in their productive capacities. As Roberto Goizueta reminds us,

> human relationships are not, at bottom, economic . . . The aesthetic celebration of life reminds us that the ultimate goal of all human action is nothing other than the active participation in relationships and the enjoyment of those relationships,

19. Shafer, *Well Played*, 130.

20. Harvey, *A Brief Theology of Sport*, 113.

> wherein the particularity of each person can be affirmed and allowed to flower.[21]

The idea of the aesthetic celebration of life can certainly extend to sport, noting again the aesthetic aspects of sport, mentioned in the previous chapter. And it is clear here that people and human activities are not graded and judged by their output. Second, the Catholic understanding of sport's instrumentality is largely based on an antiquated theological anthropology. The legacy of Platonic dualism, of the divisibility of body and soul, has been heavily critiqued by scholarship for decades.[22] The notion that proper maintenance of the body, through sport, benefits the higher faculties of the soul, appears to ignore too much of the joy that comes from sport.

And perhaps the biggest allure away from instrumentality, to the sensitive theologian, is the misuse of sport by Christian evangelicals. Harvey makes it clear that he opposes sport as a platform for evangelism, stating that, "As with idolatrous self-importance, instrumental use of sport to the 'glory of God' should be resisted. Christians should simply play sport for sport, not for the opportunities it presents, be they health, wealth or evangelistic stage."[23] Shirl J. Hoffman, in a discussion of sport-based evangelism, argues that sport, as a medium for evangelism, has never undergone criticism. Sport itself, as lived out in the professional arena, very well might be contrary to the character of God. He claims that sport has been

> variously described by those inside it and outside it as narcissistic, materialistic, self-interested, violent, sensational, coarse, racist, sexist, brazen, raunchy, hedonistic, body-destroying, and militaristic, [so] the culture of sports is light years removed from what Christians for centuries have idealized as the embodiment of the gospel message. The Christian worldview is based on an absolute, immutable, justice-loving God. The worldview of sports is based on material success.[24]

Granted, Hoffman makes some oversimplifications, but his point is correct: the evangelical Christian church has failed to criticize sport and therefore the message of the gospel has been tainted by the medium with which it is dispensed. It is no wonder then that a responsible theologian

21. Goizueta, *Caminemos Con Jesus*, 130.

22. See Merleau-Ponty and Landes, *Phenomenology of Perception*; Brown, Murphy, and Malony, *Whatever Happened to the Soul?*; Murphy, *Bodies, Souls, or Spirited Bodies?*

23. Harvey, *A Brief Theology of Sport*, 113.

24. Hoffman, *Good Game*, 11.

would want to find the value of sport outside of instrumentality, outside of what sport produces.

But there are a number of problems with the allure of the intrinsic argument. First, it is evidence of the continual project, founded at the Reformation, to move the locus of spirituality from the cosmos, the outside world, to the inward self. Calvin located the "primary seat of the divine image" in the mind and the heart,[25] as opposed to some visible part of the body, and theologians continue this march inward as we search for the essential or intrinsic value of a cultural phenomenon. Why is this a problem? Because it neglects the reality that everything people do happens in particular contexts and in particular situations. As Christian Smith puts it, every "persons' basic and non-basic motivations for action are never directly applied from nature to action, but rather are mediated through multiple modes of human particularity . . . people's natural motivations are always meditated through culture."[26] So, to find the intrinsic good of sport is to ignore the culture through which it is mediated. And the Christian theologian, who looks for that intrinsic good, draws near to the problem of divorcing the Christian faith from culture—that is, insisting that some nugget of the Christian faith exists outside of culture. As Dyrness puts it,

> much conversation about Christianity and culture would be helped by the initial recognition that we don't start with two things, something called Christianity . . . and something called culture, which we then need to bring together. This way of putting things seems to assume that Christianity is something "pure" that either will become contaminated by culture or will enter it as a cleansing agent. This approach is simply a version of the purity that Descartes sought in his darkened room, when he sought to locate fundamental reality in certain indubitable ideas. Neither Christianity nor culture can be adequately approached this way.[27]

So, a Christian discussion of sport cannot enter into an ethereal realm of absolutes and essential tenets. It must be rooted in real experience.

And finally, what the theologians who support the intrinsic argument really miss is the question of God's purposes for sport. I'm careful here to use the term purpose, as opposed to use, so as not to fall right back into strict instrumentalism. But the question of God's design, beyond just the intrinsic value given at creation, must be analyzed. How does sport play

25. Calvin, *Institutes of the Christian Religion*, 188.

26. Smith, *To Flourish or Destruct*, 188.

27. Dyrness, *The Earth Is God's*, 68.

a role in God's redemptive actions in the world? Dyrness points out that this is "so foreign to our modern way of thinking. We have come to take for granted that the world must be understood, and therefore life must be lived, on its own terms. We no longer believe these things exist for God. Rather, if we believe there is a God, we assume God exists to promote our happiness."[28] There is joy found in sport. How is God a part of that? How are God's purposes realized through sport?

To answer this question, and to help form a way forward for finding the good of sport, I want to turn to another medium entirely: modern art. There is a helpful parallel that can be drawn here, in that the autotelic argument for the good of sport posits that sport must be enjoyed for its own ends. Put simply, we must play sport for sport's sake. Sport however is not the first cultural medium to reach, what we might call, full-autotelicity. For over a century now many critics have argued for "art for art's sake." Modern art especially is held only to autotelic standards. It is helpful then, as we look at God's purposes and the Christian's role in sport, that we look at Christianity's relationship with this other autotelic medium, and more specifically, the problems that are raised for the faithful practitioner. Note here, this is not a discussion of the aesthetics of sport, or how sport is, or is not, an art form. That has been done well by others.[29] Rather, this is a discussion of modern art, an autotelic activity, and the problems it presents for the faithful Christian, which will enlighten how we approach sport and its ends in God's Kingdom.

The Problems of Modern Art

Philosopher Nicholas Wolterstorff, in his classic commentary on aesthetics, *Art in Action*, gives a lengthy proposal on how the Christian should approach modern art. First, he acknowledges that art has historically played a large role in the church, particularly in the liturgy. This includes music, painting, architecture, sculpture and many other forms that are both present in and commissioned by the church. But what makes this art in this context special, and what presents a problem for the modern artist, is that liturgical art is at the service of the liturgy. It is therefore not for its own sake but for the sake of worship, for the intent of drawing the person upward toward God. Art, in terms of the liturgy, has a purpose and a responsibility.[30]

28. Dyrness, *The Earth Is God's*, 59.

29. See chapter 5 in Hyland, *Philosophy of Sport*; Gumbrecht, *In Praise of Athletic Beauty*.

30. He has returned to this idea more recently in Wolterstorff, *Art Rethought*. But for our purposes here, his argument in *Art in Action* will suffice.

Modern art though, in many of its expressions, is divorced from any outside responsibility, or rather, any perceived or deliberate instrumental use. It is art for art's sake. It exists for and is judged by the ends of aesthetic contemplation. The primary goal of the modern artist is to advance the art form. Because of this, modern art has become a deeply secularized institution, often showing outward hostility to the Christian church, warranted or unwarranted. One can see here then how liturgical art and modern art have very different *teloi*, very different ends and purposes. Liturgical art exists to serve the liturgy while modern art exists solely for its own end, that is, aesthetic contemplation. Wolterstorff shows that the modern Christian must be both aware of art's claims to autotelicity and must remove him or herself from the demands of pure aesthetic contemplation. But this is difficult. He argues that

> the liberation experienced as the result of looking head-on at our institution of high art and then going on to formulate a perspective on the arts generally is, in large part, the liberation of no longer carrying over to art outside the institution the attitudes and evaluations appropriate to the institution. Once we have seen the institution of high art for the idiosyncratic thing it is, and once we have developed a general perspective on art in human life, then we are in a position to acknowledge practically, and not just theoretically, that art is not all for the sake of the aesthetic and that not all of the aesthetic is to be found in art, certainly not high art.[31]

So there are different ends for liturgical art and modern or high art, and the Christian must be aware of these and must respond appropriately. Wolterstorff gives a three-pronged approach for the Christian artist. First, he or she must never divorce art from responsibility. High art claims no allegiance other than itself. The Christian practitioner though is allied with God. Therefore, the

> Christian artist must constantly be engaged in the difficult, precarious task of assessing priorities as he (or she) determines the direction of his endeavors—of assessing relative importance. He recognizes that art for contemplation can serve human fulfillment. But equally he recognizes that art for other purposes can serve human fulfillment. He refuses automatically to give priority to either of these over the other.[32]

31. Wolterstorff, *Art in Action*, 178.

32. Wolterstorff, *Art in Action*, 194.

The Christian artist is defined by responsibility, which is ultimately found in God's purposes, and God's redemptive plans for creation. This does not mean that the Christian artist cannot create for pure aesthetic enjoyment, but that is not the only avenue. There are other purposes as well, namely God's purposes. Second, the Christian artist must always work for wholeness. There cannot be the "art-life" and the "church-life." There cannot be what H. Richard Niebuhr labels as Christ and culture in paradox.[33] For the Christian knows that "to answer the call to be a disciple of Jesus Christ is to commit his life as a whole, not just some fragments thereof, to God's cause in the world."[34] And finally, Wolterstorff advises the Christian artist to resist high art's claims to ultimacy. He puts it nicely, saying, "Art does not provide us with the meaning of human existence. The gospel of Jesus Christ does that. Art is not a way of rising toward God. It is meant instead to be in service of God."[35] Anyone who has spent time in the institution of high art has certainly heard the medium's claims for transformative power and enlightenment. Certainly, there is much good to be found there, but not at the expense of God's ultimate plans for redemption. Art is not an end in itself, but an avenue for God's purposes.

In this context then, of God's plans, "art now gains new significance. Art can serve as instrument in our struggle to overcome the fallenness of our existence, while also, in the delight which it affords, anticipating the shalom which awaits us."[36] Art, as an autotelic activity, holds many problems for the Christian. Art, as a piece in God's larger plan for new life and redemption, holds tremendous value.

What This Means for Sport

As mentioned before, this discussion of art, autotelicity, and God's purposes, should help us gain some insight into the nature of sport. For those who argue for sport's instrumental value, they want to assure that sport is doing something, that time is not wasted, and that that something has been produced. For those arguing for sport's intrinsic value, they want to find a way to avoid sport's destructive aspects by rooting it in sport's internal value, that is, allowing sport to be for sport's sake. But, I would argue, neither of these proposals fully captures the good of sport, at least in a theological sense. Modern art shows us that autotelicity is a highly secular principle.

33. Niebuhr, *Christ and Culture*.

34. Wolterstorff, *Art in Action*, 195.

35. Wolterstorff, *Art in Action*, 196.

36. Wolterstorff, *Art in Action*, 84.

It is a product of secularity and a symptom of modernity. Having been appreciated for its autotelicity for over a century now, art has divorced itself from outside responsibility and made its own claims to ultimacy. It stands to reason then that if sport finds its meaning and value in its autotelicity, that it too will fall prey to these same problems. One might argue that it already has. For the theologian, who wants to find the good of sport and eliminate its destructiveness, autotelicity is not the ultimate answer.

What I propose then is that the real good of sport lies in its abundant capacity to be an avenue for God's redemptive purposes in creation. Sport is an excellent means by which God is working for the shalom of the world, and in that work, there is joy to be had. This proposal does not ignore the needs of the instrumentalists. Something is happening in sport, but it's bigger than just a conversion or some restful benefit. And it does not ignore those who uphold the intrinsic argument. Sport is a cultural manifestation rooted in God's good creation. Humanity was created by God in freedom, not for God to accomplish something, but purely for the abundant joy of creating. And creation is also to engage in play. As the Psalmist says:

> Yonder is the sea, great and wide,
> creeping things innumerable are there,
> living things both small and great.
> There go the ships,
> and Leviathan that you formed to sport [שָׂחַק] in it.
> (Ps 104:25–26)[37]

So sport can be enjoyed for its own sake, its own needlessness—just as the Christian can appreciate art solely for the sake of aesthetic contemplation. But instead of rigidly focusing on the autotelicity as a defining aspect of play, one must see play in conversation with the goods that it brings about. Robert Ellis coins the term that is useful here: "autocharatic,"[38] that is sport is not an end in itself, existing for its own sake, but rather it is something *enjoyed* for its own sake. What's more, the theologian cannot ignore the fall and the Trinitarian principle that God is present in the world through the Holy Spirit and actively working, through culture, to bring about God's ultimate plan for redemption—a plan which both utilizes and includes sport. Things are happening! So the responsible Christian must anchor sport's

37. The root word, שָׂחַק, in other English versions is translated as "romp" (The Message), "frolic" (NIV), and of course "play" (KJV).

38. Ellis, *The Games People Play*, 270.

good in these plans—especially, as I will argue—because sport is so effective at bringing about God's plans for human flourishing.

How Sport Brings Human Flourishing

How then is sport part of God's redemptive plan for the world? To answer that, I would like to turn to sociologist Christian Smith. While not a theologian, he often works alongside theologians, and his sociological work serves as an excellent complement to theology. For our purposes here, I want to focus on his ideas about human flourishing.[39] Flourishing is more than just human happiness, or more than just a reductionist understanding of God as a provider of contentedness. Smith opposes that.[40] For Smith, flourishing is a "natural teleological good,"[41] or, I would add, God's design for human beings. As Jesus says in the Gospel of John, "I came that they may have life, and have it abundantly" (10:10). The argument I propose here then is that sport is an excellent means for promoting human flourishing and thereby engaging in God's redemptive purposes for creation.

To begin, Smith notes that "basic human motivations for action do indeed exist in a finite set . . . Human being involves certain natural, universal, basic goods. Some specific things are by nature simply good for human persons, what constitute 'the good' for them. The basic interest of human persons is to realize those basic goods."[42] After an exhaustive look at sociological theories about human goods, Smith settles on six basic ones. These are:

1. Bodily Survival: avoiding bodily death, injury, sickness, disease, and sustained vulnerability to harm; maintaining physical and bodily health and safety; sensual enjoyment, satisfaction, delight, or gratification of appetitive and perceptual desires of the body; and the absence of physical pain and suffering.
2. Knowledge of Reality: learning about the world and one's place and potential in it; increasing awareness and understanding of material and social realities; developing or embracing believed-in truths about

39. Flourishing is a topic that has received great attention recently amongst Christian sociologists, psychologists, and theologians, evidenced by the existence of the Thrive Center at Fuller Theological Seminary and the God and Human Flourishing Program at Yale Divinity School, whose mission is "cultivating and resourcing a new theological movement grounded in the conviction that Jesus Christ is the key to human flourishing." See "God & Human Flourishing."

40. See Smith and Denton, *Soul Searching*.

41. Smith, *To Flourish or Destruct*.

42. Smith, *To Flourish or Destruct* 180–81.

what exists and how it works that provide order, continuity, and practical know-how to life experience.

3. Identity Coherence and Affirmation: developing and maintaining continuity and positive self-regard in one's sense of personal selfhood over time and in different contexts and situations.
4. Exercising Purposive Agency: exerting influence or power (broadly understood as transformative capacity) in the social and material worlds, through the application of personal capabilities for perception, reflection, care, evaluation, self-direction, decision, and action, which causes desired (and unanticipated) effects in one's environment.
5. Moral Affirmation: believing that one is in the right or is living a morally commendable life, by being, doing, serving, thinking, and feeling what is good, correct, just, and admirable; avoiding moral fault, blame, guilt, or culpability.
6. Social Belonging and Love: enjoying recognition by, inclusion and membership in, and identification with significant social groups; loving and being loved by others in significant relationships.[43][/NL 1-6]

These are the six basic goods of personhood, and each benefit from significant explanation, but that is beyond the scope here. What's important is that "the proper human telos of flourishing as persons requires the significant realization of all six basic goods, since they constitute flourishing itself. The failure to achieve any one of the goods severely limits the prospects for realizing personal flourishing."[44] As humans, we are created with potential, and flourishing means growing into and realizing powers, capacities, and limitations. When realizing all six, people flourish, and, I would argue, live into God's purposes for creation, thereby getting a glimpse of the as-yet-unrealized fullness of God's design.

So, how does sport play a role here? Even a quick overview of the six basic human goods, backed by anecdotal evidence, shows how effectively sports can play a role in realizing these goods. But a cursory overview of select psychological research also shows how these ends are being born through sports and physical education. Compiled below are some empirical studies that show how sport has yielded one of the basic goods.

1. Bodily survival includes health and physical well-being. In 2005 the Ministry of Education in El Salvador, a country plagued by a thirteen-year civil war, enacted a new education program that put a heavy

43. Smith, *To Flourish or Destruct*, 181–82.

44. Smith, *To Flourish or Destruct*, 198.

emphasis on physical education. Current research notes that "it would appear that appropriately structured PE delivered by competent teachers holds a particular promise in being part of the solution toward a more peaceful generation of Salvadoran youth."[45] Sports can possibly lead to peace and development, and subsequent health.

2. Knowledge of reality includes understanding of the physical world and one's place in it. Sports are particularly adepts at creating procedural knowledge, that is "knowing how" as opposed to "knowing what."[46] Knowing about something, that is the facts that surround it, does not guarantee procedural knowledge and the control of complex cognitive and motor skills. We see here the limits to the Enlightenment understanding of knowledge and how sport can expand how we know the world.

3. Identity coherence includes developing positive self-regard, and it is not hard to find an athlete who locates their identity in their athletic pursuits. There is ample evidence that sport can lead to a diminished sense of self-worth when self-worth is tied to performance, especially amongst elite athletes.[47] However, research shows that recreational marathon runners who hold their athletic pursuits as a cornerstone of their identity, do not become neglectful of other important areas of life.[48] It's easy to find identity in athletics, but it doesn't have to become all-consuming—it can be very positive.

4. Exercising purposive agency means seeing how one's actions can change the environment. Physical exercise through sports has long been t[outed as a means for changing body composition, and this is certainly the truth when done with proper eating habits.[49] Much more will be said on this in future chapters.

5. Moral affirmation means seeing that what one is doing is the right thing to do. Many scholars have written on how sport brings about character building,[50] but simply receiving praise or affirmation for following the rules can help realize this good. More will be said about this in the next section.

45. Young and Okada, *Sport, Social Development and Peace*, 122. See also Holt, *Positive Youth Development through Sport*.

46. Young and Okada, *Sport, Social Development and Peace*, 112.

47. Verkooijen, van Hove, and Dik, "Athletic Identity and Well-Being."

48. Horton and Mack, "Athletic Identity in Marathon Runners."

49. Kerksick et al., "Effects of Popular Exercise Program."

50. This contention is debatable, and will be discussed in the next chapter.

6. Social belonging and love include finding a place in a group of people. Many athletes recognize their teammates as some of their closest friends and research shows that athletic teams can offer ample opportunities for validation and affiliation.[51]

This is just a cursory and brief examination of these goods and their relationship to sport. In the next chapter I will go into much more depth on these goods and show how they are manifested in the lives and faiths of the adolescents and young adults who participated in Team World Vision marathons. But even this brief look reveals that sport has the power to manifest these basic human goods.

However, we must still take into account the earlier objections to sport, that is, how sport often leads to destruction, or rather, the opposite of human thriving. Why do so many athletes damage their bodies with steroids, and why did Michael Phelps, arguably one of the greatest athletes ever to live, have to seek out rehabilitation for substance abuse? Are sports sometimes evil? sFor this, we can look again at Smith, who notes that yes, there is a such thing as evil, but not as a force in and of itself. Rather,

> ontologically, evil has only a "shadow" existence that is parasitical on the good. Ultimately, only good is independently real, and all of reality is innately good in being. So to try to find the substantive source of what is bad or evil is like trying "to see darkness or hear silence." Badness and evil come into being only in the absence of the good.[52]

Smith affirms the goodness of God's creation, and that evil is simply an absence of these human goods. All six goods are needed for human flourishing, so the neglect of one for the benefit of another can lead to hurt. I would add to this too that evil or wrongdoing is a misdirection or disordered mutation of the good. The man who has an affair is seeking out something good, such as social belonging, love, and identity coherence, but is doing so in a disordered manner, in a misdirected way that results in destruction. Again, we see how sin is a violation of relationships. The theologian must recognize that the goods of human life can become idols.[53] Returning to Michael Phelps, we can see how a teenaged boy with divorced parents and an estranged father, found knowledge of reality, identity coherence, and social belonging in swimming.[54] However, while meeting the demands

51. Allen, "Social Motivation in Youth Sport," 561–62.
52. Smith, *To Flourish or Destruct*, 234.
53. Dyrness, *Poetic Theology*, 30.
54. Layden and Layden, "The Rehabilitation of Michael Phelps."

of an Olympic athlete, he failed to find those goods elsewhere as well, and neglected other goods. So, to make clear here, this understanding of the good of sport as part of God's redemptive plans for human flourishing, does not deny or ignore the destructive powers of sport, but rather shows how all human goods, when disordered or ignored, lead to destruction.

What's more, there is ample evidence that sports, in order to yield these beneficial goods, must be actively guided toward the good—they must be properly ordered through skilled leaders.[55] In other words, good coaches are crucial for bringing about the goods of sport. So, "despite the claims that participation in sport facilitates positive youth [and adult] development, there is nothing about sport itself that is magical."[56] Sports in and of themselves do not yield these basic human goods, but when properly guided—or we might say, ordered—they do, and they do so abundantly. This is further evidence against that claim that to redeem sports we must get back to its autotelic value, to its essential goodness rooted in play. Granted, playfulness should be a cornerstone of all sport participation, but for sports to be a positive experience for those involved, activities must be guided and led by people interested in human development and thriving.

Conclusion

God has a redemptive purpose for all of creation, which is realized in Jesus Christ and is being fulfilled by the work of the Holy Spirit, mediated through the goods of human culture. Sport is an excellent means for realizing the goods of personhood and yielding human flourishing, and therein lies the good of sport. It has the power to bring about God's purposes when properly guided. And that, I believe, is why humankind resonates so deeply with sport, why humankind loves it so much. Granted, it has the capacity like all goods to become disordered, but under the care and auspices of faithful people who want to realize all human goods, it can serve as part of God's redemptive plan for the world.

55. Fraser-Thomas, Côté, and Deakin, "Youth Sport Programs," 30.

56. Danish et al., "Enhancing Youth Development Through Sport," 39.

5

Human Thriving in Team World Vision Marathon Runners

In the previous chapter, I argued that sport, when rightly ordered by good coaches and leaders, has tremendous capacity for promoting human thriving. In this chapter I will give examples, by showing how thriving is manifested in adolescent athletes who participated in marathons with Team World Vision. I will look particularly at the qualitative interview data that was gathered by myself and another researcher and will identify common themes that emerged. Through the lens of Smith's ends for human flourishing, I will show that in many cases the marathon experience was not just physically or even morally meaningful, but deeply spiritual, creating experiences of God's presence and activity.[1] Furthermore, using this data, I will elaborate on sport's capacity, when rightly directed, to promote thriving and, when in a particular context, faith formation.

About the Team World Vision Study[2]

As mentioned before, research indicates that for athletic participation to promote character development, to be a positive experience for participants, and eventually to yield flourishing, it must be situated in a context that values those good ends. This study intended to look at just such an athletic activity: The Team World Vision (TWV) marathon program. TWV is a non-profit Christian relief and development organization which solicits adolescents and adults to raise money for clean water, sanitation, and hygiene programs in African countries by training for and running half or full marathons (13.1 and 26.2 mile runs, respectively). TWV is a part of World Vision, one

1. This discussion is not a critique of Smith's categories. That is beyond the scope here. His categories rather present an accessible way to analyze manifestations of flourishing in the TWV runners.

2. For the full Protocol Description, see Appendix A.

of the largest humanitarian organizations in the world. It encourages runners to dedicate their race to helping others in Africa through sponsorship fundraising. That is, participants seek out sponsors who will donate money to World Vision should the runner complete the race. Previous runners for TWV have reported anecdotally an increase in physical and athletic ability as a result of their training, but they also recount that their experiences are profoundly spiritual and transformative. This study enacted a thorough quantitative and qualitative investigation, through multiple questionnaires and one-on-one interviews, in order to examine those claims.[3]

The data here comes from interviews that were designed, conducted and analyzed by the research team.[4] We conducted twenty-two interviews with eight completed after the 2015 Chicago Marathon, and fourteen completed after the 2016 Los Angeles Marathon. The qualitative approach of the six-phase thematic analysis was used, which includes an in-depth coding process of collected data to identify broad themes within research interviews.[5] The interview questions remained relatively consistent across the interviews, with little spontaneous interaction.[6] Interviewees were all 15 to 21 years old, and all were either high school or college students. A large portion of the college participants attended private Christian institutions while the adolescents attended both private and public high schools.[7]

3. It came about as part of a grant from the John Templeton Foundation that looks more broadly at the effect of sports participation on virtue development and was led by Fuller School of Psychology Professors Ben Houltberg and Sarah Schnitker.

4. The team consisted of Benjamin Houltberg, Amanda Williams (Assistant Professor of Child and Family Studies at University of Southern Mississippi), Fuller School of Psychology doctoral students Daniele Hand and Rachel Falco, and myself.

5. See Braun and Clarke, "Using Thematic Analysis in Psychology." Themes are discovered when a researcher carefully analyzes data through transcription and note taking, actively coding, searching for, reviewing, and naming themes that exist across the entire data set.

6. For the full list of questions, see Appendix B. The questions revolved around five themes: Purpose, Relationship to Others, Dealing with Adversity, Relationship to Body, and Relationship to God. All interviews were transcribed and coded based on the six human goods of Smith. I have removed "likes," "ums," and other speech disfluencies from the interview transcripts in order to improve readability. However, I have tried to stay as true as possible to the students' original, oral answers. I encourage the reader to look past their youthful manner of speaking.

7. Specifically, there were fifteen adolescent participants interviewed (nine females and six males) and six of them attended public schools located in area of socioeconomic disadvantage while six reported going to a private high school and two students were part of a local church youth group. Four of the adolescents reported their ethnicity as Caucasian, five self-identified as Hispanic and five reported being Asian. The college-aged participants all reported their ethnicity as Caucasian with three males and four females.

It should be noted that TWV is an explicitly Christian organization, and their recruitment and training methods reflect Christian commitments. All of the participants were aware of this. While not all identified as Christian, all knew that they were working with a Christian organization. Most interviewees however had significant church backgrounds. While not all confessed to well-formed faiths, nearly all were comfortable with age-appropriate theological discussion.

The thematic analysis presented here was based on Smith's six basic human goods and I will show how interviewees realized or did not realize these goods. Overarching themes from the data will be shown, and I will conclude with some evidence of spiritual formation that was manifested in the runners.

Good 1: Bodily Survival, Security, and Pleasure

Smith defines the first basic human good as "avoiding bodily death, injury, sickness, disease, and sustained vulnerability to harm; maintaining physical and bodily health and safety; sensual enjoyment, satisfaction, delight, or gratification of appetitive and perceptual desires of the body; and the absence of physical pain and suffering."[8] Obviously, all those interviewed had completed a full or half marathon, which are undoubtedly difficult athletic events and require a good amount of pre-existing physical health. These adolescents, by default, were not dealing with imminent threats of bodily harm or disease. That being said, the marathon led to many insights for the students about the physical self and bodily health.

First, there was increased physical awareness. One of the questions that we asked of all the runners was: "Before you learned about the marathon, did you ever think your body would have been able to finish a marathon?" Almost every single runner replied, "No." This included students who participated in other sports, including track and cross county. For even the experienced athlete, the marathon presented a challenge beyond perceived abilities. One student remarked, "I feel like I learned more about what I can do."[9] This increased awareness of physical abilities was seen in many students, while others in turn also learned about their physical limits. Another runner stated that, "I learned not to push myself too much, or I need to know how much I can take, [and] how much I can't."[10] For others,

8. Smith, *To Flourish or Destruct*, 181.

9. Interview 5 (LA)

10. Interview 3 (LA)

the challenge of a marathon led to greater discernment with diet and its connection to performance.

> When it came to a marathon, that's when I really started thinking about food and that's when I started thinking about everything. Oh man, my body got skinnier. I started to notice I had more energy because of the stuff that I was really paying attention to. I downloaded an app that counted my calories. I did everything I could to make sure my nutrition was on top, that I was drinking enough water.[11]

Another common theme was the physical pleasure that came from training for and running in the marathon. Many students truly enjoyed the process, even as it was rigorous. One noted, "I felt like it was . . . it was getting better. I felt like this was good for me, this was good for my body, and it would help in the future."[12] Another stated, "I feel like running makes you so focused, makes you focus, makes you serene, makes you calm."[13] This physical pleasure often led to greater desire to care for the body.

> I mean you feel good when you exercise every day. Endorphins or whatever it is. Just you feel stronger, and I think you want to take care of your body more. When you run so much, like you want to eat well, because it affects how you run or it affects how you feel when you run, so you eat better. Yeah, so you just feel better.[14]

Another remarked about the resiliency of her body, and the pleasure derived there.

> I feel like my body is in a shape now where I ran a marathon, and I'm back to the point where I'm not in any pain [from training and running]. It's kind of encouraging—my body was capable of running a marathon, and finishing a marathon, and then going back to normal functioning, completely normal without any issues. So, I guess it makes me feel pretty good about myself.[15]

This student mentions pain, as did many others. Smith's definition of the first good includes absence of physical pain and suffering, which is appropriate, but it should be pointed out here that many students got injured

11. Interview 12 (LA)
12. Interview 2 (LA)
13. Interview 14 (LA)
14. Interview 5 (Chicago)
15. Interview 4 (Chicago)

during training or had to push through great pain to finish their race. Is this then contrary to the definition of the first good? I would argue, no. To be fair, many runners admitted to the inconsistency in their training. TWV provides training plans, group runs, and a great deal of coaching, all to help students form realistic expectations for their performance. That being said, marathon training takes a great deal of consistency, planning, and maturity should a runner hope to avoid injury. With busy schedules and conflicting commitments, many of these young people were not consistent in their training, and therefore reported numerous injuries. However, their management of their pain and injuries was quite remarkable, and I believe a sign of fulfillment of the first good. One student saw finishing the race as an adequate justification for the pain, stating, "there was definitely [a time where I thought] wow, I am in a lot of pain right now, why am I doing this to myself? But I think it was just cool, especially right when you finish, you're just like, I just did that. I just ran twenty-six miles. What in the world?"[16] For many of the students who identified having a strong faith, these moments of physical pain were times for reaching out to God for help.

> I wasn't able to do this by myself. I really, really had to rely on God to get through all of my runs because it just, it takes a really big toll on a person's body and it's just so hard to try to do it with only your own strength that you have to really rely on God to give you strength to get through it.[17]

Another runner put it quite succinctly:

> Interviewer: How often did you seek God's support or guidance when you were feeling weak or in pain?
>
> Respondent: Every time![18]

God was also seen as playing a role in managing pain and giving endurance. One runner remarked, "I don't think that God took the pain away. But he just helped me deal with it."[19] Another mentioned that "when I asked God for strength, that's when I really did feel those little rushes of adrenaline and just that strength to just push through rather than the weakness that I had felt before."[20] One runner even saw a direct correlation between his faith and his marathon training and running.

16. Interview 5 (Chicago)
17. Interview 1 (Chicago)
18. Interview 8 (Chicago)
19. Interview 5 (Chicago)
20. Interview 1 (Chicago)

> Once the marathon started getting closer, that's when my faith started getting stronger. And in the marathon, you know, the times that I was hurting I was really looking towards God. I was suffering. And when I got to mile twenty-five, I kind of just talked to myself. You know what, you're not gonna walk. You're not gonna stop. You're gonna run this thing, and you're gonna finish. And that's when I really started praying as I started running. I was praying, let's go God. And I started singing worship songs in my head. I was like let's go. And I felt myself get stronger and stronger and stronger and I ended up clocking my fastest mile time at the last mile of the marathon. So, it definitely was like my faith and my body were just all one. [21]

In sum, the TWV participants acknowledged an increase in health and feelings of physical wellness and pleasure. Even though the training and running often caused injuries and pain—which some described as suffering—there was a strong sense that the pain was not insurmountable, or that the pain was for a greater purpose, which often connected to God.[22]

Good 2: Knowledge of Reality

Smith defines this good as "learning about the world and one's place and potential in it; increasing awareness and understanding of material and social realities; developing or embracing believed-in truths about what exists and how it works that provide order, continuity, and practical know-how to life experience."[23] As mentioned before, TWV runners are recruited for expressly instrumental purposes—water projects in Africa—not for enjoying sport for sport's sake. Their team meetings and methods for motivating runners revolve around this end. You are running for another purpose. The interviewees all showed this foundation for their running, some to greater extents than others, but in their responses were many signs of manifestation of this second good. One student noted, "I was stunned by the fact that how she [the school's TWV recruiter] showed us that water and other resources, [are] so absent from Africa. And I kind of realized that how every day in America we have it [water] and [it's] so accessible and in Africa, it's like a

21. Interview 12 (LA)

22. Recent psychology research shows that spirituality and religious involvement predict higher patience, even through times of suffering. See Schnitker et al., "The Virtue of Patience"

23. Smith, *To Flourish or Destruct*, 181.

luxury for them."[24] Another noted that involvement with TWV showed her "a different side of just a struggle. I would never be able to ponder just not having water and kids in my village dying every single day just because they don't have access to that."[25] Multiple students found a stark contrast between their lives and the lives of those they were helping. As one student said,

> In spite of me being where I am and growing up where I have and being blessed the way I have been blessed, it seemed like the cause itself—providing clean water for people that didn't have it—when I have a faucet, just about in every place I go, or free water anywhere I go, was enough to run.[26]

And another found that the race

> made me realize that . . . there's more people that need more than just what I need. Like I complain about new pairs of shoes, while there're people in other parts of the world where they don't even have water on a daily basis. So, it puts it into perspective.[27]

This greater understanding of hardships in the world left many feeling changed. One student remarked that "when I signed up for the marathon, a lot of people told me it would change my life, and I don't know if I necessarily believed them, but it really has, and it's really just changed the way that I see so many things."[28] While a few students shared that their original intent in signing up for the marathon was personal—to improve health, become more active, or accomplish something difficult—they often stated that through training their motivations shifted toward philanthropy. One student mentioned that after weeks of training with TWV, "my motivations changed. I was doing this for a different purpose now. . . it humbled me a lot because you realize that I'm not, I shouldn't be doing these [races]. I mean, I should be doing it, but I shouldn't be doing it for myself."[29]

While it may seem from these quotes that the students gained a deeper understanding of the material realities of the world, it could be argued that they were in fact handicapped by TWV in terms understanding worldwide poverty. As the student's statements show, they were taught about water crises in Africa, without any indication of the vast expanse of the continent, not to mention the economic diversity present there. Journalists are

24. Interview 13 (LA)
25. Interview 11 (LA)
26. Interview 2 (Chicago)
27. Interview 4 (LA)
28. Interview 1 (Chicago)
29. Interview 4 (Chicago)

becoming more aware of language that presents Africa as one unified place, where poverty is omnipresent. This kind of language neglects the distinctions between the continent's fifty-five coutries. In fact, references solely to "Africa" occur most frequently when paired with "global-development."[30] TWV's own website—which works as a recruitment tool—gives no indication as to what countries are actually served, but rather gives broad statements like "6 kilometers is the average distance people in Africa walk for water."[31] This language about poverty in "Africa" could be seen as a narrowing of social realities, and therefore counterproductive to the second good. I however would argue that this is not the case. Should one look at the website of World Vision, the parent organization of TWV, one will find a map with all of the clean-water work being done on the African continent.[32] It is clear that World Vision is doing work all throughout sub-Saharan Africa, and that donations may go to any numbers of countries. It makes sense then that recruitment materials, as well as motivational rhetoric for TWV runners, would refer only to Africa—although, greater focus on particular countries, when presenting information to runners, would certainly serve TWV well. I would also argue that the runners interviewed showed an age-appropriate understanding of the global reality of poverty, and a true desire to make a difference. Nearly every single runner stated that they would like to be involved with World Vision again, a desire that could lead to a more thorough integration and knowledge of world development issues, and an opportunity to see more of their life in a larger perspective.

Good 3: Identity Coherence and Affirmation

Smith defines this good as "developing and maintaining continuity and positive self-regard in one's sense of personal selfhood over time and in different contexts and situations."[33] As mentioned under Good 1, many of the students felt healthier and more aware of their lifestyle choices, as well as a pride in their previously unrealized ability to run a great distance. In the interviews, every student was asked, "Is there something about yourself that you're especially proud of?" Many had difficulty with this question, as it requires a great deal of self-reflection. They had even more difficulty with the follow-up question, "Is there anything about yourself that you're

30. Kayser-Bril, "Africa Is Not a Country."

31. Team World Vision. "Home," accessed April 25, 2017, https://www.teamworldvision.org/.

32. World Vision website. "Our Work," https://www.worldvision.org/our-work.

33. Smith, *To Flourish or Destruct*, 181.

not especially proud of?" Some students chose to skip these questions by just saying, "No." However, one runner, a college student, did find a distinct connection between her running, training, and her sense of self-regard, stating pride specifically in

> having the determination to just like stick with the things that I commit to. Whenever I make a commitment I always try to fulfill that commitment and do the best that I can to succeed while doing that too. So, I guess I'm just proud to have that determination and ability to stay committed to what I agree to do.[34]

This aspect of her personality was revealed through the disciplined work of marathon training. She also found a deeper sense of life purpose through running.

> Interviewer: Did running this race make you think about yourself differently?
>
> Respondent: It really did. It made me think more about how the things that I'm doing shouldn't be . . . I shouldn't be doing them for me, but I should be doing them to help out other people, to help out my neighbors and to just spread the love of God to others, and I've been a runner for quite some time. I ran track in high school and stuff but this was the first time that I had actually run for something other than myself, and it just really made a difference.[35]

Another question, that was deliberately highly theological, asked, "What do you think it means to be 'made in the image and likeness of God?'" Many of the youth struggled to give an answer to this question—which is understandable considering professional theologians struggle with this question (and there will be significant discussion of this doctrine, the *imago Dei*, in the following chapters). But many connected it back to love, acceptance, and purpose given by God. One runner stated that,

> I think that when we were created in the image of God, that we were created for a purpose . . . I think that we were all given the ability to do something . . . it's not going to be the same from someone else, but I think we were born with a creativity to tell our own story how we want it.[36]

34. Interview 1 (Chicago)
35. Interview 1 (Chicago)
36. Interview 3 (LA)

Another noted that, "God put a lot of potential in us, and God put a lot of faith and trust in us when he first created us."[37] Others showed a connection between the *imago Dei* concept and the ends of the TWV marathon. "We are created to do works like Mother Theresa . . . to do work that he [God] wanted us to do. To be his hands and feet, and to serve. In his image."[38] And just like the TWV coaches teach, being in God's image meant for one runner that "you could endure things that you think you can't."[39]

Even as the runners struggled with self-reflection, they showed that their training and running helped with forming a positive self-regard, which many connected back to a purpose endowed by God.

Good 4: Exercising Purposive Agency

Smith defines this good as "exerting influence or power (broadly understood as transformative capacity) in the social and material worlds, through the application of personal capabilities for perception, reflection, care, evaluation, self-direction, decision, and action, which causes desired (and unanticipated) effects in one's environment."[40] There are two main ways this good manifested itself in the runners: change in physical ability and change in another's life.

First, many runners remarked about the incredible change they saw in their own abilities. For many of the students, this was their first marathon, but a few others had participated with TWV in the past. Finishing a marathon requires incremental training, where mileage is increased each week, allowing the runner's lung and heart capacity to grow over time. TWV provides a highly effective training program, which includes group runs with benchmarks (a ten-mile run and a twenty-mile run). When a training plan is properly followed, even non-runners can become marathon ready in a relatively short amount of time. Granted, not all of the students followed the plan as diligently as needed—and injuries ensued—but many remarked on the physical transformations they underwent as a product of their training. Through training, they became able to do something that was previously thought impossible. When asked, "Did running and training in the race make you think about yourself differently?" one student responded, "Yes, because I didn't think I would be able to do something like this!"[41] Another

37. Interview 5 (LA)
38. Interview 13 (LA)
39. Interview 7 (LA)
40. Smith, *To Flourish or Destruct*, 181.
41. Interview 7 (Chicago)

noted, "I had a limited idea of what I could accomplish physically. So, I feel a lot more confident in my ability to do any sort of physical activity."[42] For one student, training yielded a greater understanding of the physical body. "Running the race and training and stuff, I learned new things. I learned how to control my breathing and breathing techniques, and how to control my pace and my breaths, and different things like that."[43] Multiple students reflected on their progress made through incremental training.

> I could kind of see myself getting stronger, you know, each week, I was like oh seven [miles], that's not too bad, and then the next week, oh I can do this. I did this last week. And so, it was cool to see the progress as time [went by]. Being willing to put in the miles actually paid off.[44]

> I could just keep running further and further and further, and I knew that, I looked ahead at the overall training schedule and I'm like wow, at some point I'm going to have to run twenty miles in one day. And now, and I look at that at a time when one or two miles was a lot. Well, we'll get there. But yeah, I started feeling better and I could reach those higher numbers, and [thought] alright, this is awesome!"[45]

An older student, who had previous marathon experience, remarked that, "I ran 15 miles straight this year without taking a break or anything, and that in my mind was just, holy cow! I can't believe I just did that!'"[46]

What is seen here is the realization of physical abilities, through training, that for many were unanticipated. These runners exercised their own purposive agency, followed a training plan, and were able to finish a full or half marathon. Granted, all of the runners interviewed completed the race.[47] But for these runners, they recognized that they brought about changes in their physical bodies through diligent and measured action.

The second way this good was manifested was in the students' feelings of impacting the life of another, particularly in this case the children in African countries who are receiving water. TWV is very clear in its recruitment campaigns that for every fifty dollars raised, one person will receive clean

42. Interview 1 (LA)

43. Interview 2 (Chicago)

44. Interview 6 (LA)

45. Interview 3 (Chicago)

46. Interview 2 (Chicago)

47. 400 runners began the study (including the quantitative and qualitative sections), and 239 completed the marathon and the study questions. The qualitative participants were only taken from the group of finishers.

water for a lifetime. For many, this became a very real and tangible result of their running and fundraising. One student mentioned that she raced because, "I knew I was helping these people that really, really needed it and I could actually see the impact that it was having."[48] Granted, that might be an overstatement, but others took a more measured view. "I ended up realizing that it was for a good cause, and so I was glad about that, and I was glad that I was actually able to make some difference whether [or not] I can really see it at the moment."[49] Many used language of potential impact. "It just brings me joy to actually do that [race] because I know that I'm doing something, and that I'm actually making a difference in the world."[50] One student connected her running and fundraising directly with her faith, saying,

> There were a lot of times where during training or definitely during the marathon where I would pray and I would tell God, I was like God, I know I'm doing this for a greater purpose, and I know I'm doing this for myself as well, but, I just want to do it to, I want to do it ultimately for you, and so, for me, doing it for him was raising the money for clean water. [51]

TWV races are framed around this concept of exerting positive influence on the life of another. Through running, which is of course tied to fundraising, people know, or at least perceive, that they are able to bring about change in another's environment.

Good 5: Moral Affirmation

Smith defines this good as "believing that one is in the right or is living a morally commendable life, by being, doing, serving, thinking, and feeling what is good, correct, just, and admirable; avoiding moral fault, blame, guilt, or culpability."[52] We've already seen how the runners saw the marathon as a means for bringing change to the world, so it's no surprise that they couched this activity in language of morally commendable actions. One youth said, "I want to do more good in the world, so I think that I did good by doing it [running the race]."[53] And another said, "It's good for other people, it's

48. Interview 11 (LA)
49. Interview 3 (Chicago)
50. Interview 11 (LA)
51. Interview 4 (Chicago)
52. Smith, *To Flourish or Destruct*, 181.
53. Interview 2 (LA)

good for you. It's a like a win-win."[54] One runner, when asked, "How does running a marathon fit in with your sense of purpose?" responded, "If I can do something to better other people, why wouldn't I do it?"[55] These quotes highlight the feelings of moral affirmation that the TWV runners experienced. Since many of the runners identified strongly as Christians, some also incorporated their faith language into their moral framework, citing that this experience was for God's glory.

> The whole reason is that I want to do good, and I think that's what it is, I want to do good because I'm guessing that's what God wants, to do good in life for other people, to not be selfish, to think of others, and because I mean we're all humans, and that's our purpose, like just keep each other alive to keep the [human] race going. [56]

> We're doing something for him. We're doing something that we believe is right and you know all of this was for the glory of God and to also spread God's word to these kids in Africa. It's not just water we're giving them. We're trying to give them new life in God. And so, I feel that while God was watching [us] putting ourselves through [physical] pain [associated with training and running], he was also proud. "They're doing this for me."[57]

> As the miles got longer . . . running for a charity and running for a cause became more of an important factor because it wasn't just running for myself. Because at like mile fifteen to twenty, it is just hard to get up and run for no reason. So, knowing that you're doing something for a reason is a cool part of it.[58]

We can also see here echoes of the previous discussion on the good of sport. The majority of the interviewees reported that they ran the race, and did the fundraising, for a very specific reason. That is, they had an instrumental purpose. While many admitted that they received other benefits, like improved health, weight loss, or increased self-esteem, these were ultimately secondary to the task of helping someone in need. Some were even hesitant to admit that training made them feel good, possibly because that sentiment would appear selfish. I would argue that what is evident here is a tension about the value of sporting activities in the Christian context. This was

54. Interview 2 (LA)
55. Interview 4 (LA)
56. Interview 2 (LA)
57. Interview 12 (LA)
58. Interview 5 (Chicago)

discussed in the previous chapter, but here we see a real manifestation of the need for richer theological language about sport, particularly as it relates to purpose and God's redemptive work in the world.

One runner though, a college student, presented an incredibly mature assessment of his participation, building a bridge between his own perceived suffering in the race and the suffering of others.

> I think, in the midst of that suffering [from running], you get a glimpse into what it's like to walk miles and miles to get water that's not even clean. But I think that's why I run, because I want to get to feel that, to know what it's like. I want to be able to join with those people, and then in the end to relinquish that from them, give them the opportunity not to have to feel that anymore.[59]

This quote represents a form of moral affirmation and philanthropy that is not colonial or demeaning but rather incarnational. He suffers to know the suffering of others, all for the sake of ending suffering. He is referencing a more inclusive narrative that makes sense of both the lack of water in Africa and the pain of running a race in America.

Overall, the moral affirmation that is produced in TWV runners is connected almost exclusively to the fundraising component, that is, to helping those in need. There was little sense from these interviews that moral affirmation arose from the actual act of running, from the sporting event itself. That is to say, these runners did not find any implicit value in running—they were wary of the potential selfishness evident in viewing running as something that exists for its own sake. Their ends were instrumental, and often tied to God's purposes for the world. And yet, they did find enjoyment in the sporting activity, a feeling that wasn't well reconciled for many participants.

Good 6: Social Belonging and Love

Smith defines this good as "enjoying recognition by, inclusion and membership in, and identification with significant social groups; loving and being loved by others in significant relationships." One question, that every interviewee was asked, was whether or not they formed any new relationships while training and running. Surprisingly, not everyone said "yes." Many who said "no" appeared to myself and the other interviewer, Danielle, as shy and reserved, not people who actively seek out new friendships. But I would argue

59. Interview 2 (Chicago)

too that relationship building through TWV happens primarily in the context of group training and group runs. All participants are encouraged to participate in group runs, but because of schedules and locations, not everyone does. This has an impact on whether or not new friends are made. One runner, who had run with TWV throughout high school, commented that,

> Because the training I did with the Saturday group run—or years ago we had Tuesday after school group run with all the members—it's spiritually inspiring for a lot of us and also creates a connection between us. And that was great. The first times I ran [with TWV] and I didn't train [with the group]—I trained on my own a little bit—and it was horrible. So, I changed that in the next two races and you feel much better.[60]

From the accounts of the runners, close relationship building came out of participation in team training activities, or very deliberate scheduling of training with other friends. For those who identified as Christian and who did build new relationships, there was often a spiritual component to these relationships. One runner remarked,

> I love just being able to build relationship with people and then invest in those relationships, too. And then training with the team from [name of university] really helped me to build relationships with other people who were experiencing the same things that I was, and it really helped me to grow in my faith as well, just being able to train with these people and pray with these people about not only just running but about other things in our lives. We were able to build relationships where we were truly concerned about each other and about what everybody was going through.[61]

Other students found inspiration and a sense of community with people they didn't know, but who were at the race. TWV has thousands of runners of all ages and they are highly visible on race day, as team members wear bright orange jerseys. There are also TWV-specific support teams that hand out water and food to runners, all while cheering them on. Many interviewees found these people particularly inspiring.

> There's just all these strangers along the road that come out every year to hold up signs and hand out water and snacks. And they keep you motivated. You don't even know them. And I wrote my

60. Interview 13 (LA)

61. Interview 1 (Chicago)

> name on my jersey, so they just called out my name and kept me motivated. So that was just, it was great. It kept pushing me.[62]

Another connected with a TWV supporter from his own church.

> I hit the wall at mile twenty, there's where I really hit the wall hard. And what was really cool was that a lady from my church was at a Team World Vision cheering station, and she ran with me from [mile] twenty to twenty-one and she was really cheering me on and making sure I had everything, making sure I had hydration and just [enough] fuel in me.[63]

For those who run with TWV, there is a tremendous amount of support and camaraderie that comes from the "mutual suffering" of marathon training and racing. The good of social belonging manifests itself in the close relationships that are built and the encouraging environment that is cultivated.

TWV and the Good of Sport

Previously, I argued that the good of sport should not be located in its intrinsic value or in its autotelic nature, but in its capacity to promote human thriving in line with God's redemptive purposes for the world. Those who argue for an intrinsically valuable understanding of sport—that is, sport for sport's sake—are hoping to move away from the instrumental argument for sport, that its good lies in its capacity to produce or affect something else. This is understandable, as agendas external to sport often corrupt both the game and the hoped-for outcome. One need look no further than the damage done to the East German Olympic swim team. In the hope to show communism as the dominant economic system (an agenda outside of sport), East German coaches gave steroids to their swimmers, without the swimmers knowing it, and thereby did irrevocable damage on many of the swimmers' bodies. From the evidence above though, I believe that basic human goods are being manifested in the lives of TWV runners. And TWV has an explicitly instrumental understanding of racing—marathons are for raising money for another cause.

What I would argue, which becomes even clearer here, is that the shaping of the sporting event, and everything around it, is what is truly important. Sport never exists in a vacuum. If the shaping of the sporting event is about economic dominance, it will become destructive. I would also argue that if the shaping of the event is for purely evangelistic reasons, without

62. Interview 11 (LA)

63. Interview 12 (LA)

opportunity for criticism of the sport itself, there will be destruction. TWV is highly shaped around self-sacrifice, and this message is communicated by coaches, volunteers, and even those cheering on the sidelines of the races. And because of this, human flourishing is manifested. Is the intent of TWV instrumental? Absolutely. But this evidence shows that growth and thriving also occur within the runners. Something happens to the participants, both apart from and because of the instrumental purposes.

I've already pointed out a number of instances where interviewees saw intersection between their running and their faith. But I would argue that TWV participation has a powerful capacity for faith formation. Many of the runners found direct correlations between their running and the state of their faith.

> Training was kind of where my faith was just all over the place so my training was all over the place. My training was some days I woke up and I just won't go and went back to sleep. And some mornings I'm like, you know I'm gonna go, and I went. And that was just like my faith. I'd be like, you know today I think I'm gonna read the Bible.[64]

> I really have just been more aware of the things that I'm doing and whether I'm doing that for myself, or whether I'm doing that to fulfill God's purposes for my life and doing it out of love rather than because I want to personally. So, I guess since throughout my training and since the marathon I've just been more aware of trying to fulfill God's purpose in my life and trying to understand what that means.[65]

One interviewee even mentioned that when she is training and racing—that is, serving, because all of her races have a philanthropic component—her faith goes up. She noted a direct correlation between her service through racing and her faith.[66] Another mentioned the lasting impact racing had on her faith and understanding of call.

> I think definitely after the race, I feel more like I've been using my body for the purpose that God designed me to. I feel like before the race I was using my body more to glorify God and try to spread his love but not necessarily listening to God the way that he wanted me to use my body to glorify him. I was more using it for my own purposes, but since the race, I've been more aware

64. Interview 12 (LA)
65. Interview 1 (Chicago)
66. Interview 13 (LA)

> of the way that I use my body in trying to use it for God and listen to the things that he wants me to do or the places that he wants me to go, and use my body for that rather than just kind of making decisions on my own and using my body in that way.[67]

Again, many of these runners had a pre-existing Christian faith. The marathon running itself did not impact their faith, but when running in the context of TWV, with its ends pointed toward God's work in the world, their faith grew.

Conclusion

So, does marathon running—or by extension any athletic activity—have an intrinsic capacity to draw someone closer to God, or even bring about human thriving in line with God's redemptive work? I would argue, not necessarily. That is not what is shown here. Through marathon racing, people can just as easily destroy their bodies, alienate their families and friends, and fracture their identities. Now, when marathon training is rightly ordered toward human thriving and the purposes of God, by diligent, caring, and compassionate coaches and leaders, will human thriving and faith formation come about? Absolutely. That is what this evidence shows. These students put their faith into embodied action. They utilized their God-given physical gifts, enacted their beliefs in a thoroughly physical way, and thriving and faith formation manifested.

Sport has an amazing, although not intrinsic, capacity to yield human flourishing and God's redemptive purposes. The stories of these young marathon runners show that a program directed toward and defined by Christian self-sacrifice yields an extrinsic product (donations for clean water projects) as well as human thriving and further faith formation. Returning to my central thesis—that the pursuit of physical fitness is an integral part of the life of Christian discipleship, and it can serve as cooperation with God's redemptive purposes in creation—we can see from this data how God's purposes are enacted through TWV marathon running. Many of these aspects of flourishing and God's purposes are seen not just in the sporting event, or just in World Vision and its ends, but rather in the two working together. One might ask, why does World Vision bother with marathon running? Why not just recruit people to fundraise, and forget about the travails of marathon running? I would argue, because marathon running—as a sport and fitness related event—and philanthropic fundraising enhance and

67. Interview 1 (Chicago)

amplify one another, as they share the same ends of human flourishing, when rightly ordered. There is kinship there. There is cooperation in God's redemptive purposes for the world. And so, it makes sense to engage in fundraising through marathon running.

6

Groundwork for a Theology of Physical Fitness

In the previous chapter, I argued that sports, when rightly ordered by coaches and leaders, have a tremendous capacity for promoting human flourishing. One could argue however that this theological framework applies to many other pursuits as well: music, the visual arts, architecture, and so many other pleasing cultural forms, when rightly ordered, lead to human flourishing. The question might be then, is there a particular part of human flourishing that sports are especially suited at promoting? The answer I wish to present here is bodily well-being, what also might be called physical health. Physical health is often sought through physical fitness activities and these activities, like lifting weights, jogging, aerobics classes, and many others, are a subset of sport that have elicited little theological analysis.[1] The task of doing so however immediately faces many attendant questions, particularly in terms of understanding bodily shape and weight.

What I propose to do here is to unearth some historical understandings of exercise, bodily shape, and food, especially as they intersect with issues of morality and virtue. By bringing these to light, and assessing them adequately, I believe it will prepare the way for a more robust and measured theology of physical fitness, which I will present in the next chapter. Giving historical context will provide a critical perspective that will avoid simplistic generalizations and theological understandings of fitness that are either too uncritical, or overly dismissive of the goods of exercise.[2] To

1. See Watson and Parker, *Sport and the Christian Religion*, who identify reflection on exercise, health, and well-being as an area of emerging research.

2. One extreme example of the uncritical stance might be Kybartas and Ross, *Fitness Is Religion—Keep the Faith*. Kybartas was Madonna's personal trainer, who apparently, when inquiring about training schedules, would ask, "What time is church?" For an analysis that is dismissive of exercise, see Hoverd, *Working out My Salvation*. While Hoverd presents a valuable entry into theological conversation, he ultimately associates the gym with Foucault's understanding of the prison and the correctional institution, thereby missing much of the joy and meaning-making that people find at the gym.

do this, I will outline what I would call the two main common theologies of physical fitness and bodily shape that are currently present in twenty-first-century American culture. A common theology is a framework of commitment and devotion that a majority of people use, including religious and non-religious commitments.[3] Common theology is general and often non-critically-minded speech about God or transcendent realities. What I will show here is how these theologies spring from wider American culture—and the moral system embedded there. These theologies are sometimes explicitly Christian and sometimes not, sometimes emanating from the church and at other times from outside the church. I would make the argument that there is a vacuum of responsible discussion about physical well-being in the church, and that these theologies arise out of an unspoken need for theological language regarding well-being.

So, first, consider the common theology that one's bodily shape is indicative of personal morality. In this, one's bodily shape and physical fitness are determined by one's choices, which are dependent on the will. One's body is shaped by personal agency, and therefore one's shape reveals morality and the strength of the will. On the opposite side of this is the second common theology: one's shape is in no way indicative of moral standing. One's bodily shape and physical fitness are predetermined—perhaps by God— and outside of personal control, and therefore cannot indicate morality. After showing how these two theologies have come about in our culture, I will argue that neither is fully true nor fully false, and I will offer a third way to understand physical fitness and bodily well-being, highlighting especially the issues of institutional sin that affect bodily shape and physical well-being.

Common Theology One: One's Bodily Shape Is Indicative of Morality

The first common theology that I want to outline is that one's bodily shape depends on personal choices and is therefore an indicator of personal morality. One is thin (healthy and fit) or overweight (unhealthy and out of shape) because of personal agency and willpower. Fitness celebrity and former host of *The Biggest Loser* Jillian Michaels says that willpower "is a not a myth or a genetic trait you either have or you don't, it's a skill. This means that anyone can develop it at any point! It's like a muscle it can grow stronger or it can become weaker."[4] That is, it comes from human

3. "Common theology" is an unpublished term coined by William Dyrness.

4. Michaels, "The Truth About Will Power."

agency. This common theology is even integrated into American language surrounding food. It's not unusual to hear someone refer to a sweet or dessert as a temptation, as something from which one must abstain or offer resistance. And this abstention is often considered "good." Someone chooses to be good by skipping dessert. But questions arise: How is it that abstaining from dessert is "good?" What is the good that is being realized or achieved? Is it that eating more dessert might add to one's waistline? If so, that reveals one's belief that a large waistline is inherently bad, or that perhaps God has a particular waist size in mind for each of us, and anything that would contest that design is a "temptation." What is also seen in this language is the belief that one's choices determine one's bodily shape. The thin person maintains that shape by not eating dessert. The overweight person therefore has made a conscious choice to be that size—perhaps by consistently ordering dessert. In both cases their bodily shape is their fault. The skinny person has greater willpower and an ability to resist temptation, and because of this has made better, more virtuous choices. The overweight person then is visibly guilty of what we might label as sloth and gluttony. This narrative of personal responsibility as the primary factor in forming one's bodily shape is highly prevalent in American culture, as will be shown. But still, how did we come to associate virtue, even Christian virtue, with food and our physical shape? And what, if any, are the theological implications to what and how much we eat?

To begin to answer these questions, let us look at the United States in the nineteenth century, when many substantive changes were happening in the country, especially in relation to food and fitness. Before the twentieth century, fatness was a prerogative of very few and it carried with it a sense of wealth and even health.[5] One who had extra girth had ample means to buy food and was free of common wasting diseases. Political cartoons of the time, in popular magazines like *Life* and *Harper's Weekly*, often showed wealthy people as portly and round.[6] In the 1890s though, what we now know as the fitness industry was being born under the guidance of Eugen Sandow, a bodybuilding showman from Prussia who wowed American audiences with his muscular physique at the 1893 Chicago World's Fair and toured the United States under the label "the World's Most Perfect Man." In 1897 he published *Strength and How to Obtain It*, a fitness guide with explanations of various exercises. It was so widely read that a copy of it appears on Leopold Bloom's bookshelf in James Joyce's *Ulysses*. Sandow began to bring fitness and the muscular, lean, body to the public consciousness

5. This is still true today in many developing nations.

6. Farrell, *Fat Shame*, 27.

as something for which to strive. R. Marie Griffith notes that at this time bodily understandings, informed by the budding fitness industry and people like Sandow, along with New Thought movements and fringe Protestant leaders like Sylvester Graham,[7] created an American environment that was "a bewildering milieu in which older hierarchies of flesh and spirit were upended, [with] carnal aversions masking not only terror and anxiety but also rapt adoration."[8]

The Progressive Era of the early twentieth century saw many developments in food science, including the discovery of vitamins and macronutrients: proteins, fats, and carbohydrates. Most notably was the discovery, or we might say invention, of the calorie, the basic unit of food energy. Food science pushed forward the then radical idea that foods from different cultures and economic classes could in fact have the same nutritional value.[9] Calories helped form a view of food as fuel, as that which sustains the body, which was not a common belief at the time. It was not unusual to think that life was sustained by a 'vital force,' supplied by heaven, which determined one's lifespan.[10]

The United States involvement in World War I arguably had the greatest impact on the American understanding of food and bodily shape. European food shortages during the war showed the Western world that balances of power would be decided by food and its distribution. The goal then was to make food more rational, to use the lessons of the Enlightenment for its production and distribution. Winning the war and maintaining world power depended on food availability and volume. One result, as Helen Zoe Veit notes, was that Progressive food reformers, concerned about the war, "imbued their quest for rational food with a profound sense of morality."[11] Winning the war meant making rational and moral decisions about food. This era then saw tremendous growth in industrial food production, what we would call today processed food. Shoppers had myriad new options for buying canned and boxed food, and this advance in factory-made food was heralded as a great achievement in the rationalizing of production.[12] The American diet began to see substantive changes, with movement away from whole and locally sourced food to boxed and

7. Graham was a Presbyterian minister and the inventor of the Graham Cracker. His radical ideas about food were designed to keep people from masturbation. See Tompkins, *Racial Indigestion*.

8. Griffith, *Born Again Bodies*, 310, Kindle edition.

9. Veit, *Modern Food, Moral Food*, 1.

10. Veit, *Modern Food, Moral Food*, 46–47.

11. Veit, *Modern Food, Moral Food*, 4.

12. Veit, *Modern Food, Moral Food*, 44.

industrially produced foods, and this was understood, counterintuitively, as a moral move. I will return to this point below.

In 1917, the United States founded the Food Administration under the leadership of Herbert Hoover. Hoover was given tremendous amounts of power to determine food prices and rations in order to support the war effort. However, he chose largely not to use these powers, and instead sought to boost volunteerism in Americans, urging the country to eat less and make lower-calorie substitutions so that higher-calorie foods could be shipped overseas to deployed troops, who needed the energy. To promote this plan, the Food Administration initiated a massive marketing campaign that stressed the need for good personal choices around food. Their arguments carried a clear moral tone, as personal food choices were done for the good of the war effort. So, "a growing number of Americans expressed the idea that self-discipline around food was a moral virtue. And it was a virtue not only in its own right but also because it bespoke a general ability to forego immediate gratification and to control animal impulses in the interest of what people knew, intellectually, to be good and right."[13] The campaign also highlighted the differences between the citizen of an autocratic state (that is, who the United States was fighting in the war) and the citizen of a democracy. Dictators could tell people what to eat and what not to eat. In a democracy, people could make the right decision for themselves. Therefore, "a nation able to conserve food voluntarily was a nation composed of disciplined individuals willingly following a centrally organized plan, people who did not need external control because they were in control of themselves."[14] So, a person who made good food choices was both a moral person and a worthy citizen in the democracy.

Hoover, having been raised a Quaker, understood the similarities between the ends of the Food Administration and American Protestantism's preferences for simplicity. The Food Administration therefore actively sought out support from religious leaders. Celebrity preacher Billy Sunday is quoted as having said during a sermon, "Oh, heed the appeal of the government to the people that ought to stop gourmandizing, and stop eating four pounds of beefsteak, when you can get along with half a pound. Do something for other people!"[15] Hoover himself coined the term "The Gospel of the Clean Plate," that is, a plate with no wasted food, and many Americans

13. Veit, *Modern Food, Moral Food*, 4.

14. Veit, *Modern Food, Moral Food*, 35.

15. "Billy Sunday's Sermon Yesterday," March 28, 1918 folder. "Chicago Herald News," box 554, Headquarters Organization, Educational Division, Press Clipping Section, Press Clippings (12HJ-A2), 1918 (Ill), RG 4, NARA. Thanks to Helen Zoe Veit for retrieving and sharing this quote with me.

interpreted the Food Administration's appeals as an opportunity to exhibit religious devotion, ascetic discipline, and enactment of neighborly love toward Europeans wracked by war. Here we see that food-related morality is being born and explicated.

What is becoming clear is that during WWI the American cultural imagination surrounding food and eating started to take on a moral dimension. To eat smaller amounts was a moral act, wrapped up in issues of citizenship, democracy, and faith. Your own willpower, your ability to govern yourself, which is made manifest in your food choices, qualifies you as a worthy citizen of the democracy and a moral person. So then, the overweight or fat body, previously considered a sign of good health and prosperous living, took on a new meaning: the overweight person was now showing "physical evidence of gluttony and a lack of self-control."[16] What's more, the overweight person, having made a bad choice, was perhaps not even worthy to be a member of the democracy. Thus began the idealization of thinness, the dominant view of beauty throughout the twentieth century—and up until today. It's no surprise then that what was considered the ideal female form in the 1920s was the flapper, the curveless woman.

Now, it should be noted that issues of health, in relation to food choices, were not a large part of the dialogue in the early twentieth century. Previously, public nutritional concern had focused largely on undernourishment, that is, not getting enough to eat. It wasn't until 1911 that the word "malnutrition" was coined to describe a state where not enough of the *right* foods were being eaten, and the concept took many years to reach the public consciousness.[17] So, eating less in order to improve health or physical well-being was not part of public consciousness during the early days of the Food Administration. Health issues surrounding weight would enter the conversation later.

Within this new understanding of food and its role in shaping thin and virtuous bodies, the fitness industry began to take shape. One of the industry's top leaders in the 1920s and beyond was Bernarr McFadden, a bodybuilder and health activist who published *Physical Culture* magazine as well as *SPORT*, a predecessor to *Sports Illustrated*. McFadden was an outsized character and his publications pushed the boundaries of contemporary respectability, showing pictures of scantily clad women along with barely-dressed men. He advocated the cultivation of the body, and employed the phrases "Sickness is sin; don't be a sinner," and "Weakness is crime; don't be a criminal."[18] Later in the decade arose Charles Atlas, whose exercise

16. Veit, *Modern Food, Moral Food*, 8.

17. Veit, *Modern Food, Moral Food*, 25.

18. Black, *Making the American Body*, 20.

program of isometrics, termed "Dynamic Tension," was cleverly marketed through comic strips about the "97-pound weakling" who built up his body and defended his girl at the beach. As Jonathan Black puts it, "At a time when the nation was reeling from the 1929 stock market crash and its aftermath, Atlas's ads promised to restore a million battered male egos."[19] Both McFadden and Atlas stressed the need for personal initiative and personal responsibility in forming one's body. A person's body could become strong and capable through diligent exercise.

After WWII, the United States entered a period of rapid economic development and increased wealth. But the Cold War era also saw the first national crisis surrounding physical fitness. In 1953, two American physicians, Hans Kraus and Ruth Hirschland, travelled to Austria and Italy where they performed fitness tests (toe-touching, sit-ups, and leg lifts) on children aged six to nineteen, hoping to find a reason for prevalent back aches in adults. Having previously tested American children, these tests were just for comparison and they expected the results to be the same. What they found though was that 56 percent of American children failed the tests while only 8 percent of European children failed.[20] Experts rushed to figure out why the American children were physically inferior to their European counterparts, and they soon reached the consensus that American children had become weak because of post-WWII abundance. This led to national anxiety about future American military strength. Thus was created the Presidential Council on Youth Fitness, a government task force designed to bring the concepts of physical fitness and exercise to the wider American public.[21] Again, this was largely a government sponsored marketing campaign, and "the council embedded its physical fitness message within a more complex rhetoric of reform that envisioned children as future parents, citizens, and soldiers whose moral, mental, and physical capabilities were key to maintaining the superiority of the nation both at home and abroad."[22] Again, notice that the government took a role in shaping the populace's understanding of bodily shape and strength, once more framing it as a moral issue. This time though, the stakes were raised, as the notion "that Americans were becoming unfit, soft, weak, or flabby—adjectives the news media employed in the wake of the fitness report—represented nothing less than the destruction of a national myth."[23] To be flabby, to be overweight, is to be un-American. The

19. Black, *Making the American Body*, 22.

20. McKenzie, *Getting Physical*, 14.

21. The President's Council on Physical Fitness, which administers tests to elementary school students, wasn't formed until the Kennedy administration.

22. McKenzie, *Getting Physical*, 15.

23. McKenzie, *Getting Physical*, 17.

very abundance that justified American democracy and capitalism (and its supremacy), was interpreted as leading to this softening of the youth. Therefore, much of the PCYF's "rhetoric cast economic prosperity and increased leisure time in terms of sin, sloth, and gluttony and warned that without intervention, the nation would be in jeopardy."[24]

Just as the Food Administration did during WWI, the PCYF reached out to churches and religious organizations to help promote their goal of fitness awareness. They suggested topics for sermons, distributed posters for bulletin boards, and even wrote a youth fitness prayer.[25] But though the PCYF was promoting the idea of fitness, they were not giving specific instructions on how to achieve fitness, much less an explanation of what defines physical fitness. Their leadership, while effective in some sense, was vague. Still, in this milieu, the fitness industry saw another season of tremendous growth, as it provided what the PCYF did not. Vic Tanny, a savvy businessman, had a vision for creating fitness clubs that were welcoming and inviting to middle class Americans. Previous gyms had a reputation as rough places, with dark and dank interiors, attracting primarily immigrant body builders. Tanny opened his first club in 1939 in Santa Monica, capitalizing on the Muscle Beach scene.[26] By the 1960s, his franchise expanded to one hundred locations in the U.S. and Canada. Also active in the 1950s was Jack LaLanne, who led workouts on TV, primarily for housewives. LaLanne stressed personal transformation and described his own pre-fitness state in graphic terms:

> At 15 I knew the tortures of the damned . . . I was a sick shut-in! I wouldn't go out and see people. I had pimples, boils, flat feet, bad eyes, bony arms and legs and my overall disposition was rotten to the core. I lived on sugar. I was a sugarholic. I was so weak I couldn't participate in sports. I didn't want anyone to see me. But in a way, I'm thankful. It was these very liabilities that got me straightened out.[27]

Physical fitness, as both a concept and an industry, took off in Cold War America. However, this era also saw a sharp rise in heart attacks and heart disease, most publicly around white-collar men, although that wasn't the

24. McKenzie, *Getting Physical*, 41.

25. McKenzie, *Getting Physical*, 50.

26. While the current Muscle Beach, made famous by Gold's Gym and Arnold Schwarzenegger, is in Venice Beach, the original was in Santa Monica, and was frequented by acrobats and circus performers.

27. Horn, "Lalanne," accessed August 4, 2016, http://www.si.com/vault/1960/12/19/585930/lalanne-a-treat-and-a-treatment.

only demographic. Considered by some to be a badge of honor for the successful executive, heart attacks became part of the national conversation, and curing them became linked to diet and exercise. Physical fitness had become irrevocably tied to health.

By the 1960s though, people were asking for a more tangible definition of physical fitness. Kenneth Cooper, who was given the job of getting astronauts into top physical shape, created the VO2 max test, which gauged the amount of oxygen an individual's heart can pump to the body. For the first time, notions of fitness were reaching for scientific accuracy. In 1968, Cooper published *Aerobics*, which saw the coining of the now popular word. The book was later followed by a workout guide for improving aerobic capacity.

By the 1970s, physical fitness and bodily shape had become enmeshed in all these strains of thought. The thin body is a virtuous body, capable of making moral choices for the good of others. The muscular body is one that is cultivated and strengthened toward peak health. The fit body is one worthy of American citizenship. The 1970s saw the rise of jogging as a fitness pursuit, but jogging carried a unique symbolism as countercultural. It "was exercise, but it could also function as a political statement, a rite of environmental solidarity, or an expression of disapproval of an unhealthy world."[28] Yoga, while it had been in the United States for decades, saw a spike in participation in the seventies and eighties. For many, yoga is a spiritual pursuit, but one rooted in non-Western traditions. By the 1980s, being physically strong and capable became a requirement for the ambitious professional. Ronald Reagan's administration made sure to show his physical strength and vitality, highlighting his White House weightlifting routine.[29] As Shelly McKenzie puts it, "the career-minded workforce had transformed exercise from a leisure hobby grounded in health to a statement of personal and professional competence written on the body."[30]

What I've attempted to show here is the long tradition in the United States of integrating moral and religious language and concepts into notions of food choices, physical fitness, and bodily shape. In this common theology, the fit body represents restraint and moral uprightness. In contrast, the fat body represents sloth, gluttony, and unfitness for democracy. In this common theology, the individual—not the community—must make the decision to live either a healthy and fit life—which is a moral and righteous life—or a sick and fat one. Fitness and a subsequent agreeable bodily shape must come through personal agency and personal choices. We've also seen

28. McKenzie, *Getting Physical*, 119.

29. McKenzie, *Getting Physical*, 45.

30. McKenzie, *Getting Physical*, 159.

a recurring theme: abundance and plenty will lead to softness and ill health, just as they did in the Progressive and Cold War eras. I have called this stream of thought a common theology, as it has not come from a specific group of Christians and makes little reference to the will of God. But it has utilized the resources of the church, especially its language and ideas of morality, to disseminate its message. There is however a growing dissent to this common theology of physical fitness and personal agency, an alternative theology, to which I turn next.

Common Theology Two: My Bodily Shape Is Pre-Determined

Meghan Trainor's 2014 song "All About That Bass" spent eight weeks atop the Billboard Hot 100 and was nominated for the Song of Year Grammy. It's also intensely catchy. In the song, Trainor sings, with great presence and confidence, that curvy bodies are beautiful and perfect, and that the practice of digitally editing photographs of models should be stopped. The song encapsulates the contemporary movement toward what's known as "positive body image." Fitness obsession and fat denigration have arguably yielded a culture wracked by eating disorders, self-esteem issues, and radical plastic surgeries. The positive body image movement seeks to reorient our culture's understanding of physical shape, moving toward acceptance and diversity. But lying underneath this is an unspoken sense that bodily shapes are pre-determined, that the shape of one's physical body lies outside of one's direct control and should therefore be accepted as is. This is an understandable conclusion to reach: while the fitness and diet industries continue to grow and expand, the obesity rate continues to rise (more will be said about this later). And for those who do desire to lose weight, the task often seems impossible. Even after extreme lifestyle changes, weight comes back. Even when personal agency is exercised, and seemingly good personal choices are made, fat sticks around. What should be made of this? Well, one answer is that we may not be in control of our physical shape. And if this is so, then there is no reason to judge someone for his or her shape, or to consider someone slothful or gluttonous for carrying extra weight. Here lies the second, currently emerging, common theology: one's bodily shape is predetermined, possibly by God or genetics, and lies outside the capacities of personal agency. In a time where sensitivity is key, this theology might even make more sense for the Christian community. Timothy J. Voss, former professor of Human Performance and Wellness at Trinity International University, declares that,

> Your body pattern was intentionally made by God and he loves your body pattern . . . Passing judgment on another's body pattern and envying someone else's is second nature for many. It's wrong! It may even be an affront to the God who created us. Our whole body image value system is in need of a transformation. We need to rewrite the rules from God's point of view. Let us each look to our own body and what we do with it and with a breath of kindness accept and enjoy the diversity found in others.[31]

Perhaps all of our bodily shapes, whether big or small, are part of God's good design for creation.

I've outlined above how sloth and gluttony became associated with overweight people in the American consciousness. Amy Erdman Farrell gives a thorough explanation of the product of this way of thinking: fat shame, a form of direct discrimination against overweight people. She states that,

> The various forms of discrimination that fat people experience, in schools, at doctors' offices, in the job market, in housing, and in their social lives, means that, effectively, their life chances—for a good education, for fair and excellent health care, for job promotion and security, for pleasant housing, for friends, lovers, and life partners . . . in other words, for a good and safe life—are *effectively reduced.*[32]

She argues that fat shaming intertwines with notions of racism and racial categorization. The fat body is not just a sign of moral laxity, but may also be a sign of primitiveness, a sign of racial and ethnic inferiority. She recounts the story of Saartjie Baartman (Anglicized as Sarah Baartman), a Khoikhoi woman of South Africa who exhibited extremely large buttocks and breasts, most likely due to the genetic condition called steatopygia, which was common amongst women of the area. In 1810 she travelled to England with her employer/owner and was forced to appear in stage shows and country fairs. She was labeled the missing link between humans and animals. After her death at twenty-six, she was dissected by George Cuvier, who then published evidence of her low-level status in the chain of human development. A plaster cast was made of her body and put on display in Paris' Museum of Man until the 1970s, when feminist and South African protesters demanded it be taken down. Sarah Baartman, and other enslaved people like

31. Timothy J. Voss, "Transforming Wellness" in Byl and Visker, *Physical Education, Sports, and Wellness*, 61.

32. Farrell, *Fat Shame*, 7. Emphasis in the original.

her, helped push the notion of the fat body as the primitive body, the poor body, the colonized body. As Farrell notes,

> A fat body can threaten to unravel all the best efforts at upward mobility, conjuring up historical and cultural memories of that Great Chain of Being in which fatness was considered to be a characteristic of the most primitive, the most "ethnic," the most sexually loose females, the most *inferior* people. A thin body, in contrast, promises to hoist a person into the realm of the "most civilized body" and to erase the cultural meaning of other stigmatized physical characteristics.[33]

While phrenology, criminal earlobe-reading, and mental illness' association with spiritual possession have all died out, the idea that we can "read" someone's physical shape and see indicators of morality still persists in fat shaming. And this, at least for the progressively-minded Christian community, should end.

So, what's being done to eliminate fat shaming? One response was the National Association to Advance Fat Acceptance, a non-profit civil rights organization, founded in 1969, with the mission to end "size discrimination in all of its forms . . . [to] help build a society in which people of every size are accepted with dignity and equality in all aspects of life . . . [and to] pursue this goal through advocacy, public education, and support."[34] The new academic discipline of fat studies has produced a large literature, and like other progressive disciplines before it,[35] seeks to reclaim pejoratives: "Rejecting the term 'obesity' either as a euphemism or as a medical term that objectifies fat people, fat studies reclaims the term 'fat,' arguing that it should become a common term freed of negative connotation, no more controversial than describing someone as tall or brown haired."[36] And there we see again this sense of determinism. One does not choose height or hair color, so fat studies advocates argue, one does not choose body shape.

But this more permissive perspective also has its opponents. Critics would argue that fat acceptance ignores health issues. Isn't obesity, and the obesity epidemic, a crisis of health? Farrell responds that fat shaming, or categorizing the fat person as lazy and gluttonous, predates any association between health and weight.[37] As was shown above, Progressive Era weight discrimination arose out of perceived democratic readiness. Further, she

33. Farrell, *Fat Shame*, 131.

34. www.naafaonline.com

35. Namely Queer Studies, which reclaimed the pejorative "queer" in the 1990s.

36. Farrell, *Fat Shame*, 22.

37. Farrell, *Fat Shame*, 4.

argues, the obesity epidemic and its association with health has in fact lent potentially invalid scientific credence to discrimination, just as phrenologists did in earlier centuries. Fat people therefore may receive inadequate health treatment and are unfairly assumed to be health risks, while thin people, who might also be unhealthy despite their outward appearance, do not receive discrimination by the health industry. Questioning the health implications of weight also attacks what Farrell calls the "diet-industrial complex,"[38] the multi-billion-dollar fitness and diet industry that profits off of people's fear of fat. Stemming from this notion then is the Health at Every Size movement, which stresses that people can be healthy at any weight. HAES grew out of fat-positive conversations emerging in the United States in the 1960s, in tandem with other Civil Rights projects. The goals of the HAES, according to their literature, are:

1. Enhancing health—attending to emotional, physical and spiritual well-being, without focusing on weight loss or achieving a specific "ideal weight."
2. Size and self-acceptance—respecting and appreciating the wonderful diversity of body shapes, sizes, and features (including one's own!), rather than pursuing an idealized weight, shape, or physical feature.
3. The pleasure of eating well—eating based on internal cues of hunger, satiety, and appetite; individual nutritional needs; and enjoyment, rather than on external food plans or diets.
4. The joy of movement—encouraging all physical activities for the associated pleasure and health benefits, rather than following a specific routine of regimented exercise for the primary purpose of weight loss or management.
5. An end to weight bias—recognizing that body shape, size, or weight are not evidence of any particular way of eating, level of physical activity, personality, psychological issue, or moral character; and confirming that there is beauty and worth in every body.[39]

Perhaps the fat acceptance and positive body image movements, with their presupposition of bodily determinism, can be summed up in the words of fat activist Marilyn Wann, who's work *Fat! So?* is considered a crucial mass market entry into the national conversation. She writes,

38. Farrell, *Fat Shame*, 13.

39. Burgard, "What is 'Health at Every Size,'" in Rothblum and Solovay, *The Fat Studies Reader*, 42–43.

> The revolution starts with a simple question: You're fat! So what? There's nothing wrong with being fat, just like there's nothing wrong with being short or tall, black or brown. These are facts of identity that cannot and should not be changed. They are birthright. They are heritage. They're beyond cures or aesthetics. They provide the diversity we need to survive. [40]

After a century of viewing fat bodies as lazy and morally inferior, these fat acceptance movements have sprung up, revealing a view that bodily shape is not determined by personal choice or willpower. It just is what it is and should be accepted, or even treated as a (potentially God-given) gift. This common theology has high appeal for churches seeking not to be offensive. If bodies are determined by God (or genetics, or any other means that is beyond one's agency), then inflicting judgment is unjust, immoral, and for the believer, un-Christian. But, just like the first theology of personal morality and bodily shape, this narrative fails to describe adequately how human bodies are shaped and what moral issues may truly be present. What is needed, I argue, is a third way that looks at the strengths and weaknesses of each theology in order to move the conversation forward.

The Sensitive and Scientific Way Forward

In the 1960s in the United States, when data was first collected, overweight and obese people made up about 10 percent of the population, as determined by the Body Mass Index (BMI), a ratio of a person's height to weight.[41] A BMI off twenty-five to twenty-nine is considered overweight, while over thirty is considered obese. It is an inelegant and imprecise metric, as it does not account for muscle mass, but it does serve to measure trends in populations.[42] The American obesity rate rose just slightly after the 1960s until 1980, when rates began to rise sharply. In 2010, 33 percent of adult Americans were overweight and 36 percent were obese—over two-thirds

40. Wann, *Fat! So?*.

41. The equation behind the BMI (mass kg/height m squared) was developed by Adolphe Quetelet in the mid-nineteenth century. The term Body Mass Index was coined by Ancel Keys in a 1972 issue of the *Journal of Chronic Diseases*. BMI is a quick and inexpensive way to judge body mass.

42. Using BMI as a metric is coming under increased scrutiny. As mentioned, it does not take into account muscle mass. Trained athletes often have a BMI that places them in the overweight category. Many companies use BMI to determine employer health care costs, so there is financial incentive to find an affordable metric that looks more closely at actual body composition (bone mass, lean mass, water mass, and fat mass).

of the adult American population is carrying excess weight. And one third of all children were categorized as overweight or obese. Obesity rates have therefore tripled since the 1960s.[43] Moreover these figures are projected to continue to rise. Treatments for obesity-related illnesses in 2008 were estimated to cost over $147 billion.[44] The United States is not alone in this. Other developed nations have also seen rates rise. The worldwide overweight and obesity rate in 2014 stood at 39 percent. Something has changed in our society and it would be negligent to ignore these statistics or advocate that our perception of overweight bodies is the only thing that needs to change. Fat advocates, while their call for increased sensitivity is admirable, do not take into account the massive systemic shifts that have happened in recent decades that are now becoming manifest on our bodies.

So, what has changed? As I mentioned earlier, the Progressive Reforms of the early twentieth century sought to rationalize food production, that is stabilize it, make it readily available so that people no longer suffer food shortages. This meant advances in industrial agriculture and food preservatives. While it was a morally commendable move, the unintended consequence was that food, particularly processed food, has become too prevalent, and it now takes up the majority of the American diet. In 1980, epidemiologist Ancel Keys, while trying to discover the source of the heart attack epidemic of the previous decades, released the "Seven Countries" study that claimed excessive fat consumption caused heart disease. His data was highly biased and later found to be erroneous.[45] What's more, in the 1960s the sugar industry, working as the Sugar Research Foundation, paid scientists to play down the link between sugar and heart disease and instead put the blame on fat.[46] One of the scientists who was paid by the sugar industry was D. Mark Hegsted, who later went on to become the head of nutrition at the U.S. Department of Agriculture, where he helped draft governmental dietary guidelines. So, the government and food manufactures, believing that fat causes heart disease and that sugar is relatively harmless, started eliminating fat from foods. The low-fat diet became the understood means for health in the 1980s. Fatless food though has little palatability, so food companies replaced fat with highly refined sugar. Sugar, especially high fructose corn syrup, is inexpensive due to prices artificially lowered by the Farm Bill. In the last thirty years then, sugar consumption has doubled,

43. National Institute of Diabetes and Digestive and Kidney Diseases.

44. Finkelstein et al., "Medical Spending Attributable To Obesity."

45. Lustig, *Fat Chance*, 111.

46. O'connor, "How Sugar Industry Shifted Blame." O'connor is reporting on Kearns, Schmidt, and Glantz, "Sugar and Heart Disease Research."

and for most Americans, sugar makes up 20 to 40 percent of daily calorie intake. This is fivefold what it was in the early twentieth century.[47]

This leads into another pervasive myth about food: a calorie is a calorie. A calorie, the unit used to measure the energy density of food, has the same value across all foods when burned in a beaker. But all calories eaten do not all affect the body in the same way—in particular, calories from processed sugar are especially powerful at causing metabolic syndrome, which is an imbalance in the body's insulin levels, which determine fat storage. And here lies a key in understanding obesity's relation to health. As physician and obesity expert Robert Lustig states,

> People don't die of obesity per se. They die of what happens to their organs. On the death certificate, the medical examiner doesn't write down "obesity"; instead it's "heart attack;' "heart failure;' "stroke," "diabetes," "cancer," "dementia," or "cirrhosis of the liver." These are diseases that "travel" with obcsity. They are all chronic metabolic diseases. But normal-weight people die of these as well. *That's the point.* It's not the obesity. The obesity is not the *cause* of chronic metabolic disease. It's a *marker* of chronic metabolic disease, otherwise known as metabolic syndrome. And it's metabolic syndrome that will kill you.[48]

So, bodily shape is not an immediate indicator of health, but neither is it unrelated to health. Fat activists have been vocal in trying to remove health from the conversation, and they are right to do so. Fat is not what is causing health crises. Fat and health are not directly linked. Slender people can have metabolic syndrome too, just without it manifesting in weight gain, but the syndrome still stems from malnutrition.

What this means is that the sugar-heavy industrialized American diet—which is rapidly becoming the world's diet—causes metabolic syndrome that then causes obesity.[49] But there is more to be said: not all fat on the body is dangerous. Subcutaneous fat, which is stored in the legs and buttocks, is there to provide energy in times of need. It's crucial for survival and it's also extremely difficult to eliminate, short of starvation. Again, fat is not an immediate indicator of health, or for that matter, virtue. Visceral fat, though, which is stored around the stomach, is the fat that damages organs

47. Lustig, *Fat Chance*, 118–19.

48. Lustig, *Fat Chance*, 7. Emphasis in original.

49. It should be noted that experts estimate that 10 perecent of people have genetic predispositions to metabolic syndrome, that is, they suffer from it regardless of what they eat. This could very well explain cases of overweight people before the industrialized diet. See Lustig, *Fat Chance*, 98.

and indicates disease. When one goes on a strict diet, this is the first fat that is lost. All of this is to say that there very well can be health at every size, assuming the size isn't measured around the stomach.

I've presented this data here, although briefly, as a means for critique of the common theologies of bodily shape and physical fitness. What's now apparent is that both theologies are somewhat right and somewhat wrong. In our current situation, the narrative of personal responsibility, which means healthful food choices and lots of exercise, just doesn't work. As Lustig puts it,

> To blame obesity on the obese is the easy answer, but it is the *wrong* answer. The current formulation of gluttony and sloth, diet and exercise, while accepted by virtually everyone, is based on faulty premises and myths that have taken hold in the world's consciousness. Obesity is not a behavioral aberration, a character flaw, or an error of commission.[50]

The larger answer may lie in the food environment we inhabit, where our food choices are limited to what is available, and what is available is not good for health. Low-income neighborhoods particularly suffer from a paucity of nutritious foods. Exercise, while life-extending and valuable, cannot be done—by the average person—at a level voluminous enough to burn the excesses of food consumed. What's more, even at high-end, health-minded grocery stores like Whole Foods and Sprouts, it is difficult to find packaged foods without added sugar. But, should someone want to live a healthy life in the midst of this toxic environment, it will take tremendous willpower and resistance, but even great willpower can be diffused in a toxic food environment. Deborah A. Cohen, a medical doctor who has served on the advisory panel of the National Institutes of Health, states that "etched into our DNA is the mantra 'Eat available food,' a survival imperative passed on through evolution."[51] We are programed to eat food when it is obtainable. Our bodies have not changed much since our days as hunters and gatherers, when food was scarce and survival meant eating food when accessible—there was no guarantee that food would be available again. So, eating is automatic to survival and "is second only to breathing as a critical survival behavior, [so] it tends to be more automatic and more automatically stimulated than any other behavior we engage in. That's why eating is not a rational behavior."[52] Obesity then is not purely the fault of the obese, and until there are sweeping institutional changes, people who want

50. Lustig, *Fat Chance*, xiii.

51. Cohen, *A Big Fat Crisis*, 50.

52. Cohen, *A Big Fat Crisis*, 50.

to be healthy will need to make very conscious, deliberate—even countercultural—food choices. But the determinist view is also not wholly wrong. What's clear is that our bodies are shaped by our environment, which is not always malleable. Children are particularly vulnerable, as they are unable to exercise much agency in food choice. Bodily shape is determined by what's around a person. What's more, there is tremendous diversity in human bodies, and some people are prone to store more subcutaneous fat than others and will keep it no matter the number of trips to the gym. So yes, forces outside ourselves impact our bodies. But that does not eliminate the need for environmental critique and difficult conversation about why we are shaped the way we are and how we can make virtuous choices. Fat stigma is damaging, and communities, especially Christian communities, should work to end it. But, as we have learned from progress in social understandings of alcoholism, mental illness, and AIDS, removing stigma does not mean eliminating desire for a cure. It's perfectly reasonable to wipe out fat stigma while also working to end the obesity epidemic.

Corporate Sin

Presented here are the issues that must first be unearthed before one can form a responsible and sensitive theology of physical fitness. Going forward, both briefly here and in more depth in the next chapter, I will argue that the global obesity epidemic is rooted in corporate sin. That is, obesity and body shape myths are not solely about the sins of individuals—although there is personal sin involved—but more importantly about our collective sins, the sin that is manifested in corporate and social structure. Or, to use the previous definition of sin, there is a violation of relationships. Social scientist Julie Guthman criticizes the very nature of capitalism and neoliberal economic policies that have allowed for the massive expansion of irresponsible food companies. Inherent in the capitalist enterprise are gross contradictions. She writes that,

> Neoliberal governmentality produces contradictory impulses such that the neoliberal subject is compelled to participate in society as both an enthusiastic consumer and as a self-controlled subject. The perfect subject-citizen is able to achieve both eating and thinness . . . Those who can achieve thinness amid this plenty are imbued with the rationality and self-discipline that those who are fat must logically lack . . . Yet unlike the Puritan ethic, in which wanting less was a mark of salvation, the worthy neoliberal citizen must seem to want less

> while spending more. Spending money on becoming thin is the perfect solution for both neoliberal subjectivity and neoliberal capitalism more broadly.[53]

We are instructed to both consume and then consume that which will mitigate our consumption (manufactured diet foods and gym memberships). And to do so garners worthiness, which Guthman equates to salvation. Knowledgeable observers insist that change must occur at not only an individual level but at a community, or even societal, level. Shelly McKenzie argues that "given the grand scale of this growing problem, it's evident that the incompatibility of our bodies and our lifestyles will be rectified only through population-wide solutions, not personal health revolutions."[54] But that entails affirming that we are affected by the actions of others, by the nature of our surroundings, and that calls into question our status as, what Charles Taylor calls, a "buffered self."[55] As an independent American, able to make decisions for myself, I must deny my porousness, and that means falling back into the narrative of personal responsibility and personal sin. But as theologian and food activist Andrew Francis states, "One of the biggest theological problems the church faces is to realize that corporate sin—subjugating the poor, the alienated, and the starving—is just as serious as any individual or personal sin. Institutional and global change is just as vitally part of the church's mission as 'saving souls.'"[56] And there the Christian must stand, ready to do the more difficult work of changing institutional practices, for the furtherance of God's work in the world and the flourishing of all.

Conclusion

I have outlined these common theologies of fitness, bodily shape, and physical well-being as a preparatory measure before working toward a robust theology of physical fitness. Notions of physical fitness carry a lot of baggage, many of which must be recognized and critiqued. The food we eat and the gyms we join are inextricably linked to capitalism and neoliberal economic policies. To whole-heartedly and theologically endorse fitness, especially as part of God's plan for the world, means denying the destructive forces that are at play there even as we recognize the positive

53. Guthman, "Neoliberalism and Constitution of Bodies," in Rothblum and Solovay, *The Fat Studies Reader*, 193.

54. McKenzie, *Getting Physical*, 182.

55. Taylor, *A Secular Age*, 27.

56. Francis, *What in God's Name Are You Eating?*, 147.

values that are represented. We are told to consume and we are told that we should look like we don't consume. But to dismiss physical fitness because of these issues would be to miss out on the stories of transformation and blessing that come about from fitness pursuits, like those stories of the TWV marathon runners. In a sense, I wish to further the work of Shirl Hoffman as applied to fitness. Hoffman provides a thorough critique of evangelical Christians' engagement with sport, stating that "the saddest consequence of the Christian community's not having thought carefully about sports may be that they have missed out on the true riches that sports have to offer."[57] Fitness has a great deal to offer the Christian community, but it must be done from a place of solid critique.

57. Hoffman, *Good Game*, 19.

7

Theology of Physical Fitness

Having done the groundwork in the previous chapter, I wish now to give a theological examination of the pursuit of physical fitness as a subcategory of sport. As I have argued, sport, fitness, and health are highly interwoven. Physical fitness is needed for high performance in sports, and many people pursue sport as a means to enhance physical fitness and health. Going forward, there are a number of questions that need to be answered. Does God care about my physical fitness? If so, in what way? What are God's expectations? How does physical fitness—noting the goodness of creation and that eternal life does not consist of escape from creation—fit in with God's plans of redemption and resurrection? To answer these questions, this chapter will touch on issues related to sin, salvation, and God's concern for the human person, especially as they relate to physical fitness.

Sin, Obesity, and Fitness

In the previous chapter, I noted that our understanding of bodily shape, and its correlation to health, relates to God's larger purpose for creation and human flourishing. Impediments to this should not be exclusively located in narratives of personal sin—that is, the notion that one's bodily shape is the result of one's own morally poor choices and behavior—and instead greater weight should be given to the impact of corporate sin. Recalling chapter 1, sin is a violation of relationships and a misuse of agency, which creates a world that is contrary to God's intended design. Environmental and social forces—that is, those forces made up of complex relationships, which are therefore beyond the individual's immediate control—play a large role in shaping one's body. Sloth and gluttony are inadequate means for describing the obesity epidemic and its moral implications. But how exactly is corporate sin at play in shaping bodies? What does it look like and where is it? To answer these questions, I would like to propose a case study of an obese child, which I will analyze through the liberation theology tradition's understanding of sin and Hendrik Berkof's exegesis of the powers in Paul's letters.

According to research compiled by the Center for Disease Control, childhood obesity in the United States has doubled in children and quadrupled in adolescents in the past thirty years.[1] Rates for children six to eleven years old increased from 7 percent in 1980 to 18 percent in 2012. Again, obesity travels with a number of diseases, so these children are at a greater risk for cardiovascular disease, diabetes, bone and joint issues, and sleep apnea. There is also, of course, the greater risk of psychological distress through stigma, as described in the previous chapter. Research also shows that low personal income increases the likelihood of obesity, so low-income children are at a greater risk.[2] In all, an obese child is handicapped from living the full and flourishing life as designed by God.

So then, let us think about one obese ten-year-old, living in a low-income neighborhood. He is malnourished and at greater risk for disease. He is unable to engage in all the activities of his peers. Due to biochemical processes related to his obesity, he has low energy and he shows little excitement for school.[3] His own body is holding him back. He rarely ever eats nutritious food, as his food sources—determined in part by his parents and in part by his school and his neighborhood—are primarily low quality and highly processed.[4] Convenience stores and fast food locations are his most readily available food sources, for both him and his parents.[5] One might ask then, where is the sin? What is the sin that has caused this condition? Looking back at the first two common theologies outlined in the previous chapter—one, obesity is a sign of personal moral failure, or two, bodily shape is not determined by personal choices and all bodily shapes should be celebrated—this child's situation serves to disprove them both. One cannot say that he is slothful and gluttonous and has failed in exercising personal responsibility. As a child, he does not know the complexities of food science, or know, beyond his immediate taste reactions, what he should or should not eat. Looking at the second common theology, he is not merely in need

1."Obesity Facts | Healthy Schools | CDC." Centers for Disease Control and Prevention. https://www.cdc.gov/healthyschools/obesity/facts.htm.

2. "Obesity Facts | Healthy Schools | CDC." Centers for Disease Control and Prevention. https://www.cdc.gov/healthyschools/obesity/facts.htm. There are however many other factors at play, too.

3. See chapter 4 of Lustig, *Fat Chance*, who describes what's often called "sloth" as a biochemical process related to obesity.

4. Schools themselves, in the last 20 years, have become partners with fast food corporations. See Morse, "School Cafeterias As Fast-Food Franchisees."

5 Davis and Carpenter, "Proximity of Fast-Food and Obesity."

of a shift in the popular consciousness. Certainly, he suffers from fat stigma, and that is wrong, but the solution to his deprivation is not simply a removal of that stigma. Instead, he shows how forces beyond his control have shaped and handicapped his body. One might point to his parents, who do guide his food choices, but finances and food availability limit those choices.[6] Perhaps he doesn't exercise or actively play enough, since he does not live near a safe play space. But volume of exercise alone does not contribute to or eliminate obesity.[7] Perhaps he is the victim of aggressive food marketing targeted to children, and the corporate forces of food production. Certainly, there is wrongdoing in the streams of food production, but food companies are made up of individuals—marketers, scientists, farmers—who do not intend to handicap this child but rather earn a living for their own families.[8] In terms of personal agency, this boy can make some of his own choices, but his agency is limited and constrained by the larger factors that surround him, over which he has little or no control. In other words, healthful foods exist, and he might even want them, but he does not have the means to get them. So where is the sin? To answer this, I would like first to look at the Liberation Theology tradition and its understanding of sin.

Rising out of this oppression of Latin American peoples, liberation theology pays particular attention to sinful social structures. Note, I am not offering here a thorough and complete analysis of liberation theology, and I wish also not to equate obesity with historic Latin American oppression. What I do hope to do is borrow some of the notions of sin found in the liberation tradition and utilize them to assess our case study. To begin, Derek R. Nelson notes that, "Latin American theologians counsel against excessive individualism in articulations of sin. They refuse an arbitrary decoupling of reflection on sin and the Christian vocation to alleviate, where possible, its effects."[9] Here then, sin is not an individual phenomenon. It does not reside solely with the individual, or one person's will. Rather, it shows its effect in communities and structures, in the fracturing of these complex relationships. Gustavo Gutiérrez states,

6. The American Nutrition Association has done a great deal of work in defining and locating "food deserts," which are communities without convenient access to healthful food. See "USDA Defines Food Deserts."

7. Lustig, *Fat Chance*, 144.

8. See Niebuhr, *Moral Man and Immoral Society*. While not a focus of the discussion here, Niebuhr does argue that individuals are able to make moral decisions and consider the interests of others. But in societies and social groups, the collective egoism produces harmful structures. This was in large part a critique of the Social Gospel, and its post-millennial roots, which will be discussed later in this chapter.

9 Nelson, *What's Wrong With Sin?*, 83.

> Sin—a breach of friendship with God and others—is according to the Bible the ultimate cause of poverty, injustice, and the oppression in which persons live. In describing sin as the ultimate cause we do not in any way negate the structural reasons and the objective determinants leading to these situations. It does, however, emphasize the fact that things do not happen by chance and that behind an unjust structure there is a personal or collective will responsible—a willingness to reject God and neighbor. It suggests, likewise, that a social transformation, no matter how radical it may be, does not automatically achieve the suppression of all evils.[10]

Corporate sin then comes about because of collected personal sins. Nelson shows that "for Gutiérrez, the link between personal and social expressions of sin is therefore *causal.* Personal sins cause situations which must be named as sinful."[11] So, Gutiérrez moves beyond just personal understandings of sin, but claims that sinful social structures are a result of individual sins while still not fully reducible to those personal sins. Because of this, "Gutiérrez is able to maintain moral culpability for sin at the individual level."[12] Social institutions do not become sinful independently of the people who form them, and the ultimate removal of sin must happen on the personal level.

Using this model to look at our case study, one could argue that the food company executive, who exhibits the personal sin of greed, places sales above the health of consumers and manufactures tremendous volumes of high-margin junk food. There are personal sins in every part of the supply chain, as each individual moves that food into the marketplace, again placing his or her own profits above health, until it reaches the convenience store owner, who creates an environment where only junk food is available, which in turn leads to the obesity of the six-year-old. A sinful system has been created from the negligence of all the parties involved. While no individual is solely to blame, a sinful food distribution structure has been formed. This model however assumes the willful negligence of all involved. Each person is actively and knowingly sinning. Is this fair, though? Argentinian Methodist theologian Aldo Etchegoyen asks for a closer look at the forces that form oppressive structures, and how systems create oppressive interconnections. Analyzing the history of mistreatment and aggressive land acquisition away from indigenous populations in his home country, he states,

10. Gutiérrez, *A Theology of Liberation*, 24.

11. Nelson, *What's Wrong with Sin?*, 88. Emphasis in original.

12 Nelson, *What's Wrong with Sin?*, 91.

> For the aboriginal communities, land is property on which to live a full and abundant life. For the mentality of oppression, on the contrary, land is private, commercial, capitalist property, the object of profit. From this we can identify some of the characteristics of a structure of oppression: dominating and capitalist possession of the land, and an extermination of the community as a hindrance to control of the land. In two words, possession and reification (people treated as things). When we speak of the aboriginal communities of Latin America we should recognize our own sin, because we are participants in the structures that oppress them.[13]

Under this system of capitalist possession, people are reduced to things. All who do not combat the system are guilty of oppression. A structure formed liked this creates a "deepening of dependence" on both the oppressor and the oppressed.[14] The oppressed cannot now live without the structure put in place by the oppressor, and the oppressor's livelihood now becomes dependent on the abuse of the oppressed. Etchegoyen points out that this is a failure of true connectionalism, that is, recognition of humankind's interdependence for thriving. Connectionalism "must be seen in the service of the liberation that Jesus Christ is bringing in every place. It is a connectionalism that speaks to us of our comradeship for service and for the good of the whole people and of all peoples."[15] Looking again at our case study, the convenience store owner and the success of his business is dependent on the sale of high-margin junk foods. That is where he earns his living. While he might not willfully desire the six-year-old to be obese, he has become dependent on the child's (and other children's) consumption. So, we see here a deepening of the complexities of the sin involved: structures are formed through interdependencies that reify humans. There might not be willful and deliberate individual sin, but there are systems formed by sinful forces, the "mentalities of oppression," that push people into near-inescapable patterns of destruction.

Rebecca S. Chopp assesses the question of institutional sin from a different point of view, noting the presence of sinful and oppressive structures, but emphasizing instead the role of the Christian faith in overcoming these structures. She summarizes liberation theology as an interpretation of the Christian faith

13. Kirkpatrick, *Faith in Struggle for Life*, 108.
14. Kirkpatrick, *Faith in Struggle for Life*, 158.
15. Kirkpatrick, *Faith in Struggle for Life*, 165.

> combining spirituality and politics as part of the ongoing process of Christian conversion to God and neighbor. It understands human existence in terms of social agency, and history in terms of liberation. It reflects on a new subject, the poor, and reads the Scripture in light of a liberating God. This theology is a practical reflection, a process of discerning, judging, deciding, and becoming within a specific community.[16]

The key here is what the Christian faith does and how it works toward liberation. Sinful structures and sinful individuals both exist. The disciple of Christ then must be in active resistance, must exert social agency. God is for liberation. For a Christian to act otherwise, in favor of oppression, would be contrary to God's work in the world. The real emphasis of liberation theology is that "the Christian faith as a force in history that holds the possibility of helping all persons to become, within history, new people."[17] Under this model then, the disciple of Christ and the community of believers have numerous roles to play in the life of the obese child, particularly as they relate to God's liberating activity, which very well might include the reduction of obesity. The Christian should combat the aggressive and manipulative marketing practices of food companies, hold corporate entities to greater accountability for health, and use purchasing power to steer the market toward providing more healthful food options that are accessible to all. While the liberation tradition might not give a fully clear description of how sin works within structures, it is clear that God works toward liberation and thriving for all.

Here now, I would like to look at our case study from a slightly different perspective, specifically that of the powers in Paul's letters. In Romans 8, in a discussion of the law and freedom, Paul says, "I am convinced that neither death, nor life, nor angels, nor rulers, nor things present, nor things to come, nor powers, nor height, nor depth, nor anything else in all creation, will be able to separate us from the love of God in Christ Jesus our Lord" (8:38–39). The entity here that is hard to define today is "powers," which is in some sense a force that is different from human rulers or otherworldly beings, such as angels or demons. The powers are some form of invisible influence, which Paul mentions numerous times, using various terms (1 Cor 15:24–26; Eph 1:20, 2:1, 3:10, 6:12, Col 1:6, 2:15). These passages get a thorough exegesis in Dutch theologian Hendrik Berkhof's classic text *Christ and the Powers*.[18] Berkhof states that according to Paul,

16. Chopp, *The Praxis of Suffering*, 27.

17. Chopp, *The Praxis of Suffering*, 25.

18. This analysis here will focus primarily on Berkhof's exegetical work of Paul.

our created world "comprises a visible and an invisible, or an earthly and a heavenly part. We might better say: Creation has a visible foreground, which is bound together with and dependent on an invisible background. This latter comprises the Powers."[19] These powers have rule over earthly life. They exert control. They have however, through Christ's death and resurrection, been dethroned, stripped of their ultimate authority. While Paul never gives an exact definition of the powers, he speaks of them in relation to time (present and future), space (depth and height), life, death, politics, philosophy, public opinion, Jewish law, pious tradition, and even the course of the stars. This broad range of influencing forces exerts great control in human life. For Paul,

> apart from Christ man [sic] is at the mercy of these Powers. They encompass, carry, and guide his life, the demands of the present, fear for the future, state and society, life and death, tradition and morality—they are all our "guardians and trustees," the forces which hold together the world and the life of men and preserve them from chaos.[20]

Now, it's important to note that these powers are not implicitly evil or destructive. In fact, Paul makes it clear that they are part of God's good creation. Christ "is the image of the invisible God, the firstborn of all creation; for in him all things in heaven and on earth were created, things visible and invisible, whether thrones or dominions or rulers or powers—all things have been created through him and for him." (Col 1:15-16) All of these powers were created by and for Christ. They are not evil in themselves, but to the contrary, were made to act as a "linkage between God's love and visible human experience. They are to hold life together, preserving it within God's love, serving as aids to bind men fast in His fellowship."[21] These powers hold back chaos and maintain creation. In a sinful world though, these powers become malformed, wrongly pointed, and ultimately oppressive. That which was created for order and unity can in fact alienate humankind from God and from oneself. Berkhof states that it should not be difficult

> for us to perceive today in every realm of life these Powers which unify men [sic], yet separate them from God. The state, politics, class, social struggle, national interest, public opinion,

For a more thorough analysis of the powers, see the trilogy of books by Walkter Wink: (Wink, *Naming the Powers*; Wink, *Unmasking the Powers*; Wink, *Engaging the Powers*.)

19. Berkhof, *Christ and the Powers*, 28.

20. Berkhof, *Christ and the Powers*, 22.

21. Berkhof, *Christ and the Powers*, 29.

> accepted morality, the ideas of decency, humanity, democracy—these give unity and direction to thousands of lives. Yet precisely by giving unity and direction they separate these many lives from the true God; they let us believe that we have found the meaning of existence, whereas they really estrange us from true meaning.[22]

These powers, created to hold back chaos, are equally able to push people apart and away from God. Christ however has "disarmed the rulers and authorities and made a public example of them, triumphing over them in it" (Col 2:15). Christ is ultimately victorious, but this victory is not one of destruction. The role of the Christian is not to eliminate the powers, but rather to reorient them, "to battle for God's intention for them, and against their corruption."[23] This is a hopeful conclusion that affirms the goodness of creation of the redemptive opportunities therein, again affirming the claims of chapter 1, that God's ultimate plan for humankind is not escape from creation but rather a renewed place in the redeemed creation. Walter Wink makes the point that the powers are "simultaneously the outer and inner aspects of one and the same indivisible concretion of power."[24] The powers, like the human person, are a unified whole, known in and through their earthly manifestations. That means that encountering, or even fighting destructive powers, means engaging with real-world situations and embodied realities.

So then, let us apply this to our case study. There are many potential powers at play in the life of an obese child. There is hunger, the pleasure of eating, a parent's desire to see her child happy, and of course, capitalism, the guiding force behind food production and distribution. In and of themselves, none of these powers are implicitly evil. In fact, they all exist to bring order and stability. But we can see too how each of these can lead to obesity. A child wants and needs to eat and seeks out that which is pleasurable. A mother wants to see her child happy and gives him that which immediately makes him happy. The market economy is productive, and capitalist forces have yielded abundance in the industrialized world. And yet, that power too often becomes destructive, through reification and denigration of humankind—that is, loss of love for neighbor.[25] These powers, put in place by God, have become distorted, have become ends

22. Berkhof, *Christ and the Powers*, 32–33.

23. Berkhof, *Christ and the Powers*, 29.

24. Wink, *Naming the Powers*, 107.

25. For a thorough examination of capitalistic forces and their capacity for growth or destruction, see Harvey, *A Brief History of Neoliberalism*.

in themselves and, as Berkhof notes, they estrange us from true meaning. They are not implicitly evil, but they do in fact need redemption and reordering by the Christian community.[26]

This understanding of the powers is helpful because it sheds light on one of the perennial questions in fitness and weight loss movements: how do we make sense of the destructive power of something that brings great joy? In more specific terms, how do we understand how delicious food, which brings us together and forms fellowship, which yields joy and pleasure, must—at least for a time—be eliminated, or at least moderated? The joy that comes from an ice cream cone is a gift from God! Yet, when that power claims ultimacy, or points to itself, then it estranges one from God, the true source of meaning. Food is wonderful because it is a gift from God. A cupcake is a treat and can bring great pleasure, but an overabundance of cupcakes (or other sugary foods, which is the reality today) is harmful and destructive. Moderation, in the form of recognition and proper use of the powers, is key.

This brief overview of the multiple causes of obesity unearths the complexity of the role of sin in forming overweight bodies. What is clear is that the Christian community has a role and responsibility in alleviating oppression in all of its forms, and guiding, shaping, and critiquing the numerous powers, both visible and invisible, that are at play in shaping the human form.

The Soteriology of Physical Fitness

While a theological understanding of physical fitness might seem new and novel, it is actually a conversation that, in the United States, is nearly two-hundred years old. During the nineteenth century, American Christians heard a great deal about the value of health and well-being, particularly as they related to sports and recreational activity. What is interesting though is that these conversations were wrapped up and intertwined with Millennialism, the hope for a 1,000-year period of perfection as believed to be foretold in Revelation 20. Millennialism saw an increased interest in the nineteenth century and that perfect millennium included physical fitness. As I will show, millennial beliefs have helped form the church's relationship

26. Wink notes that when "the invisible mercantile mechanism" that is capitalism, is seen as benign, it thus "becomes the arbiter of human destiny, producing results in apparent independence of the human beings who comprise the system it governs." See Wink, *Naming the Powers*, 109.

with sports and fitness, and have contributed to what exists today: a secular and imminent soteriology of fitness.

In the early nineteenth century, bolstered by the Industrial Revolution, American society saw tremendous changes as populations moved into towns and cities and left agricultural employment for more industrial, intellectual, and metropolitan employment. Many people took up sedentary occupations, losing the physical activity associated with rural work. Unsanitary conditions in cities created abundant health crises, particularly cholera, which hit New York in 1832. For many in the Christian community, the city was seen as a place of disease, sin, and moral decay. In 1830, Charles Grandison Finney, prominent figure of the Second Great Awakening, preached to his Presbyterian congregation in Rochester, New York that if Christians united and focused, they could convert the world and bring on the millennium, the perfected society, in just three months.[27] While this obviously did not happen, his claim revealed the intense desire for dramatic social change, and it signaled a shift away from the historic Calvinist understanding of original sin which is "perverted and corrupted in all the parts of our nature,"[28] and its subsequent North American interpretation that people "could alter neither their individual spiritual states nor the shape of their society."[29] Rather, Christians could and absolutely should work in shaping the world. Harvey Green notes that, many Second Great Awakening revivalist preachers argued that

> the human race could improve itself and that Christ's reappearance would occur only after human civilization had evolved to that state of perfection that would then endure for a millennium, or one thousand years. Millennialism offered both a peril and a hope. The awesome responsibility for arriving at the state of grace and perfection rested squarely upon human shoulders—but the task was comprehensible and, therefore, possible. Good health—the avoidance of disease, debility, and "premature" death—thus took on extraordinary importance. Physical degeneration was a spiritual as well as medical or physiological problem.[30]

Thus, health and fitness took on a new, eschatological dimension in a society that was seeing rapid change. There was a new motivation to make oneself perfect, make oneself ready for the coming millennium. Prominent social

27. Johnson, *A Shopkeeper's Millennium*, 3–4.
28. Calvin, *The Institutes of the Christian Religion*, 251.
29. Johnson, *A Shopkeeper's Millennium*, 3.
30. Green, *Fit for America*, 10.

reformer and Congregationalist clergyman Henry Ward Beecher is noted to have said, "Nothing can come more properly in the sphere of Christian activity than the application of the cause of physical health in the community. If general health is not religion, if it is not Christ, it is John the Baptist; it goes before him."[31] Emerging activities like gymnastics and calisthenics, could be more than just an indicator of a this-worldly state, but also a metric of humankind's advancement toward perfection and Christ's return.

Now, early in the nineteenth century, most believers had seen sport as a competitor to the Christian faith, as it pulled upon the affections.[32] Under the drive of millennialism though, it was recognized as a powerful means for social organization and character development—it could be appropriated for societal change. It could build character, form social bonds, promote health and wellness, and alleviate the problems of city life. As Tony Ladd and James Mathisen state, sport took on

> the added goal of making the "bad of society good." By such means Christianity and sport reversed their relationship from being aliens to being allies. American revivalism helped form a symbiotic relationship, so that the eventual engagement of religion and sport infused a missionary zeal in those who participated in sports and stimulated the idealism of a generation of muscular Christians who felt called to win the world to Christ in their generation.[33]

This marriage of sports and fitness with the goals of millennialism came to be known as Muscular Christianity, a novel and alternative form of the faith defined by masculinity and self-control. One of the lasting institutions of this movement is the Young Men's Christian Association (YMCA), which was founded as Christian ministry that would promote sport, activity, and physical health. James Naismith, a physician and proponent of physical education, created the sport of basketball at the YMCA in Springfield, Massachusetts. While he invented it as game to be played indoors during the harsh New England winters, he saw basketball as a means of Christian witness and as a way to support physical and spiritual needs, believing that placing young men in a game would yield moral formation.[34] Now, the Muscular Christian movement was not without theological impact. Dominic Erdozain claims that the

31. Referenced as J. H. Sawyer, "Henry and Catherine E. Beecher" 6, in Gulick's Theses at the Springfield College Archives, Special Collection, hereafter referred to as SCA-SC.) in Ladd and Mathisen, *Muscular Christianity*.

32. Erdozain, *The Problem of Pleasure*, 69.

33. Ladd and Mathisen, *Muscular Christianity*, 13.

34. Ladd and Mathisen, *Muscular Christianity*, 71.

movement brought about "a kind of hybrid morality that was potentially independent of divine reference . . . What we see is the development of a subtle humanism of self-control and almost physically generated virtue, implicitly rather than explicitly this-worldly."[35] While unashamedly Christian, this new movement offered an alternative to staid religion, but also formed the space for an imminent soteriology, that is, a type of salvation that can be found exclusively in this world. This will be discussed later.

So far, I have described millennialism as a monolithic movement, which it is not. To this day, there are a tremendous number of strands and nuances.[36] It was during and after the Civil War that the movement split into two distinct parts: pre-millennialism and post-millennialism.[37] The post-millennialist believes that society can be made perfect through proper ordering. After it is made perfect, Christ will come and reign. In a sense, it is a movement marked by hope, particularly hope in the capacities of humanity. The pre-millennialist believes that only Christ can make the world perfect, and that the promised millennium will be ushered in by Christ's return, during the next "dispensation." The goal of the Christian then is to convert as many people as possible to faith in Christ so that they may be with him upon his return. There is a sense of distrust of humanity and culture. Again, this is an extreme simplification of the topic, but, as will be shown, what is relevant here is how the faithful Christians of both streams came to incorporate sport in ministry. Moving forward, the hopes for a perfect and righteous society were rightly questioned by the bloodshed of the American Civil War. The Southern states, lying decimated, could hardly fathom what a perfect society would look like. In the South, there was then a rejection of post-millennialism and an embrace of pre-millennialism: human progress had failed. Only Christ could fix the world. Crawford Gribben argues that after the Civil War, Southern "evangelicals were convinced by the new expectation of evangelical marginality and cultural decay, and articulated those expectations in terms of the new expansion of dispensational pre-millennial belief."[38]

As mentioned above, one of the enduring products of the Muscular Christian movement was the YMCA, which did an excellent job of promoting health and well-being for Christian purposes, perhaps even to their own detriment. Throughout the century, in large part because of its promotion by Christians, sport became popular. This then led to institutionalization

35. Erdozain, *The Problem of Pleasure*, 203.

36. See Grenz, *The Millennial Maze.*

37. Ladd and Mathisen, *Muscular Christianity*, 41.

38. Gribben, *Evangelical Millennialism in Trans-Atlantic, 1500-2000.*

and professionalization of particular sports and the lionization of sports heroes.[39] As coaches were hired and sports became more professional, "character education for muscular Christians was moving from qualitative measures of personal growth to quantitative ones marked by performance. Gradually coaching performers to win became the priority for some muscular Christians."[40] The capitalistic possibilities of sport were soon recognized, and so adult and professional sport moved away from its roots as a tool of moral development and character formation—although that continues on primarily in youth sport. As Ladd and Mathisen say, "No longer did those who led the sports movement believe the arena held unalterable divine or natural laws that provided a positive social environment for transforming both the game and the players."[41] Sport was now business and "evangelical muscular Christians, who had earlier embraced sport to accomplish God's redemptive purposes, now found themselves trapped by the values and structures of an institution rapidly moving in a different direction."[42] It could be argued that the defining moment, when sport became fully secularized, was when Billy Sunday, the future celebrity evangelist, left professional baseball.[43] In 1893, in *Young Men's Era*, the official publication of the YMCA, Sunday gave a ten-point rationale for why he could not be a professional baseball player and a Christian. Most notably he claimed that baseball "develops a spirit of jealousy and selfishness; one's whole desires are for personal success regardless of what befalls others."[44] Sport had exited the Christian faith, or, in another sense, Christians chose to exit that which they had helped create, leaving it then to sports promoters to develop humanistic explanation and motivations for sport and its goodness.

In the early twentieth century then, the post-millennial hopes of societal transformation, which included health and fitness, moved away from sport and into the Social Gospel Movement. Post-millennialism became associated with Liberal Christianity and mainline denominations.

39. Major League Baseball was founded in 1869; American Football found a place in colleges and universities in the 1870s and was professionalized in the 1890s; local professional club basketball teams came to prominence in the 1920s.

40. Ladd and Mathisen, *Muscular Christianity*, 64–65.

41. Ladd and Mathisen, *Muscular Christianity*, 77.

42. Ladd and Mathisen, *Muscular Christianity*, 78.

43. While the Muscular Christian movement certainly helped promote the advancement of sport in the United States, the use of the term "secular" is not to imply that there was ever a time when sport was exclusively part of the church, or any religious tradition. Ancient sport particularly, whether Greek or Aztec, played a part in religious devotion. But throughout the centuries, sport has had a varying relationship with religion. That is, it has never been owned by one religious tradition.

44. Ladd and Mathisen, *Muscular Christianity*, 80.

Pre-millennialism became a cornerstone doctrine for nascent Fundamentalists, who, after the Fundamentalist-Modernist controversies, chose to separate from wider culture, including sport. So then ended the early salvifically-tinged notions of sport and fitness. Health and healthcare are certainly still concerns and priorities for modern Christians, but there is little linkage to understandings of salvation or eschatological hope.

It wasn't until after World War II that sport once again became part of the Christian consciousness, but this time in a different way, divorced of notions of health and moral development. Modern evangelist Billy Graham, who was raised in a Southern, pre-millennial, fundamentalist faith, learned quickly that he could draw large crowds to his revivals if he incorporated notable athletes. Through Graham's use of athletes' testimonies, "sports became a powerful means of legitimizing the previously marginalized, accommodationist fundamentalists."[45] What's notable here, in Graham's method, is that sport is not an end in itself, or even valued for what it produces, physically or spiritually, but rather simply a tool for evangelism. Again, we see here the instrumental view of sport, as discussed in chapter 4. Its own popularity legitimizes Christian outreach. Graham's methods have been used by many other church and parachurch organizations, and it became the de facto model of mid-twentieth-century Christianity's engagement with sport—and it should be said that this is a form of engagement that is largely critique-free. That is, there is little to no critique of the sport played by the featured athlete, no critique of that which supports an evangelist's platform. We see here then the subtle manifestation of pre-millennial theology: gaining converts to Christ is the primary mission. If an athlete's celebrity can facilitate that, then the work of God is done. As Ladd and Mathisen put it,

> Evangelicals are more concerned with "making the bad of society good" and thereby preparing for the coming of the kingdom of God. Evangelicals are about correct beliefs and theology, but primarily when those affect their larger concern with evangelizing the world . . . the essential core of the modern myth must be something like "sport enhances the gospel" or "sport helps save souls."[46]

Now, this is not to say though that mainline and liberal streams of American Christianity have formed a robust doctrine of sport or fitness. What we are left with now, in a broad sense, is a liberal tradition that, while supportive of sport, does not often theologically engage with it, and an evangelical

45. Ladd and Mathisen, *Muscular Christianity*, 118.

46. Ladd and Mathisen, *Muscular Christianity*, 214–15.

tradition that has appropriated it for eschatological purposes,[47] often independently and without critique of what is happening in a specific sport.[48] Healthcare and this-world comfort are concerns of mainline Protestants, but this exists largely without reference to soteriology or eschatology. All of this is to say that what does exist today, in the realm of sport and fitness and its engagement with eschatological themes, is what can be called a flattened, or imminent soteriology of physical fitness. Becoming all you can be is the short path to heaven on earth.

The Imminent Soteriology of Physical Fitness

Dominic Erdozain argues that the evangelical engagement with sport and fitness, particularly in the nineteenth century, has today yielded a "practical, this-worldly theology of salvation-by-recreation" that "quietly occluded the classical and explicit soteriology of the 'parent' institutions" such as the YMCA.[49] I agree that this does in fact exist. Muscular Christianity brought awareness to and spiritualized physical pursuits and allowed for the formation of sporting institutions that eventually broke ties with ecclesial bodies. And so, we see today this flattened sense of salvation. As noted before, the language that people use to describe their bodies and their states of physical fitness are often coded in moral terms. Particularly today, notions of obesity carry heavy undertones of moral failure. William James Hoverd and Chris G. Sibley found through a qualitative study that "people implicitly evaluate the condition of the body using moral discourse, and that the use of such rhetoric reflects an appraisal of obesity as *immoral*, rather than as simply *negative* in a standard sense."[50] Our bodies are seen as sites of morality, and evidence of a moral state. But this moral language does not connect to any notion of transcendent existence. There is no God at work in these moral narratives. Salvation language also plays heavily in the contemporary sport of CrossFit. Founded in 2000 in Santa Cruz, California, CrossFit mixes numerous forms of weightlifting, gymnastics, and calisthenics into a new physical fitness regime and competitive sport. Its gyms are focused on

47. To be fair, not all evangelical engagement with sport is purely utilitarian, that is just "sports heroes make good evangelists." See Blazer, *Playing for God*; Neal, *The Handbook on Athletic Perfection*.

48. To see this played out in the context of Mixed Martial Arts, watch Junge and Storkel, *Fight Church*.

49. Erdozain, *The Problem of Pleasure*, 38.

50. Hoverd and Sibley, "Immoral Bodies," 401. Emphasis in original.

community, accountability, and clean eating (particularly the Paleo Diet).[51] There are now over 10,000 CrossFit gyms (or "boxes") in the world. In a recent interview, co-founder Greg Glassman said that CrossFit members are "the stewards of something," and that, "We're saving lives, and saving a lot of them . . . 350,000 Americans are going to die next year from sitting on the couch. That's dangerous. The TV is dangerous. [The weightlifting exercise] squatting isn't."[52] The follow-up question might be, "this is salvation from what, or for what?" Ostensibly, Glassman is referring to salvation from a premature death. Partaking in CrossFit means extending life. On a larger scale though, these notions of salvation might refer to a more abundant and well-lived life, that is, human flourishing.

One might ask the question then, is this form of imminent soteriology wrong? Should the Christian community condemn it? Could it possibly be celebrated as something life-giving? I would answer that yes, it can be celebrated, but criticism of this world-bound salvation must first be clearly registered. Hoverd offers a strong critique of this modern imminent soteriology of fitness by claiming that,

> The gym offers us another way to think about religion in light of the declining influence of traditional Christianity. The people who flock to the gymnasium are looking for a systemisation of life that provides them with meaning. They are implicitly participating in a theology of the ideal body, in which they are promised that through work they can transform their body and self, recreating themselves as a more successful person. When we confront the gym of today we see an institution that offers temporal salvation through discipline. Working out is your way to salvation; it is how you can 'become somebody!'[53]

This is a fair critique. As noted in the previous chapter, there is no one ideal bodily form. Humanity is created in bodily diversity. What's more, Hoverd cites a failure of the church to act as a recognizable meaning-making institution and notes that for many at the gym, self-transformation is an ultimately solitary or even selfish pursuit.

Another critique, which seems continually to arise, is the role of capitalism as a corrupting force in understanding fitness pursuits. As we've seen, capitalism helped professionalize sport and remove it from Christian mission, and it is an ever-present factor in the deleterious structures of obesity, particularly as it insists that people both consume large quantities of food

51. www.thepaleodiet.com

52. Oppenheimer, "Some to Church, Others CrossFit."

53. Hoverd, *Working Out My Salvation*, 105.

and consume products that reduce the appearance of consumption. But exercise in modern America has been for many a counter-cultural activity. In the 1960s and 1970s, joggers saw themselves as counter to car culture, and in line with environmental movements and alternative forms of health care.[54] Jogging was a pleasant form of resistance. Many people today also practice dieting and weight-loss as resistance activities, running counter to a culture of consumption. But, as was the case with jogging, consumer culture has found its way in. Michelle M. Lelwica states,

> Like the ascetic Christian disciplines that it implicitly takes as its models, the fitness ethic began as a countercultural critique. In particular, it challenged mainstream eating and dieting practices, promoting nutritious food and moderate exercise as means for mental and spiritual renewal. Before long, however, this alternative was absorbed by the very powers it meant to criticize: the giant food and weight-loss industries.[55]

Lelwica calls the culture formed by the diet and weight loss industries "Culture Lite," and notes that it offers an imminent soteriology that requires consumption. This perverse soteriology operates as a distraction from greater concerns.

> Organized around the pursuit of female slenderness, Culture Lite is a central nerve in this society's politics of distraction: the wide-scale diversion of attention away from the prevailing values and actual conditions that undermine individual and social well-being. On one level, the prominence of diet culture stems from its ability to synthesize a number of authoritative discourses and beliefs, thus offering diverse Americans what traditional religion no longer does: a common, public frame of meaning which appeals and applies across competing party lines.[56]

These are a few critiques of an imminent soteriology of physical fitness. They are strong and valid, but they should not eclipse the many stories and testimonies of the life-giving and life-affirming properties of physical fitness pursuits. Yes, pursuit of physical fitness can become an idol and occlude the meaning-making activities found in the community of Christian believers. But that does not allow for outright dismissal. I would agree with Robert Ellis that

54. See especially chapter 6, "Run for Your Life" in McKenzie, *Getting Physical.*

55. "Losing Their Way to Salvation," in Forbes and Mahan, *Religion and Popular Culture in America*, 179.

56. Forbes and Mahan, 183–84.

> a concern for fitness and health does have a proper part in a fully rounded doctrine of salvation . . . We may suggest that when salvation has become only a matter of fitness and health (or, for that matter, only a matter of eternal destiny), then a reductionist soteriology is operating; but the presence of such elements at all within a soteriology should be welcomed rather than discarded.[57]

Physical fitness can and should be one part of a doctrine of salvation. A soteriology without it, I would argue, is deficient. But, as Miroslav Volf puts it, "The greatest of all temptations isn't to serve false gods, as monotheists like to think. The greatest of all temptations, equally hard to resist in abundance and in want, is to believe and act as if human beings lived by bread alone, as if their entire lives should revolve around the creation, improvement, and distribution of worldly goods,"[58] or, for our purposes here, the maintenance and improvement of the physical body. What this reveals then, is that physical fitness is not an end in itself, as a worldly good that one should pursue. Rather, it is part of the holistic peace, the shalom, that God offers and it is a pursuit that is part of getting the world back "to the way it should be." So then, how might we move past this current imminent salvation narrative of physical fitness and locate it in God's wider plans for the Earth and humankind?

Physical Fitness in God's Wider Plan of Redemption

So far, I have shown that our physical bodies are shaped not only by our will and personal agency, but also by our environments and the created forces that surround our world, which often times become sinful. Nineteenth-century millennial movements included sport and fitness as part of the hope for a perfect world. Health took on eschatological implications, but this has left us today with a flattened and imminent soteriology of fitness that is often susceptible to the corrupting forces of consumer culture. And yet, as we have seen in the testimonies of the Team World Vision marathon runners, sport and fitness pursuits have tremendous capacity for fostering human thriving. These stories of the life-giving capacities of fitness should not be overlooked. So how then does one make sense theologically of physical fitness without falling into a purely this-world understanding of salvation? I

57. Ellis, *The Games People Play*, 271.

58. Volf, *Flourishing*, 22.

would argue that fitness must be placed into the narrative of God's larger redemptive plans for the world and all of creation, which is a fully embodied redemption, rooted in the resurrection and the recreation of the Heavens and the Earth (Rev 21). To do this, I will use a three-pronged approach that focuses on relationships: our relationship with ourselves within our physical bodies, our relationship with God in terms of our physical presence on Earth, and our relationships with other people.

First, let us look at the relationship that we have within ourselves, particularly in reference to the flesh (sarx) and the spirit (pneuma) (Rom 8, Gal 5–8). In chapter 2, I went into great detail about the value of embodiment and the problematic history of Christian dualist anthropologies. Here though, I want to say more about this antithesis of flesh and spirit, particularly as physical fitness pursuits are considered by many to be solely pursuits of the flesh. That is, they are of benefit only to the flesh and should therefore be minimized or even ignored. That, I would argue, is a misunderstanding both of Paul and of fitness. Noting again that Paul does not use a Platonist anthropology, but rather supports the historic Jewish understanding of humankind as a psychosomatic unity (a modern term, but one that fits with ancient Judaic anthropology), we can see that Paul's condemnation of flesh is not an indictment of God's good creation. Rather, as New Testament scholar Udo Schnelle makes clear, "The antithesis of sarx and pneuma results from their different goals: death and life (Rom 8:13). Because the Spirit of God or Christ is alive and at work in believers (Rom 8:9), they still live en sarki [in the flesh], of course, but no longer kata sarka [according to the flesh]. Their existence in hostility to God is abolished; they do the works of the Spirit (Gal 5:22)."[59] What is key here is the notion of different goals. Paul says works of the flesh are "fornication, impurity, licentiousness, idolatry, sorcery, enmities, strife, jealousy, anger, quarrels, dissensions, factions, envy, drunkenness, carousing, and things like these." (Gal 5:19–20). While four of those relate to the physical body, the rest do not. Rather, they are all simply works that lead toward destruction and fractured relationships, not solely bodily sin. Living by flesh means living toward death, toward that which is perishable and non-lasting, just as the human body is non-lasting without God's redemptive power. By contrast then, living by the Spirit means living toward life, and producing the fruits of the Spirit: love, joy, peace, patience, kindness, generosity, faithfulness, gentleness, and self-control (Gal 5:22–23). These are pointed toward life, toward cooperation with God's creative powers. And they are fully embodied experiences, with large implications for bodily activities.

59. Schnelle, *The Human Condition*, 62.

We might say then that living by the Spirit means living toward that which is life-giving, that which promotes life, well-being, and human thriving. Schnelle makes this point by looking at 1 Thessalonians 5:23: "May the God of peace himself sanctify you entirely; and may your spirit and soul [pneuma] and body be kept sound and blameless at the coming of our Lord Jesus Christ." Again, this is not Paul promoting some kind of fractured or trichotomous anthropology, but rather showing that "the sanctifying work of God concerns the whole person . . . in 1 Thessalonians pneuma for Paul is not a component of the human essence but the expression and sign of the new creative activity of God in humankind."[60] The Spirit, and life lived by the Spirit, means new creation, regeneration, and fulfillment of that which God has planned for the world. It is to live toward life. With this in mind, I would then argue that physical fitness pursuits, when life-giving, are in fact a manifestation of the Spirit. Pursuing the life-giving ends of fitness (noting again, that fitness can become disordered and destructive) is to live life in the Spirit. We are then to find reconciliation, a renewed relationship, within ourselves. That is the first aspect of this relational theology of fitness. We are not at war within ourselves, or in a war between mind/spirit and body, but rather in conflict between the life-giving work of the Spirit of God, and the destructive forces of "the flesh," the temporary, which is not co-equal with the physical body. Simply put, promotion of rightly-ordered physical health and well-being is the work of the Spirit. It is life-giving.

The next aspect of this relational theology of physical fitness comes in our relationship with God, particularly as it applies to the *imago Dei*. Genesis 1:26–28 reads:

> Then God said, "Let us make humankind in our image, according to our likeness; and let them have dominion over the fish of the sea, and over the birds of the air, and over the cattle, and over all the wild animals of the earth, and over every creeping thing that creeps upon the earth."
>
> So God created humankind in his image,
> in the image of God he created them;
> male and female he created them.
>
> God blessed them, and God said to them, "Be fruitful and multiply, and fill the earth and subdue it; and have dominion over the fish of the sea and over the birds of the air and over every living thing that moves upon the earth."

60. Schnelle, *The Human Condition*, 104.

This passage makes it clear that God created humankind as something different from the rest of the creatures. The underlying theological question then is, "How exactly is humankind special amongst God's creation?" The historic answers to this question are vast, and it is beyond the scope here to go into all of them. But, in short, the *imago Dei* has been applied to humankind's ability to communicate, the size of the human brain, possession of a soul, the capacity to reason, and even the ability to stand upright. In sum, the *imago Dei* is referenced as the means by which humankind does incredible feats. As we think of this in terms of sport and physical fitness then, there is a temptation to see our great achievements as a manifestation of the *imago Dei*. That, I would argue, is a mistake. John Swinton, who is pioneer in the field of theology of disability, argues that the *imago Dei* cannot be applied to any particular human attribute for achievement for fear of alienation of mistreatment of a population that does not have, or have in abundance, that attribute.

> The problem appears to be that if human beings are defined [in the *imago Dei*] by something within themselves, this inevitably leads to the exclusion and alienation of the weakest members of society. This is a very important observation. Biblically speaking, an adequate understanding of what it means for humanity to be in the *imago Dei* must be tested against the impact which particular formulations have on the marginalized and least powerful members of society (i.e. those who normally have no voice in theological construction). In other words, the authenticity or otherwise of any theological anthropology cannot be worked out on a purely abstracted and theoretical basis, but must be carved out in constructive dialogue with the ways in which it works itself out within the praxis of the church and the world.[61]

This is important for our conversation here because we have seen that God creates humankind with physical diversity. We are created with different attributes. Michael Phelps's physical abilities for swimming are far superior to Michael Jordan's, and Jordan's abilities for basketball are far greater than Phelps's. And let us not forget all those whose physical abilities do not come anywhere close to either of those athletes. That is to say also, that any theology of fitness and sport must incorporate those who are born handicapped, or become handicapped, or who are limited physically.

Swinton therefore adopts a relationist understanding of the *imago Dei*, that is "the image of God is understood as pertaining to a particular type of relationship that is available to all human beings, but unavailable to the rest

61. Swinton, *From Bedlam to Shalom*, 26.

of creation."[62] It is "God's willingness to enter into meaningful, purpose-endowing personal relationship with human beings that is the defining factor which marks them out from the rest of creation and proffers upon them a dignity and 'specialness' that is not given to other creatures."[63] Humankind, unlike other animals, has the capacity for a relationship with God. This interpretation therefore includes all people, of all abilities and capacities. The *imago Dei* speaks not of what we can do, but who we are in relation to God. That being said though, it also refers to responsibility, that is, what we are to do. Returning to chapter 1, this relationship implies an expectation of care, maintenance, and further creation. Now, that is not part of Swinton's interpretation of the *imago Dei* as presented above: how can there be an expectation of creation care or care for others on those with mental disabilities, that is, those who are in need of great care? Well, again, it is important to remember that all of humankind is part of creation, so creation care extends not just to the plants and animals, but to each other as well. There is relationality amongst all of creation. The *imago Dei* implies responsibility for care of all of God's creation, even humanity's care for humanity, however that might look. God has given the creation, set up humankind as God's image-bearers in and of creation, and in special relationship with God, and now God expects humankind to have "dominion," that is stewardship and loving care of all of creation.

As mentioned in chapter 1, this view of creation carries tremendous ecological implications. But, this care and formation must also apply to our own bodies. It is in and because of this relationship that we are able to pursue flourishing, physical and otherwise. It is because of the *imago Dei* that we are able to pursue our best selves, to reach our physical potential through the care, maintenance, and development of God's gift of our bodies. Robert Ellis acknowledges this relationist view, but also follows the Irenaean tradition of seeing the *imago Dei* as potential, that is, humankind is created in and moving toward its full, created capacity. This is why the athlete continually strives for a better performance. He states, "Humanity in the *imago Dei* is a dynamic creature of potential, reaching beyond itself to God, and sport exemplifies this human characteristic in a distinctive way. This human restlessness, this striving for better, is ultimately a striving after God."[64] I don't believe this conflicts with the relationist interpretation, and it adds to an understanding of why an athlete would desire to work hard and be the best that she can be. However, if we are talking about

62. Swinton, *From Bedlam to Shalom*, 27.

63. Swinton, *From Bedlam to Shalom*, 30.

64. Ellis, *The Games People Play*, 243–44.

athletic and physical ability and how that fits in with our relationship with God and the relational mandate to steward and form creation, we must be careful with this idea of potential.[65] Lurking behind this sense of *imago Dei* and human potential, particularly as it relates to sport and fitness, is that there is in fact a terminus to this potential, a quantifiable performance, or noticeable moment when this potential has been reached.[66] Ostensibly, an Olympic athlete, whose life has been dedicated to training, would be the most likely to find that potential, at least in physical terms. But there are hints of Platonism and Aristotelianism when discussing potential: there is an ideal form which one might be able to reach and should work to reach. Judging from his book, this is not Ellis's argument, but I do believe this is a pitfall of any theological discussion of sport and fitness. Can I reach my potential? Will I know it when I reach it? Or, worst of all, will I disappoint or even fail God if I do not reach that potential?

Again, this is where the relationist understanding of the *imago Dei* becomes important. I am created in relationship with God and given a role in the stewardship of creation. But that stewardship is highly contextual. In Jesus's parable of the talents (Matt 25:14-30), each of the servants is given a portion of the master's wealth, "each according to his ability." The servants are expected to invest the money and bring back a return. The only servant with whom the master is upset is the servant who buries his talent, who does not utilize it to create more wealth—that is, engage in stewardship. This servant acted in fear. He felt that the master was a "harsh man," an attribute that is not mentioned anywhere else in the parable and is ostensibly a machination of the fearful servant. In other words, the servant did not have a good relationship with the master. He didn't know him well and attributed him with inaccurate qualities. We see here that the Master expects stewardship to be done contextually, to be done with what is given. And when a right relationship is in place, stewardship is done, granted in different amounts by different people, but done faithfully, which pleases the master.

The proper relationship to the physical body stems from a proper relationship with God. The *imago Dei* is the sign and seal of that relationship, and it shows an expectation of contextual stewardship. Therefore, the performative capabilities of the body must always be understood as existing in context.

65. In casual conversations with former Olympic swimmers, I have often asked if they feel that they reached their full potential during their Olympic careers. I have always heard "no," tinged with a hint of sadness. I offer this not as thorough qualitative data, but merely an interesting illustration.

66. There is an opportunity, not covered here, to engage with these notions of sport and fitness with process theology. How do we understand physical potential as continual growth?

There is no quantifiable best performance. There is only the best performance in a particular place and time by a particular person, gifted with individual abilities.[67] This idea of contextuality then segues into the third relational aspect of a theology of fitness, our relationship with others.

Let us return to Dyrness's Trinitarian understanding of creation as discussed in chapter 1 and reflect further on the notion that "God's nature is communal so our life in the world is invariably relational and communal."[68] As we've seen in the discussion of the sin of obesity, our bodily shapes and our bodily health exist inside an intricate and elaborate web of relationships. My health is dependent not only on my own actions, but also on other's actions, particularly as they have an effect on the food I eat, the gym I attend, the cultural expectations I internalize, and even the air I breathe. Now, because of the relationship within the life the Trinity, God's expectation for humankind is one of loving relationship. Therefore, a theology of fitness must exist within this network of relationships. My fitness is not my own, just as my life is not my own. As mentioned before, the health care costs of obesity related illness are currently reaching toward $200 billion annually in the United States. So, take for example a person who suffers from a heart attack. The direct and indirect costs of treating a minor heart attack are estimated at $760,000 over the remaining years of life.[69] Now, the patient will most likely not pay that full cost, assuming he has health insurance. But that means then that the cost is distributed to all of the members of the health insurance plan. In other words, the community pays the cost. Ideally, if the patient in our example did not suffer a heart attack—because he took better care of himself—then the financial burden on the community would be reduced. This is a simplified example, but it shows that our physical fitness, as personal as it might be, exists within the web of community responsibilities. Pursuing the life-giving ends of physical fitness, can in fact be an act of loving the neighbor.

God's redemptive purposes in the world are highly relational, and therefore fitness must be seen in relational terms. There is the relationship within the individual, between the competing demands of flesh/death and Spirit/life, the relationship with God, which calls for stewardship of

67. Johnny Weissmuller, Olympic swimmer and later actor, broke the world record and won the gold medal at the 1922 Olympics in the 100-meter freestyle, registering a time of 58.6 seconds. In 2016, the necessary qualifying time just to attend the American Olympic Trials and compete for a spot on the Olympic team was 50.69. The gold medal in Rio in 2016 was won with a time of 47.58. This is to ask, did Weissmuller reach his full ability? He certainly did in his own context.

68. Dyrness, *The Earth Is God's*, xiv.

69. Vernon, "How Much Would Heart Attack Cost?"

creation—including the body—and the relationship with others, as one's fitness and health, however indirectly, have an impact on the community. The American Heart Association recommends about 3 hours of physical activity a week as a mean for preventing heart attack and stroke.[70] But, as I am arguing here, physical fitness is not just about maintenance of health or avoidance of illness and death. There must also be an element of creation, of utilizing one's particular set of physical gifts to build and form and give glory to God. As Dyrness puts it, "If we believe that God is creator of this world and that Christ holds all things together through the ministry of the Holy Spirit, we can insist that God has a stake in what we are making of the world." [71] So then, one might ask, does God want or expect me to have six pack abs, or to look like Arnold Schwarzenegger, or to win an Olympic medal in the decathlon? I would argue, maybe so. But that question can only be answered in context, in the particular location of responsibilities, relationships, and gifts. Does a pursuit of any of those ends lead to destruction or do they lead to abundant life for the individual as well as the community? All of this is to affirm though that God's plan for the redemption of the world includes the human body and its abilities. Again, Dyrness states that,

> As Christ offers up to God the renewed life of God's human creation, so the Holy Spirit bears up the whole created order and moves it toward the perfection to which creation is directed. Resurrection, ascension, and Pentecost are the opening up of relations between God and the creation, and, at the same time, a reaffirmation of its value to God.[72]

Humankind has a responsibility to God's creation and a role to play in its inevitable redemption and perfection. Our physical bodies are part of this grand plan, particularly as they are part of our interconnectedness.

Conclusion

I have argued here that the obesity epidemic is a product of sinful structures (however those might be construed), which are a failure of relationship, and a corruption of the good powers that God has put into creation to maintain order and peace. Stemming from this then, the understanding of sin and physical fitness is not one exclusively of personal sin, but rather a failure of the community. After an initial investment in physical fitness

70. "American Heart Association Recommendations."

71. Dyrness, *The Earth Is God's*, 11.

72. Dyrness, *The Earth Is God's*, 15–16.

as part of a millennial hope, the Christian church has unintentionally fueled an imminent soteriology that finds value in the body, but does not have a referent to God.

God's ultimate plan for creation is redemption and recreation, and this implies today a responsible use of creation, as realized through relationship with God. Our bodies are part of creation and therefore we must treat them respectfully, seeking not only good health, but physical greatness, as defined in context. It is becoming clearer now how fitness—as often realized through sport—is a critical element of the life of discipleship. Ultimately, our physical forms will only be perfected in the life to come, but the goal of physical fitness, in the here and now, does serve as an important directional marker for motivating physical practices. Growing toward God, and resisting the powers of sin, means maintaining, utilizing, and cherishing the good gift of the human body.

Conclusion

In his 2007 guidebook on a Christian approach to fitness, psychologist and Catholic leader Kevin Vost argues that one should look to Jesus as an example for the physically fit life. He asks the reader to

> close your eyes and try to imagine the physical characteristics of Jesus Christ himself. He must have been magnificently fit and strong. The Virgin Mary herself nursed him and then helped establish his eating habits. Being free of sin, his dietary practices would have been guided by perfect temperance. His earthly father, St. Joseph, a hardworking carpenter, was the young Jesus's earthly model for physical strength and endurance. And Jesus himself, working without modern power tools, would undoubtedly have developed lean, powerful muscles. After he had begun his public ministry, we can barely read a chapter of the Gospels without hearing about his long journeys, mostly on foot, over hilly, unpaved paths. In his humanity, he would not have had the stamina to carry out his exhausting public work had he been in anything less than peak physical shape.[1]

Having read this description of Jesus's physically fit body, I would ask the reader, how does that make you feel? Does it stir any feelings of discomfort? I believe there is an unintentional sensualizing of Jesus's body, as the reader is pushed to contemplate Jesus's "lean, powerful muscles." There is also a romanticizing of the pre-modern lifestyle before people spent most of their days sitting behind desks and working on computers. So, while Vost does make an understandable argument for Jesus's toned physique, it is highly anachronistic. The qualities and ends of contemporary fitness movements are read into the life of Jesus. Vost does not take into account Jesus's status as a peasant worker living under imperial occupation. Certainly, his dietary practices were guided by perfect temperance, but that also assumes that he

1. Vost, *Fit for Eternal Life*, xix.

had an abundance of food options, which as I have shown, is a modern phenomenon. The first-century peasant diet was limited, and it's more likely that Jesus faced under-nutrition. It is more possible that Jesus's body, which existed in a time without modern health care, physical therapy, or proper hygiene, was a damaged body, with scars, untreated injuries, and chronic pain. One need look no further than the bodies of contemporary colonized people to see the physical impact of oppression.

Now, this is not to say that Jesus should not be a model for the physically fit life. As I have argued, fitness pursuits should be couched in relationality, that is, they are not just personal endeavors, but ones that are motivated by love for God and love for neighbor. Jesus showed incredible concern for physical wholeness and integration into community life. In Matthew 9:14-30, Jesus heals four people in quick succession: a woman suffering from bleeding for twelve years, a young girl who had died (or nearly died), and two men born blind. Jesus shows tremendous concern for their physical well-being and for their ability to thrive in the created world. In the case of the woman with bleeding, her healing allows for a reintegration into the wider community, as she was continuously considered ritually unclean under Mosaic purity laws, and therefore limited in her contact with others. Jesus's healing brings shalom, a peace within oneself and a peace within the community. So, did Jesus have lean, powerful muscles? Perhaps. But he was more concerned about relationship, community integration, and physical wellness, which are all interwoven. And these are the same concerns that undergird the needs for physical fitness and health in the modern world.

Let us return here to my central thesis: the pursuit of physical fitness is an integral part of the life of Christian discipleship, and it can serve as cooperation with God's redemptive purposes in creation. I have argued that creation (the entire physical world, including the human body, as created by God) is good. Sin does not occlude this goodness. Sin rather is a failure to respect and honor the relationships that God has set up within creation—between God and humans, between humans themselves (and within oneself), and between humans and the rest of creation—and is a failure to use properly the agency that we have, which is a gift from God. Created in the *imago Dei*, human beings are entrusted with the responsibility of tending to and maintaining the created world. Humans have a relationship with creation, and the way we treat it is indicative of our relationship with God. The Industrial Revolution however brought about a dramatic change in food production—at the expense of the land—and therefore modern diets have shifted. The modern industrial diet has then had an impact on human health and the physical form, most notably the obesity epidemic and its related health concerns. And therein lies the failure of relationship between human beings, the failure to live the command to love one another. The systemic issues at the root of the obesity epidemic spring from institutional and corporate sin—not just personal sin, or misuse of personal agency. Institutional sin, which is the sin—sometimes small, sometimes large—that we all commit, often unknowingly, is a fracture of relationship. So then, I argue, pursuing physical fitness is a countercultural endeavor that serves as an act of creation care, and exhibits love of God and love of neighbor, lived out within the interconnectedness that we all share.

Now, this is not an attempt to romanticize the pre-industrial diet. There is no question that modern food production has eliminated hunger in many places. In 1857, Gail Borden Jr., an entrepreneur, perfected the process for creating shelf-stable condensed milk. He was troubled by the illness and death that he saw amongst children on trans-Atlantic boat trips—milk could not be properly preserved on these long journeys, and often went bad.[2] It might be argued then that Borden created condensed milk as an act of love for neighbor. Yet today, condensed milk is a perennial ingredient in confections and obesogenic sweets, having gained tremendous popularity beyond its initial intent. This is to say that humankind's relationship with, and understanding of, food and the physical body is in development. There is a journey taking place.

So, seeking physical fitness is a key component in the life of Christian discipleship—a life which entails growth and development. Certainly, there is the narcissistic, preening bodybuilder, who cares about vanity above all else. And there are those who suffer from body dysmorphia and pursue fitness as a part of a mental disorder. But these are corruptions or misappropriations of a good thing, like the man who desires the goods of love and companionship and therefore pursues an extramarital affair. It should be noted that the fitness industry, along with the sports industry, are just that, industries designed to make money, and they are pulled and distorted by the ends of capitalism over the ends of human thriving. But at its core, pursuing physical fitness means pursuing the abundant physical life for which God designed humankind.

Let us return here for a moment to the joys of the cupcake. A well-made cupcake is a treat that elicits delight. But, an overabundance of cupcakes, or an immoderate intake of any sugar-heavy snack, leads to illness. The food industry though, knowing the health problems created by adulterated foods but not wanting to deny people the delight of sweets, has offered a solution in the form of artificial sweeteners. Aspartame, for example, which is used to sweeten sodas and other shelf-stable foods, was unintentionally

2. O'Connell, *The American Plate*, 125.

discovered in 1965 by chemist James M. Schlatter who was working on an anti-ulcer drug. Aspartame is 200 times sweeter than table sugar and therefore less can be used in products and caloric content is reduced. It and other artificial sweeteners have long been studied, with mixed results, as possible carcinogens. All this is to say that people's taste for sweet foods has led to the creation of chemical compounds that mimic what we desire while hopefully mitigating health issues. Diet food products use tremendous amounts of these artificial foods. Now, I would make the argument, based on personal experience, that whole food, that is, real food that comes from proper care, maintenance, and cultivation of the land (or creation), actually tastes better than processed treats, industrially produced foods, and artificially created food. A raspberry at peak ripeness actually tastes better than a bag of Skittles, or even that cupcake. A properly roasted Brussels sprout is more delicious than McDonald's (highly adulterated) French fries. And it is the whole foods, which, in theological terms are arguable closest to how God made them, that best promote health and well-being. [3] The diet industry has long advocated for abstinence from calorically high foods and has promoted artificial foods. To go on a diet means eating bland and tasteless—or perhaps joyless—food or some synthesized food item. The diet industry has also pulled on people's ascetic impulses: if I give up these foods I will become a better person. Yet, by insisting on synthesized or highly processed foods as an alternative to tempting treats, the diet industry has missed the true power of asceticism. The Christian ascetic does not give something up just for the sake of denial, or for some perceived righteousness that comes through self-inflicted pain. Rather, the true Christian ascetic denies himself or herself something in order to gain a greater awareness and appreciation of that which has already been provided and become a new person who lives within a new and better order.[4] In other words, we shouldn't give up sugar-

3. Now, this doesn't mean that we should cease experimenting with food or stop trying to create new foods because doing so would be unnatural, or would take foods away from how God "made them." To cease doing so would deny the mandate for creativity, as discussed previously. Rather, I'm arguing that we should experiment with foods in a manner that does not deteriorate their integrity.

4. I am following the argument of Richard Valantasis in "A Theory of the Social Function of Asceticism" in Wimbush and Valantasis, *Asceticism*, 547. "At the center of ascetical activity is a self who, through behavioral changes, seeks to become a different person, a new self; to become a different person in new relationships; and to become a different person in a new society that forms a new culture. As this new self emerges (in relationship to itself, to others, to society, to the world) it masters the behaviors that enable it at once to deconstruct the old self and to construct the new. Asceticism, then, constructs both the old and the reformed self and the cultures in which these selves function: asceticism asserts the subject of behavioral change and transformation, while constructing and reconstructing the environment in which that subjectivity functions."

heavy foods for bland foods (or artificially sweetened foods) but rather give them up so that we may gain a better appreciation for the abundant and delicious foods that God has already made available.

Food then is a metonym for the wider eschatological purposes of God: human beings are not to find hope in escape from the created world (perhaps like Aspartame) but are to hope for the redemption of all things, and the revealing of the inherit goodness of God's creation (like the perfect raspberry). This then connects to the second aspect of my thesis: sport and fitness pursuits can be part of God's redemptive purposes for creation. Humans were not created to toil. Rather, we were created to play, to enjoy God's good creation and live life abundantly. And that is still God's desire for humankind. Therefore, God isn't working to remove humans from creation, or to help our souls escape into an ethereal realm, or enter into the transcendent space of God, but rather, God is working to redeem all of creation, to bring it back to its full, flourishing state. God has worked throughout history—through Noah, Abraham, Isaac, Jacob, Moses, Mary, Jesus, Paul, and all successive disciples of Christ—to bring creation back into proper relationship with God. Now, we live in the already-but-not-yet, where we have been told of what is to come in the New Heavens and New Earth, and we have been shown the path of redemption through Jesus Christ. So, in this current time, we are not to be "conformed to this world," but to discern "what is the will of God—what is good and acceptable and perfect" (Rom 12:2). We are to strive for the life to come, and part of this is human flourishing, here in the world now. As I have shown then, sport, when rightly ordered—or we might say, coached—has a tremendous capacity to promote human flourishing, which is, arguably, the ends of God. And it is particularly good at this not just because of what it produces, but because it stems from play. Sport is playful, and God created playfully and encourages humans to be playful.

Now, I want to emphasize again the contextual nature of all sporting and fitness endeavors. There are those who are gifted with a tremendous VO2 max or lactate threshold who will thrive in sport. There are those who are not given such gifts—or, perhaps, are handicapped or otherwise disabled—who will not be able to pursue traditional paths of fitness. But that does not exclude anyone from the necessity of pursuing physical fitness as an act of love for God and neighbor, and it does not deny that we are all "fearfully and wonderfully made" (Ps 139:14). Some are given ten talents, physical or otherwise, and some are given one. The master is only upset with those who bury their talents. Theologian Simon Chan makes a parallel point in his classic work *Spiritual Theology*. Contemporary Christianity, particularly in young adult evangelical circles, has put a great deal of stress on living the life that God has designed for you, living into God's "perfect will." Chan points out that many Christians

> worry themselves sick about missing God's "perfect will" and settling for God's "permissive will." What they usually mean is that at one point in their lives they felt sure that God wanted them to go into "full-time" ministry or some such calling, but they became lawyers or stockbrokers instead. A few things need to be said about this commonly encountered "case of conscience." First, a person who is really concerned about God's will is probably already in it. The willingness and desire after God *is* the will of God. Second, making a mistake in one choice does not mean forever missing out on God's perfect will. God's will for one's life is found in the process of living in love and obedience, not in one crucial choice we made or failed to make.[5]

I raise this here to show that physical fitness, as an act of obedience to God, has to be seen in proper context. There will be times when one's fitness is tremendous, and one's body is working at full capacity. But there will also be times when fitness goals are occluded by other commitments, like raising a small child or writing a doctoral dissertation (or, God forbid, both at the same time), and one's overall fitness and athletic performance will suffer. But that doesn't imply failure in God's eyes. What's more, in chapter 5, I showed that one of the basic human goods that was manifested in the Team World Vision runners was identity coherence. The marathon helped many students better understand who they are. But research shows that sport can often have a negative impact on one's identity formation, as participation in sports obstructs other avenues for finding knowledge of self and prevents formation of a well-rounded identity.[6] That is, those athletes have not been contextually minded about their athletic performance. Psychologist Benjamin J. Houltberg has done a great deal of work with youth athletes (elite and recreational) and has identified the perils of "performance-based identity." He states,

> It is the natural trajectory of a gifted adolescent to form a central part of their identity around being an athlete and, more specifically, how they perform in their sport. Coupled with the heightened sensitivity and difficulty regulating emotionality, this can lead to a performance-based identity that can undermine the emotional health of youth and ultimately prevent young athletes

5. Chan, *Spiritual Theology*, 201. Emphasis in original.

6. See Horton and Mack, "Athletic Identity in Marathon Runners"; Verkooijen, van Hove, and Dik, "Athletic Identity and Well-Being."

> from performing at their best. Even more, a performance-based identity is often celebrated in our culture and reinforced by adults within the young athlete's developmental context.[7]

So, when a young athlete fails to perform at expected levels, this impacts his or her identity. It is not just a failure of performance, but also a failure of the whole person. For the Christian athlete then, especially the one who has been lifted up as an evangelist for the faith because of their athleticism, an inadequate performance means letting down fellow believers and even letting down God! Houltberg instead encourages athletes to find a "purpose-based identity."

> A sense of identity grounded in feeling loved and based in purpose empowers youth to act on their gifts in healthy ways . . . Sports are seen as meaningful not just because of the joy experienced but also because of the productive engagement with others. As a result, the young athlete is able to experience the freedom to strive for excellence and maximize their potential on and off the athletic field . . . An alternative [to performance-based identity] is to view participation in sports as a gift from God that reflects God's unchanging love for the athlete and provides a source of joy and an opportunity to serve others. Thus, sports are another way to experience God's love and pleasure and connect to something greater than self.[8]

Houltberg's research focuses on young athletes, but I believe it is relevant to adult athletes as well, and it brings further light to the contextuality of all sporting and fitness endeavors. As I have argued, the purpose of sport and fitness can be found in God's redemptive purposes for the world, which are ultimately centered on love and reconciliation. So, the better question for the contextually-minded pursuit of sport and fitness might be, "how am I living toward the ends of human thriving by exercising my own agency, in relationship with others and with God, in the place and context where I currently reside? And how might I do so even better in the future, as an act of love toward God and neighbor?"

Now, there are a few more related points and clarifications that I would like to make. In chapter 2, I argued that if a person is a unified whole, without a separable soul then we meet God in our bodies. Our bodies are what we have for approaching God, and God approaches us as we are, in our physical, created selves. Our encounters with the transcendent God will always be mediated through creation, and this includes our bodies. If we

7. Houltberg, "Moving from Performance to Purpose."

8. Houltberg, "Moving from Performance to Purpose."

are our bodies then, and we meet God in our bodies, then physical activities are, in a sense, God-seeking activities.[9] Maintaining and honing the body is to strengthen that with which we encounter God. So then, does that mean the fastest person at the track meet, or the person with the most Olympic medals is thereby the most Godly, or the closest to God? Certainly not. There are far too many other factors that contribute to a person's relationship with God to make athletic performance a reliable metric. And again, sport and fitness contribute to the purposes of God only as they are formed and directed toward those ends, which are defined by relationships, not personal achievement. But, I do want to lift up fitness and sporting endeavors as possible entry points into relationship with God, as can be the case with many aesthetic endeavors. As Dyrness argues,

> Aesthetic and symbolic projects are also spiritual sites where the affections, the goods of the world, and religious longings meet and interact . . . they are places where, because of God's continuing presence in creation and God's redemptive work in Christ and by the Spirit, God is also active, nurturing, calling, and drawing persons—and indeed all creation—toward the perfection God intends for them.[10]

In chapter 7, I mentioned the modern phenomenon of the imminent salvation found in fitness culture. Salvation in the here-and-now comes through perfecting the body, making it impervious to illness or decay, as futile as that might be. This is of course a reductionist understanding of salvation, but, I support it, at least as a starting point. Again, if God is working through our aesthetic endeavors, then that glimpse of salvation found at the gym just might be a starting point to a wider understanding of salvation. If one has found reconciliation in the body, that might just be a beginning to finding reconciliation with an estranged parent or community group, or perhaps even reconciliation with God.

Finally, I want to argue that sport and fitness pursuits should in fact be seen as possible God-honoring creative endeavors. The artist takes the elements of the earth, of creation, and forms and molds them into awe-inspiring paintings and sculptures that can invite people to reflect on the glory of God, and that might actually be present in the New Heaven and New Earth. The architect and engineer fashion wood and stone into marvelous sanctuaries that call people into God's presence here and now. And so, I

9. I'm avoiding the phrase "spiritual activities" here, which might be the more recognized phrase, as spiritual, in some sense, implies escape from or denigration of the physical life.

10. Dyrness, *Poetic Theology*, 6.

believe, the athlete can do the same: he or she can take the elements of creation, which in this case is the human body, and lovingly fashion and mold it—or more specifically train it—to do amazing feats. The world record in the 100-meter butterfly swimming event might get broken on a regular basis, and one's time in the local 5k run might increase every year, but these are still awe-inspiring feats that speak of God's glorious work in and through creation, as made by the faithful and God-honoring athlete.

This, I believe, is the first word, from a cultural theological perspective, on the value of physical fitness and sport in the life of Christian discipleship. There are many more possibilities for in depth research. The nature of institutional sin, and the inner working of capitalistic structures in regard to food production and environmental concerns could be greatly expanded. Speaking of capitalism, it would be very interesting to analyze it as a power that influences and shapes, for good or bad, sport and bodily health. The arguments for the intrinsic value of sport, as mentioned in chapter 4, show a desire to remove sport from all other outside forces. In a way, it is an argument that asks for sport to be removed from capitalism, that it can only truly be play if it exists outside market forces. Perhaps that will never happen, but there are long-running and heated arguments about just such a move for American health care. Socialized health care programs are just that, health care removed from capitalism, ostensibly because capitalist forces have ends other than the health of the people, or at best, distort the ends of health. This could raise conversations about what other institutions should exist outside of capitalism. I have made comments about disability, but I believe there could be a further integration with the topics discussed here and current literature on the theology of disability. Overall though, I believe the next area for research is in practical theology, looking at how the theological principles expounded upon here can be integrated and utilized by congregations. How can the Platonist and body-denying culture present in many churches, evangelical and mainline, which support an escapist understanding of salvation, be reoriented toward a creation-minded and creation-appreciating understanding of God's work in the world? I pray that day comes soon.

Appendix A

Protocol Description of Team World Vision Study

Title:

Effects of Training with Team World Vision
in Adolescents and Adults

Investigators

Sarah Schnitker, Ph.D., Benjamin Houltberg, Ph.D., Nanyamka Redmond, MA., Nathaniel Fernandez, MA., TJ Felke, MA., Lyndsey Deane, M.A., Wes Kriesel, Julie Bierschenk, Daniel Mendoza, Erik Dailey, Danielle Hand.

Overview of Study

Athletic programs are popularly touted as primary conduits of character strength development in adolescents, but empirical research has yielded mixed results as to the efficacy of athletic participation in instilling virtue (Dierdorff, Surface, & Brown, 2010). It is likely that for athletic participation to promote character developm 0ent, it must be situated in a context that explicitly values moral growth. We intend to study just such an athletic program. We propose to track the character development of adolescents and adults training for half or full marathons through Team World Vision (TWV). TWV is a non-profit Christian program in which adolescents and adults raise money for clean water, sanitation, and hygiene programs in Africa by training for half/full marathons. Not only do runners for TWV report an increase in physical health as a result of their training, but they also recount that their experiences are profoundly spiritual and transformative, likely due to the spiritual meaning attached to the training. The study described in this protocol is part of a grant from the John Templeton Foundation (JTF) that will look more broadly at the effect of sports participation on virtue development. Our specific hypotheses are listed below.

Hypotheses

1. Fitness, moral, and spiritual motivations to engage in TWV training will predict increases in self-control, emotion regulation and patience, and moral and spiritual motivations to engage in TWV training will predict increases in generosity and decreases in contingencies self-worth.
2. Fitness, moral, and spiritual motivations to engage in TWV training will predict race performance.
3. Moral and spiritual motivations to engage in TWV training will predict fundraising.
4. Amount of training will predict increases in self-control and patience.
5. Fitness, moral, and spiritual motivations to engage in TWV training will predict increases in well-being (life satisfaction, depression, and positive affectivity) and health behaviors (servings of fruit/veggies, junk food).
6. Perceptions of connection with fellow training partners (adults and peers) and TWV leaders, along with team entitativity, will predict increases in patience, self-control, emotion regulation, performance, and fundraising.
7. Fitness, moral, and spiritual motivations to engage in TWV training will predict training activity two months post-race.

Participant Characteristics

Participants will be adolescents (thirteen to twenty-one years of age) and adults (N » 100–450) who are training for half or full marathons through Team World Vision (TWV). TWV (www.teamworldvision.org) is a non-profit Christian program in which adolescents and adults raise money for clean water, sanitation, and hygiene programs in Africa by training for half and full marathons. TWV is a part of World Vision (www.worldvision.org), one of the largest humanitarian organizations in the world. TWV encourages runners to dedicate their race to helping others in Africa, which they say leads to change in the runners' lives as well. In 2013, over 5,000 runners participated in the TWV training program, and 80 percent of its participants are new to running. Approximately 5 percent of TWV runners were adolescents last year, but the number of adolescent runners is expected to increase in the next two years. The largest contingent of adolescents who currently run half marathons with TWV are recruited by teachers in inner-city Chicago public high schools to run the Chicago Marathon. Many of these adolescent runners are from diverse ethnic background (especially African American) and come from low SES neighborhoods. TWV has begun to more actively recruit other adolescents to run. Many of the newest recruitment efforts are targeted to church youth groups in the LA area. Our partnership with TWV will enable them to expand their adolescent recruiting. We will focus on recruiting adolescents from diverse backgrounds in LA. Participants will need to speak English for participation in this study. Participants will be required to have a working email address to participate in this study. An adolescent population, although a vulnerable population, was selected for this study because the research questions specifically look to address how virtue development occurs within adolescent development.

Methods and Procedures

As participants sign up for TWV to run marathons in various cities across the U.S. (mostly LA and Chicago; possibly New York, Denver, Miami, Detroit, and Seattle), they will be asked to participate in a research study that is sponsored by TWV and JTF.

Research assistants will present an overview of the study and answer any questions that participants and parents might have about the study. After obtaining parental and participant consent, participants will be asked to complete a short survey (Time 1) with measures of training motivations, self-control, patience, religiousness and God concept, well-being, and training outcomes. All measures will be completed online. We will ask participants to keep running logs as they train so that we can evaluate the quantity and quality of their training. Around week twelve or sixteen of the training program (when participants have completed their largest group run), we will re-administer the initial survey materials (Time 2). In the week after completing their half/full marathon, participants will again take the survey measures (Time 3). Two months after the race, we will contact participants one last time to complete the final survey measures (Time 4). Table 1 displays the data collection timeline for "half" and "full" trainees.

In addition to collecting quantitative data from TWV participants, we will select five to ten participants with whom we will collect in-depth qualitative data. We will interview the selected participants at each of the four time points specified for survey collection. Participants will be asked about their experiences running, why they are a part of TWV, how they think training is changing their lives, and how they make meaning from the training. Interviews will be video-taped with hopes that they may be used for more engaging presentations of study findings and/or for TWV promotional materials.

Table 1. Data Collection Schedule

Week		**Task**
Half	*Full*	
0	0	Participant Recruitment and Obtaining Informed Consent
1	1	Time 1 Participant Survey (Pre-training)
2-13	2-19	Participants Complete Running Logs
12	16	Time 2 Participant Survey (Long training run)
14	20	Time 3 Participant Survey (Post-race)
22	28	Time 4 Participant Survey (2-month follow-up)

Measures

Measures to be administered to participants include measures of performance and motivational orientation (Crocker, Luhtanen, Cooper, & Bouvrette, 2003), interpersonal generosity (Smith & Hill, 2009), self-control (Tangney, Baumeister, & Boone, 2004), patience (Schnitker, 2012), general regulatory behavior (Oaten & Cheng, 2006) and emotion regulation processes (Zeman, Shipman, & Suveg, 2002), religious activity (Koenig & Bussing, 2010) God concept (Carter, McCullough & Carver, 2012; Laurin, Kay, & Fitzsimons, 2012), life satisfaction (Diener, Emmons, Larsen, & Griffin, 1985), risk behaviors (Foti, Balaji, & Shanklin, 2011), entitativity (Gaertner & Schopler, 1998), fundraising outcomes, sponsorship status, training participation (e.g., in group runs), training outcomes (e.g., race times), and demographic variables. Participants will also be asked to keep daily training logs to record daily distance ran, time, type of run or cross-training, workout difficulty, workout motivation, socialization habits during group runs, hours slept, servings of fruit/veggies, and servings of junk food/drinks.

Virtue Measures

Virtue measures are conceptualized as the dependent variables that will differentially change as a result of the training with Team World Vision (TWV).

1. *Self-Control Scale.* Tangney, Baumeister, & Boone's (2004) scale contains items measuring self-control (e.g., "I am good at resisting temptation") on a *1 (Not at All)* to *5 (Very Much)* scale. We will use the abbreviated, thirteen-item version of the scale.
2. 3-*Factor Patience Questionnaire.* The eleven-item 3-Factor Patience Questionnaire (3-FPQ; Schnitker, 2012) will be used as a measure of interpersonal ("My friends would say I'm a very patient friend"), life hardships ("I find it pretty easy to be patient with a difficult life problem or illness"), and daily hassles ("Although they're annoying, I don't get too upset when stuck in a traffic jam") patience. Items are rated from 1 (*Not Like Me At All)* to 5 (*Very Much Like Me).*
3. *General Regulatory Behavior Questionnaire.* A questionnaire was developed based on Oaten and Cheng's (2006) study items measuring everyday regulatory behaviors, including cigarette smoking, alcohol and caffeine consumption, dietary habits, self-care habits, spending habits, emotion control, study habits, obeying rules, use of social media, energy conservation, and turning in assignments. Participants were asked to rate how often they engaged in behaviors in the past week on a scale from 1 (*Not At All)* to 5 (*Almost Always).*
4. *Emotion regulation.* Participants will be assessed using three subscales (i.e., four-item anger regulation coping, four-item emotion regulation inhibition, and three-item dysregulated expression) from the Children's Sadness and Anger Management Scale (Zeman, Shipman, & Penza-Clyve, 2001. Participants will report on sadness and anger. A sample item follows: "When I am feeling mad, I control my temper," (anger/sadness regulation coping), "I hide my anger/sadness," (inhibition), and, "I attack whatever it is that makes me mad," (dysregulated coping). The response choices follow: 0 (*Not True),* 1 (*Somewhat True),* and 2 (*Very True).*
5. *Interpersonal Generosity Scale.* The 10-item Interpersonal Generosity Scale (Smith, & Hill, 2009) will be used as a measure of generosity. The items measure six identifiable dimensions of interpersonal generosity: attention ("I am known by family and friends as someone who makes time to pay attention to others' problems"), compassion ("When friends

or family members experience something upsetting or discouraging, I make a special point of being kind to them"), open-handedness ("When it comes to my personal relationships with others, I am a very generous person"), self-extension ("My decisions are often based on concern for the welfare of others"), courage ("I am usually willing to risk my own feelings being hurt in the process if I stand a chance of helping someone else in need"), and verbal expression ("I make it a point to let my friends and family know how much I love and appreciate them") on a *1 (Strongly Disagree)* to *6 (Strongly Agree)* scale.

Spirituality/Religiosity Measures

Spirituality and religiosity measures are expected to moderate the effects of running with TWV on virtue development. Religious commitment and spirituality may also change as a result of involvement in TWV.

6. *Duke University Religious Index (DUREL).* The Duke University Religion Index (DUREL; Koenig & Bussing, 2010) is a five-item measure of religious involvement that includes dimensions of religiosity (organizational religious activity, non-organizational religious activity, and intrinsic religiosity). Organizational religious activity (ORA; How often do you attend church or other religious meetings?) and non-organizational religious activity (NORA; How often do you spend time in private religious activities, such as prayer, meditation or Bible?) are both rated on a six-point scale. For ORA the response choice is as follows: 1 (*Never*), 2—*Once A Year Or Less*), 3 (*A Few Times A Year*), 4 (*A Few Times A Month*), 5 (*Once A Week*), and 6 (*More Than Once A Week*); NORA includes: 1 (*Rarely Or Never*), 2 (*A Few Times A Month*), 3 (*Once A Week*), 4 (*Two Or More Times A Week*), 5 (*Daily*), and 6 (*More Than Once A Day*).
7. *God Concept Questions.* Based on Laurin, Kay, and Fitzsimons (2012), perceptions of God's sovereignty and watchfulness. Perceptions of God's sovereignty will be rated from 1 to 5 based on the degree to which the person conceives of God as in control of their success or failure in life. "My future success in life depends . . . 1 (*Completely On Factors God Controls*), 2 (*Mostly On Factors That God Controls*), 3 (*Equally On Factors That God And I Control*), 4 (*Mostly On Factors That I Control*), and 5 (*Completely On Factors I Control*). Perceptions of God watching will be rated from 1 to 5 on a Likert scale. "If God (or some non-human spiritual being) exists, it is likely that God watches

peoples' behavior and notices when they misbehave." Additionally, the monitoring by God subscale (three items) based on Carter, McCullough & Carver (2012) will also be used. Ratings will be based on a 1 (*Not At All*) to 7 (*Very True*) scale, and include items such as, "I believe a higher power can see my behavior."

Well-Being Measures

In addition to expecting increases in virtue as a result of running for TWV, we expect that well-being will also increase. Thus, these will be used as dependent variables.

8. *Satisfaction with Life Scale.* This 5-item scale (Diener, Emmons, Larsen, & Griffin, 1985) measures global satisfaction with life. Items such as, "In most ways, my life is close to my ideal," are rated on a scale from 1 *(Strongly Disagree)* to 7 *(Strongly Agree).*
9. *Youth Risk Behavior Surveillance.* Participants will be administered sixteen items selected from Youth Risk Behavior Surveillance measure utilized by the Centers for Disease Control and Prevention (Foti, Balaji, & Shanklin, 2011). Items to be administered relate to tobacco, alcohol, marijuana, dietary habits, exercise activities, safe driving, and media/technology use.
10. *Positive and Negative Affect Schedule.* The shortened version of the PANAS-C (Ebesutani et al., 2012; Laurent, et al. 1999) will be used that includes five-item PA scale (joyful, cheerful, happy, lively, proud) and a five-item NA scale (miserable, mad, afraid, scared, sad) rated on a 1 (*Very Slightly Or Not At All*) to 5 (*Extremely*) scale.

Variables Related to Participation in TWV

These measures will be used as predictors of virtue development (group entitativity and motivations for training), or as outcomes variables (fundraising, training outcomes).

11. *Group Entitativity Measure.* The GEM-in (Gaertner & Schopler, 1998) calculates perceived interconnections between self and others. Test-takers choose between six different pictures of the self and others (pictorially represented by circles). The first picture has the greatest distance between self and others, while the last picture shows no distance between self and others, so that the group and self are completely

overlapping. Participants will be instructed to complete the measure relative to their athletic teams/extracurricular activity group (alternative instructions).

12. *Performances and Motivation Orientation.* To assess participants instrumental, moral, and spiritual motivations for training, we will ask them to rate the extent to which they are motivated to train with Team World Vision because of opportunities to improve physical fitness, raise money for clean water, and grow spiritually. At later time points, we will ask participants the extent to which they change in each of these domains as a result of training. Ratings will be made on a 1 (*Not At All True Of Me*) to 5 (*Always True For Me*) scale.
13. *Contingencies of Self-worth.* Further, participants will report on three subscales of contingencies of self-worth rated on a 1 (*Strongly Disagree*) to 7 (*Strongly Agree*) and each subscale has five items (Crocker et al., 2003; competition, virtue, God's love). Participants' competition contingencies will include statements such as, "My self-worth is affected by how well I do when I am competing with others." Virtue contingencies include statements like, "I couldn't respect myself if I didn't live up to a moral code;" God's love contingencies will include statements such as,"When I think that I am disobeying God, I feel bad about myself."
14. *Fundraising and Training Outcomes.* Data will be collected directly from TWV documenting participant fundraising. To assess sponsorship trends, participants will note their involvement in sponsorships programs before and after training for either the half or full marathon. Participants will also be asked to note how frequently they participated in TWV group runs.

Daily Training Log

Participants will be asked to fill out a daily training log, which they will complete online or fill out in paper to turn in on their Saturday group run.

15. *Daily Training Log*—The daily training log will ask participants to record their distance ran, time, type of run or cross-training, workout difficulty, workout motivation, hours slept, servings of fruit/veggies, and servings of junk food/drinks. Additionally, to assess the effects of socializing with those of different ages, participants will indicate

if they normally run with peers, or older adults, and will report on content of conversation and quality of connection.

Sources of Research Material

Sources of research material include the pre- and post-test surveys obtained from the participants and information drawn from their training logs. We will also collect fundraising outcome information directly from TWV at the completion of training season. This information will be collected from TWV administrative personnel rather than from those coaches/group leaders who work directly with participants.

TWV is the only external organization involved in this project. The specific goals of the project have been presented to the relevant staff within the organization via personal communication. Staff persons are broadly aware of the scope of the study as well as the methodology. Permission was obtained by request from these staff within the organization and is documented. Data will be collected from participants within the TWV's youth and adult programs in the form of completed questionnaires. This material will be specifically collected for the purpose of this study.

Participant Recruitment and Informed Consent/Assent

Recruitment will include meetings that participants and their parents (for adolescents) can attend in order to learn more about the study, and to receive informed consent/assent forms. Parents or participants unable to attend these meetings may schedule phone conferences or in-person meetings in order to have questions addressed. Researchers can also obtain consent and assent forms at these requested meetings. Two research assistants that are NIH certified and listed as researchers on this project will most closely interact with the participants during recruitment. The research assistants will present the research opportunity to participants during sign up meetings and will collect completed forms. The research assistants will be trained as to how they may approach participants in a non-coercive manner. Moreover, it is important to note that research assistants' primary role at TWV is recruitment. Other adults will serve as coaches/group leaders for the adolescents during training.

The forms for both informed consent for participants eighteen years and older, and parental consent and child assent for participants under eighteen years are attached. Both informed consent and assent will be obtained prior to the collection of any data for participants under eighteen, and consent will be obtained before data collection for those eighteen years and older. There will be different consent forms for adults eighteen to twenty-one years old who will receive compensation, and for those over twenty-one years old that will not receive any compensation for their time. This will be clearly stated on the consent form.

In addition, participants who hear about the study but lose their paper consent forms will also be able to: (a) obtain digital copies of the consent and assent forms via email from us; (b) print out these forms; (c) read and sign the assent; (d) have their parents read and sign the consent; and (e) fax both forms to a digital fax receipt system (i.e., http://www.efax.com/help/how-efax-works). The digital faxes will arrive at an account that is password protected and maintained by the Thrive Center. The research team will print them out and store them along with paper copies of consent received normally, and then the digital versions would be deleted. At that point, these consent/assent forms would be treated the same as before, securely stored and appropriately cataloged in case of a need to reexamine them at a later date. Both consent and assent must be obtained before the participant begins the study. This process has been previously approved in our pilot study in 2014.

Cultural Considerations

Our data will be collected in the San Gabriel Valley therefore there are no significant cultural considerations. We can provide translated consent or assent form at schools where this is needed; however, all participants must be proficient in English. We will be working with participants from diverse ethnicities, and we will be sensitive to issues of diversity. In particular, we will work to make all of our participants feel empowered during the process.

Potential Risks

There are minimal risks involved with study participation. Although we have many protections in place assuring confidentiality of survey responses, there is always a risk that data may be identified as the study is not anonymous. Records will be converted to electronic data, which will be kept secure and confidential, and paper records of the questionnaires will be locked up in a secure file drawer maintained by Sarah Schnitker, or Benjamin Houltberg. This material will be maintained for the duration of the study, which is expected to be between two to four years. Individual participants will have their data identified by name in the original file only. All data analyses will take place on files where participants are identified only by ID numbers that are assigned to them after data collection has taken place. Access to this data will be monitored and controlled by Sarah Schnitker.

Although processes are in place whereby we can confidently assure the confidentiality of responses to study surveys, protections for whether or not others can identify if a TWV training adolescent is a participant in our study are less rigorous. Adolescents training together are apt to talk about being a part of the study, so it will likely become apparent amongst runners who are participating. Although this is not ideal, we do not judge this as a major risk to participants. Discussions with a TWV leader indicate that there should be no positive or negative implications/stigma associated with whether or not a runner to chooses to participate. TWV coaches/group leaders will also be trained to discourage discussion of the study and to act in way such that they do not coerce any participants of whom they might be aware to continue participation.

Some survey questions may be somewhat uncomfortable to answer, such as questions asking about information related to drug and alcohol use or sexual history. Participants who find this to be too uncomfortable may drop out of the study at any time, or they may choose to leave these questions unanswered. Other questions on well-being measures may also bring to light participants' life dissatisfaction, but these are very common measures used in research without adverse effects. The risk of this study having a damaging effect on participants is therefore minimal, and will be further minimized by making sure adequate resources (e.g., space to talk about the study with a coach/teacher, referrals to mental health professionals, etc.) are available to participants should the survey questions cause distress. No materials will be presented to participants that are offensive, threatening, or degrading.

Finally, there are physical risks involved in commencing an athletic training program. Participants signed a separate release form with TWV related to these risks when they enrolled in the training program with TWV. These risks are minimal as TWV training leaders are highly trained and very conscious of safety.

Anticipated Benefits

First, adolescents who were interested in running with TWV but who may not have been able to afford the race fee will be able to experience all of the benefits of training for a marathon as a result of participating in our study. Adult participants may benefit from participating in the study as well. Adults may gain additional motivation for training when tracking progress and it may enhance meaning of training. Anecdotal accounts for TWV attest to the transformative nature of this training experience.

In addition, we hope that our data will illuminate the best ways to develop character strengths in adolescents and adults in real-world contexts using rigorous methodology, such that findings can influence the scholarly community and be directly applied to youth programs and character education. The scholarly community will benefit from an increased understanding of the psychological processes underlying character development, particularly the development of patience and self-control. Our work with TWV will have direct applications for best practices in youth-serving and athletic organizations.

Compensation

We will pay for adolescent participants' race fee and twenty dollars to complete the final survey as compensation for study participation. The race fee will range from $150–185 depending on which city race they enter. Adults over the age of twenty-one will not receive payment for participating in this study, which will be clearly communicated as a part of the informed consent.

Certification

NIH Certification or equivalent is on file and current for Dr. Sarah Schnitker, Dr. Benjamin Houltberg, Nanyamka Redmond, Nathaniel Fernandez, Thomas Felke, Lyndsey Deane, Wes Kriesel, Julie Bierschenk, Erik Dailey, Danielle Hand, and Daniel Mendoza.

Appendix B

Team World Vision Study Qualitative Questions

Interview Introduction

Hi, my name is ____________ and I work with Dr. Ben Houltberg who helped coordinate research for the LA marathon for World Vision. Today I'm going to ask you questions about the marathon—what it was like training for, and running in it. This interview will help us understand what young people think about running races and what it means in their lives. You will receive a ten dollar gift card that will be sent to your email upon completion of this interview for your time today. Everything we say here is private and there are no "right" or "wrong" answers. You can ask to skip questions or stop the interview whenever you want. If it is OK with you, I need to record our interview so I can make sure I hear everything correctly.

Interview Question Set A (Purpose)

Question A1: First, tell me why you chose to train for and run in the marathon.

- Probe 1: Did you feel motivated to run the race for a specific reason? Describe what that felt like.
- Probe 2: Who else said or did something that motivated you to run in the race?
- Probe 3: Did your reason for running the race change at all as you trained?

Question A2: Tell me more about you. Who are you? How do you see yourself? Prompts if they are silent or "don't know": OK well, would you consider yourself outgoing/private? . . . happy/sad? sure of yourself/unsure? more spiritual/less spiritual? driven/relaxed?

- Probe 1: How would you describe yourself?
  - What are you especially proud of about yourself?"
  - If you feel comfortable can you share, "What are you not so proud of?"
  - "What do you like the most about yourself?"
  - If you feel comfortable can you share, "What do you like the least about yourself?
- Probe 2: Who do you hope to be in the future? What do you hope to be like? What are your goals? (If no goals: What would be different about your life if you had goals?)
  - What do your friends and family hope for your future? What might they be afraid of about your future?
- Probe 3: What are you afraid of being like in future?

Question A3: Would you say your life has purpose?

- Probe 1: How would you describe it?
- Probe 2: Where does this sense of purpose come from?
- Probe 3: How does it affect the way you live your life?
- Probe 4: Do you think people in your life are aware of this purpose? If so, how do they respond?

Question A4: How do you think training for and running the race made a difference in your life? You described your purpose in life as . . . (fill in from above). Is that what you meant?

- Probe 1: How does running a marathon fit in your sense of purpose?
- Probe 2: Did it make you think about your purpose differently? How so?
- Probe 3: Was there a time during training or in the race that you felt this purpose more strongly?
  - Can you describe one of the times when you felt particularly spiritual?
  - How would you describe your faith life, spirituality, or religion?

Interviewer Note

If participant is in clear distress when responding to these items, please read the following: "It may be that this part of the interview connected with some difficult feelings. It is normal for people to experience emotions like sadness, anger, and embarrassment in these types of interviews. If this is a time in your life when you are facing difficulty, it may be helpful to think about ways to find some support. Often, talking with someone can be a big help. Here are some possibilities: talking with family, with friends, or with spiritual supports. We can connect you with a safe person to talk to at the end of this interview—either Dr. Ben Houltberg at Fuller Theological Seminary, who is in charge of this study, or a local professional. We can talk more about finding support at the end of the interview. Are you ready to continue?"

- No: Go back through the options for getting support & provide contact email addresses for Ben. (Local contacts and Ben's email are on the Local Informants Referral Sheet). Discontinue interview and read final thanks and debriefing script at end of interview.
- Yes: Continue below.

Interview Question Set B (Relationship to Others)

Question B1: Now I would like to ask you about the people that you feel support from in your life. If I were to talk with an adult in your life—like a teacher or coach who knows you, how would he or she finish the following sentence: "I think the most important thing in (participant's name)'s life is . . . "

- Probe 1: How do adults like these support you in this area that is most important to you?
- Probe 2: How did adults support you running this race?

Question B2: If I were to talk with a friend who knew you well, how would he or she finish the following sentence: "I think the most important thing in (participant name)'s life is . . . "

- Probe 1: How do your friends support you in this area that is most important to you?
- Probe 2: How did your friends support you running this race?

Question B3: If I were to talk with your parents, how would he or she finish the following sentence: I think the most important thing in (participant name)'s life is . . . "

- Probe 1: How do your parents support you in this area that is most important to you?
- Probe 2: How did your parents support you running this race?

Question B4: What kinds of new relationships did you make during training for and running this race? With whom?

- Probe 1: Who helped you or motivated you the most to complete the race? How did you keep each other on track? Can you think of a specific example?
- Probe 2: Did you find yourself making comparisons to other people while training for the race? How about while running the race? Tell me more about that.
- Probe 3: How would the race have been for you without their support?

Interview Question Set C (Adversity/Suffering)

Question C: When you were training for the race, did you ever feel especially discouraged, frustrated, or that it was difficult?

- Probe 1: Describe moments during training when you were suffering or felt like giving up. How about during the actual race? What did you feel while running?
  - Yes: How did you deal with this suffering? . . . physically . . . emotionally . . . socially. Was there any meaning to be found in it?
  - No Suffering: Tell me about the last time you remember experiencing suffering. Why do you think the race was easier for you?
- Probe 2: Can you describe a time when you felt inspiration in a particularly difficult moment?
- Probe 3: What or who did you rely on to get through that difficult time?

Interview check-in by saying- "I want to take a moment to see how you are doing so far with this interview. How are you doing?" If there are any signs of discomfort follow the above protocol in the Interviewer Note. Otherwise say, "Would you like to keep going?"

Interview Question Set D (Relationship to Body)

Question D1: Training and running a marathon takes a huge commitment and sacrifice of your own time and body. I would like to ask you a bit more about the impact of training on your body and your thoughts about your body during training and running the marathon. Can you describe some of the feelings or thoughts (if any) that you had about your body before starting to train for the marathon?

- Probe 1: When you think about your body, what words come to mind? What are some feelings you have about your body?

(Pay particular attention to the level of discomfort here because it may be a trigger when you ask these questions. If any discomfort, be sure you give referral information or check in with the student.)

- Probe 2: Before you learned about the TWV marathon, did you ever think your body would have been able to handle running a marathon? Why or why not?

Question D2: Have your feelings toward your body changed during the process of training for and running in this marathon?

- Probe 1: During your training, how did you feel about your body?
- Probe 2: What thoughts about your body did you have while you were running the marathon?

Question D3: Did you find any limits to your physical abilities? What were they?

- Probe 1: Describe a time when you were surprised by what you were able to do physically.
- Probe 2: Were you ever surprised by what you were not able to do? Tell me about that . . .

Question D4: We are also interested in what you think about the connection between your body and your "mind" or "spirit?" Do you know what I mean by that? Like with how you felt emotionally during training for or running in the race?

- Probe 1: How about feelings you had in your body that connected to how you felt spiritually or how connected you felt to something greater than yourself?
- Probe 2: How did preparing for and running the marathon deepen your understanding of your body? What did you learn about your body or yourself that you didn't know before?

Interview check-in: "We are almost done with the interview. We only have one more set of questions but I wanted to check-in with you again to see how you were doing. Are you OK to keep going?" If there are signs of distress, go back to interview note for script.

Interview Question Set E (Relationship with God or Beyond Self)

Question E1: What do you think it means to be "made in the image and likeness of God?"

(skip to final question series if they do not believe in God)

- Probe 1: How do you think God felt about your body before the race? . . . during . . . after the race?

Question E2: How would you describe your relationship with God?

- Probe 1: How does God feel about us when we do things that are physically difficult or cause us to suffer?
- Probe 2: How does God measure "success?"
  - How do you think finishing the race seemed in God's eyes?
  - If you did not complete the race, what would God think?
  - What about your family and friends? What would they think?

Question E3: How did your relationship with God change while you were training for the race? . . . during the race? (additional prompts as needed: Feel closer? More distant?)

Final Question Series

What would you tell someone your age who was thinking about running a marathon, but was afraid or embarrassed that they couldn't do it?

Now I have a few final questions you can answer quickly, with just one word (*Yes* or *No*):

- Was asking your friends and family to donate money for the race easy or hard?
- Would you run in another marathon?
- Will you be involved with World Vision again?

Is there anything else you want me to know about your experiences with the World Vision Marathon?

Referral Information

Interviewer: "Thank you for being willing to share about your experience during this interview. Sometimes when people are interviewed like this, it causes them to have strong feelings. There is nothing wrong with these feelings and, in fact, they are normal. However, if these feelings are too strong, last a long time, or begin to disrupt someone's life, then it is important to deal with them. A good way to help deal with such feelings is to talk about them with someone. Do you feel like you need to talk with someone about any feelings you have had during this interview? (If yes, make sure they are connected with a counselor; if no, continue). Well, if you do become upset or have strong feelings about this experience in the future, here is a list of counseling centers in the area and a contact person at your school (if applicable) that you can call and set up a time to talk with someone. (Hand them a referral sheet and show them the agencies and the numbers to call). If you have any problems, questions or concerns about the interview, please contact Dr. Benjamin Houltberg at Fuller Theological Seminary in Pasadena, California at (626) 584-5345 or bhoultberg@fuller.edu. Thank you. We really appreciate your participation."

End Interview

Bibliography

"2017 Reebok CrossFit Games Tickets." *Games* (blog), *CrossFit.com*, June 13, 2017, https://games.crossfit.com/article/2017-reebok-crossfit-games-tickets/regionals/2017.

Allen, Justine. "Social Motivation in Youth Sport." *Journal of Sport and Exercise Psychology* 25 (2003) 551–67.

"American Heart Association Recommendations for Physical Activity in Adults." *Fitness Basics* (blog). *Heart.org.*, accessed May 16, 2017, http://www.heart.org/HEARTORG/HealthyLiving/PhysicalActivity/FitnessBasics/American-Heart-Association-Recommendations-for-Physical-Activity-in-Adults_UCM_307976_Article.jsp#.WRs-_FKZP-Y.

Anderson, Jonathan A., and William Dyrness. *Modern Art and the Life of a Culture: The Religious Impulses of Modernism*. Downers Grove, IL: InterVarsity, 2016.

Aquinas, Thomas. *Summa Theologica*. New York: Benziger, 1947.

Augustine, Saint. *The Confessions of St. Augustine*. Translated by E. B. Pusey. New York: Dutton, 1951.

Bahrami, Naeim, et al. "Subconcussive Head Impact Exposure and White Matter Tract Changes over a Single Season of Youth Football," *Radiology* 281 (October 2016) 919–26. https://pubs.rsna.org/doi/full/10.1148/radiol.2016160564.

Baker, William J. *Playing with God: Religion and Modern Sport*. Cambridge: Harvard University Press, 2007.

Barth, Karl. *The Epistle to the Romans*. London: Oxford University Press, 1963.

Berkhof, Hendrik. *Christ and the Powers*. Scottdale, PA: Herald, 1977.

Berry, Wendell, and Norman Wirzba. *The Art of the Commonplace: Agrarian Essays of Wendell Berry*. Washington DC: Counterpoint, 2002.

Black, Jonathan. *Making the American Body: The Remarkable Saga of the Men and Women Whose Feats, Feuds, and Passions Shaped Fitness History*. Lincoln: University of Nebraska Press, 2013.

Blazer, Annie. *Playing for God: Evangelical Women and the Unintended Consequences of Sports Ministry*. New York: New York University Press, 2015.

Bottomley, Frank. *Attitudes to the Body in Western Christendom*. London: Transatlantic Arts, 1979.

Bouma-Prediger, Steven. *For the Beauty of the Earth: A Christian Vision for Creation Care*. Kindle edition. Grand Rapids: Baker, 2001.

Braun, Virginia, and Victoria Clarke. "Using Thematic Analysis in Psychology." *Qualitative Research in Psychology* 3 (January 2006) 77–101. https://doi.org/10.1191/1478088706qp063oa.

Brown, Frank Burch. *Religious Aesthetics: A Theological Study of Making and Meaning*. Princeton: Princeton University Press, 1993.

Brown, Warren S., et al. *Whatever Happened to the Soul?: Scientific and Theological Portraits of Human Nature*. Minneapolis: Fortress, 1998.

Brown, Warren S., and Brad D. Strawn. *The Physical Nature of Christian Life: Neuroscience, Psychology, and the Church*. Cambridge: Cambridge University Press, 2012.

Burns, J. Patout. *Theological Anthropology*. Philadelphia: Fortress, 1981.

Byl, John, and Thomas L. Visker. *Physical Education, Sports, and Wellness: Looking to God as We Look at Ourselves*. Sioux Center, IA: Dordt College Press, 1999.

Bynum, Caroline Walker. *The Resurrection of the Body in Western Christianity, 200-1336*. Lectures on the History of Religions New Series 15. New York: Columbia University Press, 1995.

Caillois, Roger. *Man, Play, and Games*. Translated by Meyer Barash. Urbana: University of Illinois Press, 2001.

Calvin, Jean. *Institutes of the Christian Religion*. Edited by John T McNeill. Translated by Ford Lewis Battles. Louisville, KY: Westminster John Knox, 1960.

Carter, Evan C., Michael E. McCullough, and Charles S. Carver. "The Mediating Role of Monitoring in the Association of Religion with Self-Control." *Social Psychological and Personality Science* 3 (March 2012) 691–97. https://doi.org/10.1177/1948550612438925.

Chan, Simon. *Spiritual Theology: A Systematic Study of the Christian Life*. Downers Grove, IL: InterVarsity, 1998.

Chauvet, Louis-Marie, and François Kabasele Lumbala. *Liturgy and the Body*. Maryknoll, NY: Orbis, 1995.

Chopp, Rebecca S. *The Praxis of Suffering: An Interpretation of Liberation and Political Theologies*. Maryknoll, NY: Orbis, 1986.

Chupungco, Anscar J. *Liturgical Inculturation: Sacramentals, Religiosity, and Catechesis*. Collegeville, MN: Liturgical, 1995.

Cohen, Deborah. *A Big Fat Crisis: The Hidden Forces behind the Obesity Epidemic—and How We Can End It*. New York: Nation Books, 2014.

Corrigan, Kevin. *Evagrius and Gregory: Mind, Soul and Body in 4th Century*. Farnham, UK: Ashgate Publishing, 2009.

Cortez, Marc. *Theological Anthropology a Guide for the Perplexed*. New York: T. & T. Clark, 2010.

Cowan, Douglas E. *Sacred Space: The Quest for Transcendence in Science Fiction Film and Television*. Waco, TX: Baylor University Press, 2010.

Crocker, Jennifer, Riia K. Luhtanen, M. Lynne Cooper, and Alexandra Bouvrette. "Contingencies of Self-Worth in College Students: Theory and Measurement." *Journal of Personality and Social Psychology* 85 (November 2003) 894–908. https://doi.org/10.1037/0022-3514.85.5.894.

Cronin, Zach. "3 Things That Made Kobe Bryant Transcendent." Los Angeles Lakers (blog). Thebasketballnetwork.com, November 30, 2015. http://www.thebasketballnetwork.com/3-things-that-made-kobe-bryant-transcendent/.

Crouch, Andy. *Culture Making: Recovering Our Creative Calling*. Kindle edition. Downers Grove, IL: InterVarsity, 2013.

Csikszentmihalyi, Mihaly. *Flow: The Psychology of Optimal Experience*. New York: Harper & Row, 2009.

Danish, Steven, et al. "Enhancing Youth Development Through Sport." *World Leisure Journal* 46 (January 2004) 38–49. https://doi.org/10.1080/04419057.2004.9674365.

Davies, J. G. *Liturgical Dance: An Historical, Theological, and Practical Handbook.* London: SCM, 1984.

Davis, Brennan, and Christopher Carpenter. "Proximity of Fast-Food Restaurants to Schools and Adolescent Obesity." *American Journal of Public Health* 99 (March 2009) 505–10. https://doi.org/10.2105/AJPH.2008.137638.

Deardorff, Donald L., and John White. *The Image of God in the Human Body: Essays on Christianity and Sports.* Lewiston, NY: Edwin Mellen, 2008.

Defrantz, Thomas F. *Dancing Many Drums: Excavations in African American Dance.* Madison: University of Wisconsin Press, 2001.

Detweiler, Craig, and Barry Taylor. *A Matrix of Meanings: Finding God in Pop Culture.* Grand Rapids: Baker, 2003.

Diener, Ed, Robert A. Emmons, Randy J. Larsen, and Sharon Griffin. "The Satisfaction With Life Scale." *Journal of Personality Assessment* 49 (June 2010) 71–75. https://doi.org/10.1207/s15327752jpa4901_13.

Dierdorff, Erich C., Eric A. Surface, and Kenneth G. Brown. "Frame-of-Reference Training Effectiveness: Effects of Goal Orientation and Self-Efficacy on Affective, Cognitive, Skill-Based, and Transfer Outcomes." *The Journal of Applied Psychology* 95 (November 2010) 1181–91. https://doi.org/10.1037/a0020856.

Dillenberger, Jane. *The Religious Art of Andy Warhol.* New York: Continuum, 2001.

Doctor Who. "Forest of the Dead." Directed by Euros Lyn. Written by Steven Moffat. BBC One, June 7 2008.

Dreyer, J. S. "Practical Theology and Human Well-Being : An Exploration of a Multidimensional Model of Human Action as Conceptual Framework." *Practical Theology in South Africa* 23 (January 2008) 3–22.

Dunn, Geoffrey D. *Tertullian.* London: Routledge, 2004.

Durkheim, Émile. *The Elementary Forms of the Religious Life.* New York: Free Press, 1965.

Dyrness, William. *Poetic Theology: God and the Poetics of Everyday Life.* Grand Rapids: Eerdmans, 2011.

———. *The Earth Is God's: A Theology of American Culture.* Maryknoll, NY: Orbis, 1997.

Ellis, Robert. *The Games People Play: Theology, Religion, and Sport.* Eugene, OR: Wipf & Stock, 2014.

Engel, Mary Potter. *John Calvin's Perspectival Anthropology.* Atlanta: Scholars, 1988.

Erdozain, Dominic. *The Problem of Pleasure: Sport, Recreation and the Crisis of Victorian Religion.* Woodbridge, UK: Boydell, 2010.

Evans, Christopher Hodge, and William R. Herzog, eds. *The Faith of Fifty Million: Baseball, Religion, and American Culture.* Louisville: Westminster John Knox, 2002.

Farrell, Amy Erdman. *Fat Shame: Stigma and the Fat Body in American Culture.* New York: New York University Press, 2011.

Faulconer, James E., ed. *Transcendence in Philosophy and Religion.* Bloomington: Indiana University Press, 2003.

Feeney, Robert. *A Catholic Perspective: Physical Exercise and Sports.* Marysville, WA: Aquinas, 1995.

Fellowship of Christian Athletes. "Vision & Mission." *Who We Are* (blog). *FCA.org*. Accessed March 14, 2016. http://www.fca.org/aboutus/who-we-are/mission-vision.

Fenton, John Y., et al., eds. *Theology and Body*. Philadelphia: Westminster, 1974.

Fight Church. Directed by Daniel Junge and Bryan Storkel. Santa Monica: Lionsgate, 2014.

Finkelstein, et al. "Annual Medical Spending Attributable To Obesity: Payer-And Service-Specific Estimates." *Health Affairs* 28 (September 2009) w822–31. https://doi.org/10.1377/hlthaff.28.5.w822.

Fishbein, Rebecca. "Pastor Gives His Congregation a Workout for Body and Soul." *Good News* (blog). *Today.com*, October 16, 2016, http://www.today.com/news/pastor-gives-his-congregation-workout-body-soul-6C10981348.

Forbes, Bruce David, and Jeffrey H. Mahan. *Religion and Popular Culture in America*. Berkeley: University of California Press, 2000.

Foti, Kathryn, Alexandra Balaji, and Shari Shanklin. "Uses of Youth Risk Behavior Survey and School Health Profiles Data: Applications for Improving Adolescent and School Health." *The Journal of School Health* 81 (June 2011) 345–54. https://doi.org/10.1111/j.1746-1561.2011.00601.x.

Foucault, Michel. *The Birth of the Clinic: An Archaeology of Medical Perception*. New York: Vintage, 1994.

Francis, Andrew. *What in God's Name Are You Eating?: How Can Christians Live and Eat Responsibly in Today's Global Village?* Eugene, OR: Cascade, 2014.

Fraser-Thomas, et al. "Youth Sport Programs: An Avenue to Foster Positive Youth Development." *Physical Education & Sport Pedagogy* 10 (February 2005) 19–40. https://doi.org/10.1080/1740898042000334890.

Fujimura, Makoto. *Culture Care: Reconnecting with Beauty for Our Common Life*. New York: Fujimura Institute, 2014.

Gadamer, Hans-Georg. *The Relevance of the Beautiful and Other Essays*. Edited by Robert Bernasconi. Translated by Nicholas Walker. Cambridge: Cambridge University Press, 1986.

Gaertner, Lowell, and John Schopler. "Perceived Ingroup Entitativity and Intergroup Bias: An Interconnection of Self and Others." *European Journal of Social Psychology* 28 (December 1998) 963–80. https://doi.org/10.1002/(SICI)1099-0992(199811O)28:6<963::AID-EJSP905>3.0.CO;2-S.

Geertz, Clifford. *The Interpretation Of Cultures*. New York: Basic Books, 1977.

Gill, Jerry H. *Mediated Transcendence: A Postmodern Reflection*. Macon, GA: Mercer University Press, 1989.

"God & Human Flourishing." *God & Human Flourishing* (blog). *Yale.edu*. Accessed March 17, 2016. http://faith.yale.edu/god-human-flourishing/god-human-flourishing.

Goizueta, Roberto S. *Caminemos Con Jesus: Toward a Hispanic/Latino Theology of Accompaniment*. Maryknoll, NY: Orbis, 2013.

Gonzalo de Abreu. "Julie Moss Competing in the 1982 Hawaii Ironman Triathlon." Youtube Video, 2:54. March 29, 2007. https://www.youtube.com/watch?v=VbWsQMabczM.

"Got Your Back." This American Life, accessed April 25, 2015, http://www.thisamericanlife.org/radio-arc hives/episode/531/got-your-back.

Green, Harvey. *Fit for America: Health, Fitness, Sport, and American Society*. New York: Pantheon, 1986.

Green, Joel B. *Body, Soul, and Human Life: The Nature of Humanity in the Bible*. Grand Rapids: Baker, 2008.

Grenz, Stanley J. *The Millennial Maze: Sorting out Evangelical Options*. Downers Grove, IL: InterVarsity, 1992.

Grenz, Stanley J., and Roger E. Olson. *Who Needs Theology?: An Invitation to the Study of God*. Kindle edition. Downers Grove, IL: InterVarsity, 1996.

Gribben, Crawford. *Evangelical Millennialism in the Trans-Atlantic World, 1500-2000*. New York: Macmillan, 2011.

Griffith, R. Marie. *Born Again Bodies: Flesh and Spirit in American Christianity*. Kindle edition. California Studies in Food and Culture 12. Berkeley: University of California Press, 2004.

Grumett, David, and Rachel Muers. *Theology on the Menu: Asceticism, Meat and Christian Diet*. London: Routledge, 2010.

Gumbrecht, Hans Ulrich. *In Praise of Athletic Beauty*. Cambridge: Belknap, 2006.

Gunton, Colin E. *The Triune Creator: A Historical and Systematic Study*. Grand Rapids: Eerdmans, 1998.

Gutiérrez, Gustavo. *A Theology of Liberation: History, Politics, and Salvation*. Maryknoll, NY: Orbis, 1973.

Haldeman, Scott. *Towards Liturgies That Reconcile: Race and Ritual among African-American and European-American Protestants*. Liturgy, Worship, and Society. Burlington: Ashgate, 2007.

Harvey, David. *A Brief History of Neoliberalism*. Oxford: Oxford University Press, 2007.

Harvey, Lincoln. *A Brief Theology of Sport*. Eugene, OR: Cascade, 2014.

Hatch, Nathan O. *The Democratization of American Christianity*. New Haven: Yale University Press, 1991.

Heintzman, Paul. *Leisure and Spirituality: Biblical, Historical, and Contemporary Perspectives*. Engaging Culture. Grand Rapids: Baker, 2014.

Hoffman, Shirl J., ed. *Sport and Religion*. Champaign: Human Kinetics, 1992.

Hoffman, Shirl James. *Good Game: Christianity and the Culture of Sports*. Waco: Baylor University Press, 2010.

Holt, Nicholas L., ed. *Positive Youth Development through Sport*. London: Routledge, 2008.

Horn, Huston. "Lalanne: A Treat and a Treatment," accessed August 4, 2016, http://www.si.com/vault/1960/12/19/585930/lalanne-a-treat-and-a-treatment.

Horton, Robert S, and Diane E Mack. "Athletic Identity in Marathon Runners: Functional Focus or Dysfunctional Commitment?" *Journal of Sport Behavior* 23 (June 2000) 101–19.

Houltberg, Benjamin. "Moving from Performance to Purpose in Youth Sports." November 8, 2016. https://fullerstudio.fuller.edu/moving-performance-purpose-youth-sports/.

Hoverd, William James. *Working Out My Salvation: The Contemporary Gym and the Promise of "Self" Transformation*. Oxford: Meyer & Meyer Sport, 2005.

Hoverd, William James, and Chris G. Sibley. "Immoral Bodies: The Implicit Association between Moral Discourse and the Body." *Journal for the Scientific Study of Religion* 46 (2007) 391–403.

Huizinga, Johan. *Homo Ludens: A Study of the Play-Element in Culture*. Boston: Beacon, 1950.

Hurston, Zora Neale. *The Sanctified Church*. Berkeley: Turtle Island, 1981.

Hyland, Drew A. *Philosophy of Sport*. Paragon Issues in Philosophy. New York: Paragon House, 1990.

"Inside Look: Reliving the Cubs' World Series Parade." NBC Sports. http://vplayer.nbcsports.com/p/BxmELC/chicago_article/select/media/V4CleUAvviaS.

Johnson, Paul E. *A Shopkeeper's Millennium: Society and Revivals in Rochester, New York, 1815-1837*. New York: Hill and Wang, 2004.

Johnston, Robert K. *God's Wider Presence: Reconsidering General Revelation*. Grand Rapids: Baker, 2014.

———. *The Christian at Play*. Grand Rapids: Eerdmans, 1983.

Kayser-Bril, Nicolas. "Africa Is Not a Country." *The Guardian* (January 2014) sec. World news. https://www.theguardian.com/world/2014/jan/24/africa-clinton.

Kearns, Cristin E., et al. "Sugar Industry and Coronary Heart Disease Research: A Historical Analysis of Internal Industry Documents." *JAMA Internal Medicine*, (November 2016). https://doi.org/10.1001/jamainternmed.2016.5394.

Kerksick, Chad, et al. "Effects of a Popular Exercise and Weight Loss Program on Weight Loss, Body Composition, Energy Expenditure and Health in Obese Women." *Nutrition & Metabolism* 6 (May 2009) 1–17.

Kim, DaeHwan, and John Paul Leigh. "Estimating the Effects of Wages on Obesity." *Journal of Occupational and Environmental Medicine* 52 (May 2010) 495–500. https://doi.org/10.1097/JOM.0b013e3181dbc867.

Kirkpatrick, Dow, ed. *Faith Born in the Struggle for Life: A Re-Reading of Protestant Faith in Latin America Today*. Grand Rapids: Eerdmans, 1988.

Koenig, Harold G., and Arndt Büssing. "The Duke University Religion Index (DUREL): A Five-Item Measure for Use in Epidemological Studies." *Religions* 1 (December 2010) 78–85. https://doi.org/10.3390/rel1010078.

Kybartas, Ray, and Kenneth Ross. *Fitness Is Religion—Keep the Faith*. New York: Simon & Schuster, 1997.

Kyle, Donald G. *Sport and Spectacle in the Ancient World*. Ancient Cultures. Malden, MA: Blackwell, 2007.

Ladd, Tony, and James A. Mathisen. *Muscular Christianity: Evangelical Protestants and the Development of American Sport*. Grand Rapids: Baker, 1999.

Laurent, Jeff, et al., "A Measure of Positive and Negative Affect for Children: Scale Development and Preliminary Validation." *Psychological Assessment* 11 (1999) 326–38. https://doi.org/10.1037/1040-3590.11.3.326.

Laurin, Kristin, Aaron C. Kay, and Gavan J. Fitzsimons. "Reactance versus Rationalization: Divergent Responses to Policies That Constrain Freedom." *Psychological Science* 23 (February 2012) 205–09. https://doi.org/10.1177/0956797611429468.

Layden, Tim, and Tim Layden. "The Rehabilitation of Michael Phelps." http://www.si.com/olympics/2015/11/09/michael-phelps-rehabilitation-rio-2016.

Lehrer, Jonah. "Blame It on the Brain." *Wall Street Journal* (December 2009) sec. Life and Style. http://www.wsj.com/articles/SB10001424052748703478704574612052322122442.

Linville, Greg. *Christmanship A Theology of Competition and Sport*. Canton, OH: Oliver House, 2014.

Long, Kimberly Bracken. *The Worshiping Body: The Art of Leading Worship*. Louisville: Westminster John Knox, 2009.

Lustig, Robert H. *Fat Chance: Beating the Odds Against Sugar, Processed Food, Obesity, and Disease*. New York: Plume, 2013.

Mallett, Jef. *Trizophrenia: Inside the Minds of a Triathlete*. Boulder: VeloPress, 2009.

Matuszewski, Erik. "Rory McIlroy's Weightlifting Prompts Fears He's Headed Down Same Injury Road As Tiger Woods." Forbes. http://www.forbes.com/sites/erikmatuszewski/2016/02/17/rory-mcilroys-weightlifting-prompts-fears-of-injury-tiger-woods-repeat/.

Mazza, Carlo "Sport as Viewed From the Church's Magisterium," in Catholic Church, ed., "The World of Sport Today: A Field of Christian Mission: International Seminar," *Vatican, 11-12 November 2005*. Laity Today 10. Vatican City: Vatican Publishing Library, 2006.

McKenzie, Shelly. *Getting Physical: The Rise of Fitness Culture in America*. Lawrence: University Press of Kansas, 2013.

Mehta, N., and S. C. Davies. "The Importance of Psychiatry in Public Mental Health." *The British Journal of Psychiatry* 207 (September 2015): 187–88. https://doi.org/10.1192/bjp.bp.115.169003.

Merleau-Ponty, Maurice, and Donald Landes. *Phenomenology of Perception*. Edited by Taylor Carman. London: Routledge, 2013.

Michaels, Jillian. "The Truth About Will Power—And How to Get More!" Glamour. http://www.glamour.com/story/the-truth-about-will-powerand.

"Mind over Matter? The Central Governor Theory Explained." *Runners Connect* (blog) *RunnersConnect.net*, accessed May 30, 2013, https://runnersconnect.net/running-training-articles/central-governor-theory.

Morse, Dan. "School Cafeterias Enroll As Fast-Food Franchisees." *Wall Street Journal* (July 29, 1998) sec. Marketplace. http://www.wsj.com/articles/SB901574891620347000.

Mouw, Richard J. *When the Kings Come Marching in: Isaiah and the New Jerusalem*. Grand Rapids: Eerdmans, 1983.

Muir, Edward. *Ritual in Early Modern Europe*. Second edition. Cambridge: Cambridge University Press, 2005.

Murphy, Michael, and Rhea A. White. *In the Zone: Transcendent Experience in Sports*. New York: Penguin, 1995.

Murphy, Nancey. *Bodies and Souls, or Spirited Bodies?* Cambridge: Cambridge University Press, 2006.

National Institute of Diabetes and Digestive and Kidney Diseases. "Overweight and Obesity Statistics." https://www.niddk.nih.gov/health-information/health-statistics/Pages/overweight-obesity-statistics.aspx.

Neal, Wes. *The Handbook on Athletic Perfection*. Milford, MI: Mott Media, 1981.

Nelson, Derek R. *What's Wrong with Sin?: Sin in Individual and Social Perspective from Schleiermacher to Theologies of Liberation*. London: T. & T. Clark, 2009.

Niebuhr, H. Richard. *Christ and Culture*. San Francisco: Harper & Row, 1975.

Niebuhr, Reinhold. *Moral Man and Immoral Society: A Study in Ethics and Politics*. London: Continuum, 2005.

Novak, Michael. *The Joy of Sports: End Zones, Bases, Baskets, Balls, and the Consecration of the American Spirit*. Lanham, MD: Hamilton, 1988.

Oaten, Megan, and Ken Cheng. "Longitudinal Gains in Self-Regulation from Regular Physical Exercise." *British Journal of Health Psychology* 11(November 2006) 717–33. https://doi.org/10.1348/135910706X96481.

"Obesity Facts | Healthy Schools | CDC." Centers for Disease Control and Prevention. https://www.cdc.gov/healthyschools/obesity/facts.htm.

O'Connell, Libby. *The American Plate: A Culinary History in 100 Bites*. Naperville, IL: Sourcebooks, 2015.

O'connor, Anahad. "How the Sugar Industry Shifted Blame to Fat." *The New York Times* (September 12, 2016). http://www.nytimes.com/2016/09/13/well/eat/how-the-sugar-industry-shifted-blame-to-fat.html.

Oppenheimer, Mark. "When Some Turn to Church, Others Go to CrossFit." *The New York Times* (November 27, 2015). http://www.nytimes.com/2015/11/28/us/some-turn-to-church-others-to-crossfit.html..

Parry, S. J., ed. *Sport and Spirituality: An Introduction*. London: Routledge, 2007.

Parry, S. J., Mark Nesti, and Nick Watson, eds. *Theology, Ethics and Transcendence in Sports*. London: Routledge, 2011.

Plantinga, Cornelius. *Not the Way It's Supposed to Be: A Breviary of Sin*. Grand Rapids: Eerdmans, 1999.

Pollan, Michael. *The Omnivore's Dilemma*. New York: Penguin, 2006.

Powell, Samuel M. *Embodied Holiness: Toward a Corporate Theology of Spiritual Growth*. Eugene, OR: Wipf & Stock, 2012.

Putney, Clifford. *Muscular Christianity: Manhood and Sports in Protestant America, 1880-1920*. Cambridge: Harvard University Press, 2003.

Rayner, Geof, et al. "Why Are We Fat? Discussions on the Socioeconomic Dimensions and Responses to Obesity." *Globalization and Health* 6, no. 7 (2010). http://www.biomedcentral.com/content/pdf/1744-8603-6-7.pdf.

Reid, Heather Lynne. *Introduction to the Philosophy of Sport*. Kindle edition. Lanham, MD: Rowman & Littlefield, 2012.

Reynolds, Philip Lyndon. *Food and the Body: Some Peculiar Questions in High Medieval Theology*. Leiden: Brill, 1999.

Rothblum, Esther D., and Sondra Solovay. *The Fat Studies Reader*. New York: New York University Press, 2009.

Sanmartín, Ricardo, et al. "Positive and Negative Affect Schedule-Short Form: Factorial Invariance and Optimistic and Pessimistic Affective Profiles in Spanish Children." *Frontiers in Psychology* 9 (March 2018). https://doi.org/10.3389/fpsyg.2018.00392.

Schnelle, Udo. *The Human Condition: Anthropology in the Teachings of Jesus, Paul, and John*. Minneapolis: Fortress, 1996.

Schnitker, Sarah A., Benjamin Houltberg, William Dyrness, and Nanyamka Redmond. "The Virtue of Patience, Spirituality, and Suffering: Integrating Lessons from Positive Psychology, Psychology of Religion, and Christian Theology." *Psychology of Religion and Spirituality* 9 (August 2017) 264–75. https://doi.org/10.1037/rel0000099.

Scholes, Jeffrey, and Raphael Sassower. *Religion and Sports in American Culture*. New York: Routledge, 2013.

Schnitker, Sarah A. "An Examination of Patience and Well-Being." *The Journal of Positive Psychology* 7 (July 2012): 263–80. https://doi.org/10.1080/17439760.2012.697185.

Schrader, Paul. *Transcendental Style in Film*. New York: Da Capo, 1988.

Schwarz, Hans. *The Human Being: A Theological Anthropology*. Grand Rapids: Eerdmans, 2013.

Seligman, Adam B. *Modernity's Wager: Authority, the Self, and Transcendence*. Princeton: Princeton University Press, 2000.

Shafer, Michael. *Well Played: A Christian Theology of Sport and the Ethics of Doping*. Eugene, OR: Pickwick, 2015.

Silvas, Anna. *The Asketikon of St Basil the Great*. Oxford: Oxford University Press, 2005.

Smith, Christian. *To Flourish or Destruct: A Personalist Theory of Human Goods, Motivations, Failure, and Evil*. Chicago: University of Chicago Press, 2015.

Smith, Christian, and Jonathan P. Hill. "Toward the Measurement of Interpersonal Generosity (IG): An IG Scale Conceptualized, Tested, and Validated." Unpublished Monograph, 2009. https://generosityresearch.nd.edu/assets/13798/ig_paper_smith_hill_rev.pdf.

Smith, Christian, and Melinda Lundquist Denton. *Soul Searching: The Religious and Spiritual Lives of American Teenagers*. Oxford: Oxford University Press, 2005.

Smith, James K. A. *Imagining the Kingdom: How Worship Works*. Kindle edition. Grand Rapids: Baker, 2013.

Smith, James K. A., and James H. Olthuis, eds. *Radical Orthodoxy and the Reformed Tradition: Creation, Covenant, and Participation*. Grand Rapids: Baker, 2005.

Stoyanov, Yuri. *The Other God: Dualist Religions from Antiquity to the Cathar Heresy*. New Haven: Yale University Press, 2000.

Swinton, John. *From Bedlam to Shalom: Towards a Practical Theology of Human Nature, Interpersonal Relationships, and Mental Health Care*. New York: P. Lang, 2000.

Tangney, June P., Roy F. Baumeister, and Angie Luzio Boone. "High Self-Control Predicts Good Adjustment, Less Pathology, Better Grades, and Interpersonal Success." *Journal of Personality* 72 (April 2004) 271–324.

Taylor, Charles. *A Secular Age*. Cambridge: Belknap, 2007.

Team World Vision. "Home," accessed April 25, 2017, https://www.teamworldvision.org/.

Tertullian. *Ante-Nicene Fathers: Volume III: Latin Christianity: Its Founder, Tertullian*. Edited by Paul A Boer Sr. Translated by Peter Holmes and S Thelwall. Veritatis Splendor, 2014.

Tompkins, Kyla Wazana. *Racial Indigestion: Eating Bodies in the 19th Century*. New York: New York University Press, 2012.

Torrance, Thomas F. *Calvin's Doctrine of Man*. Grand Rapids: Eerdmans, 1957.

USA Swimming. "2016 U.S. Olympic Team Roster." http://www.usaswimming.org/ViewNewsArticle.aspx?TabId=1&ite`mid=15731&mid=14491.

"U.S. Masters Swimming Fact Sheet." U.S. Masters Swimming. http://www.usms.org/news/content/factsheet.

"USDA Defines Food Deserts." American Nutrition Association. http://americannutritionassociation.org/newsletter/usda-defines-food-deserts.

Uzukwu, E. Elochukwu. *Worship as Body Language: Introduction to Christian Worship : An African Orientation*. Collegeville, MN: Liturgical Press, 1997.

Van Vliet, Jason. *Children of God: The Imago Dei in John Calvin and His Context*. Göttingen: Vandenhoeck & Ruprecht, 2009.

Veit, Helen Zoe. *Modern Food, Moral Food: Self-Control, Science, and the Rise of Modern American Eating in the Early Twentieth Century*. Chapel Hill: University of North Carolina Press, 2013.

Verkooijen, Kirsten T., et al. "Athletic Identity and Well-Being among Young Talented Athletes Who Live at a Dutch Elite Sport Center." *Journal of Applied Sport Psychology* 24 (January 2012) 106–13. https://doi.org/10.1080/10413200.2011.633153.

Vernon, Steve. "How Much Would a Heart Attack Cost You?" http://www.cbsnews.com/news/how-much-would-a-heart-attack-cost-you/.

Volf, Miroslav. *Flourishing: Why We Need Religion in a Globalized World*. New Haven: Yale University Press, 2015.

Vost, Kevin. *Fit for Eternal Life: A Christian Approach to Working out, Eating Right, and Building the Virtues for Fitness in Your Soul*. Manchester, NH: Sophia Institute, 2007.

Wann, Marilyn. *Fat! So?: Because You Don't Have to Apologize for Your Size!* Berkeley: Ten Speed, 1998.

Watson, Nick J., and Andrew Parker. *Sport and the Christian Religion: A Systematic Review of Literature*. Newcastle upon Tyne, UK: Cambridge, 2014.

———. "The Mystical and Sublime in Extreme Sports: Experiences of Psychological Well-Being or Christian Revelation?" *Studies in World Christianity* 21 (December 2015) 260–81. https://doi.org/10.3366/swc.2015.0127.

Westphal, Merold. *Suspicion and Faith: The Religious Uses of Modern Atheism*. New York: Fordham University Press, 1998.

Wimbush, Vincent L., and Richard Valantasis, eds. *Asceticism*. New York: Oxford University Press, 1995.

Wink, Walter. *Engaging the Powers: Discernment and Resistance in a World of Domination*. Minneapolis: Fortress, 1992.

———. *Naming the Powers: The Language of Power in the New Testament*. Philadelphia: Fortress, 1984.

———. *Unmasking the Powers: The Invisible Forces That Determine Human Existence*. Philadelphia: Fortress, 1986.

Winson, Anthony. *The Industrial Diet: The Degradation of Food and the Struggle for Healthy Eating*. New York: New York University Press, 2014.

Wirzba, Norman. *Food and Faith: A Theology of Eating*. New York: Cambridge University Press, 2011.

Wolterstorff, Nicholas. *Art in Action: Toward a Christian Aesthetic*. Grand Rapids: Eerdmans, 1987.

———. *Art Rethought: The Social Practices of Art*. Oxford: Oxford University Press, 2015.

World Health Organization. "Basic Documents: Forty-eighth edition." 2014. http://apps.who.int/iris/handle/10665/151605.

World Vision website. "Our Work," https://www.worldvision.org/our-work.

Wosien, Maria-Gabriele. *Sacred Dance: Encounter with the Gods*. London: Avon Publishers of Bard, 1974.

Young, Kevin, and Chiaki Okada. *Sport, Social Development and Peace*. Bingley, UK: Emerald Group Publishing, 2014.

Zeman, Janice, Kimberly Shipman, and Cynthia Suveg. "Anger and Sadness Regulation: Predictions to Internalizing and Externalizing Symptoms in Children." *Journal of Clinical Child and Adolescent Psychology* 31 (September 2002) 393–98. https://doi.org/10.1207/S15374424JCCP3103_11.

Zeman, Janice, Kimberly Shipman, and Susan Penza-Clyve. "Development and Initial Validation of the Children's Sadness Management Scale." *Journal of Nonverbal Behavior* 25 (September 2001) 187–205. https://doi.org/10.1023/A:1010623226626.